CW00525280

Live Fire

*Seasonal Barbecue Recipes
and Stories of Live Fire
Traditions Old and New*

Helen Graves

Hardie Grant

BOOKS

Contents

What comes to mind when you think of 'barbecue'? Here are some of my own favourite scenarios: sitting cross-legged in the park idly twiddling grass as my mate snaps off a can of beer and hands it over; turning up late, clammy and relieved at someone's house to find music, laughter and a grill in full summer swing; catching an allspice-scented gust from the jerk drum hidden behind my favourite takeaway's façade; hearing the approach of a sizzling mixed grill at the best East End Pakistani restaurant; turning fat spears of asparagus to find them zebra striped with grill marks; splitting a smoked aubergine (eggplant) to reveal its creamy flesh; taking the first bite of a hot dog, fat spurting, ketchup dripping; heaving a thick steak onto the grill and waiting for the sizzle; chatting around still-glowing embers as the night turns cool.

There often seems to be two faces to the 'British barbecue'. The first is its unfortunate association with poorly cooked food – or what I call 'burnt bangers and boob aprons' – while the second is that of an exclusive private members' club accessible only to those with expensive, high-tech kit. This is due to the recent resurgence of barbecue as a 'trend', but I've always believed that barbecue should be accessible to anyone with outdoor space, or access to a park that allows grilling. Barbecue is something humans have been doing around the world for millenia.

There is a lot of off-putting messaging surrounding live fire cooking and it's something I hope I've started to contribute towards changing with *Pit*, the independent magazine I edit with my friends Holly and Rob. *Pit* aims to celebrate global live fire traditions by platforming diverse voices in barbecue – the real experts in their field.

In London, where I live, there are multiple diaspora communities that contribute to an eclectic barbecue scene. Visiting pockets of the city, it's possible to taste food cooked expertly over fire by people from many cultures: a firecracker sumac-soured Adana kebab still spitting hot from the grills of Green Lanes; a shiny ghee-slicked naan blistered in moments on the walls of an East End tandoor; an all-spice scented chicken leg from a jerk drum in Thornton Heath. In summer, our parks are filled with spiralling smoke amidst gatherings of families and friends; a million backyard parties pump with familiar flavours, whatever those might be.

I want to show you how wonderfully eclectic British barbecue is today and how the tips and tricks I've been taught by so many generous hosts and restaurateurs can work just as well for you in your back garden or local park.

I want to combine these eclectic flavours with those of our best homegrown produce, which includes so much world-class veg, seafood and meat – why limit ourselves to various iterations of 'meat in a bun'? The recipes in this book are simple, seasonal and characteristically big on flavour. Let it be known from the start that I do not 'do' timid when it comes to cooking and neither does barbecue cookery lend itself to a delicate approach. If you're into bold flavour, colourful platefuls and joyful gatherings, then hopefully you'll be on the same page – literally. In fact, I think we could probably be friends.

I also want to briefly make a point about the recipes I've written that borrow flavours – or in some cases recreate entire dishes – from other cultures and how I've gone about developing them. You won't find a recipe representing every diaspora cuisine in London within this book, only those that have had an influence on my personal cooking style through people I've met and the food they have introduced me to. By telling you the stories of some of these people in their own words, I hope you can understand where these influences have come from and how they have integrated themselves into my personal food story. This is a book about my favourite flavours, my favourite people and my favourite way to cook: in the open air over live fire.

The Barbecue Year

For me, barbecuing is a year-round activity and I've been known to stand over the grill with a brolly in hand. Top tip: if you do this, the brolly will smell so strongly of smoke it will become unusable, but on the plus side, you'll have a dedicated umbrella for cooking. Year-round barbecue doesn't mean standing in the rain, dripping and miserable, it means adapting techniques and ingredients to suit: it's more wrapping up warm to roast a whole pumpkin stuffed with beer fondue (page 156), for example than feeling the grass tickling your toes as the lamb chops sizzle (page 51).

I want to show you how to make the most of your grill through the seasons. If it's summer, then most likely I've got butter shining on my chin from the last corn cob I chomped and I'm still working on that stubborn corn skin stuck between my teeth. You could safely bet your house that I will cook many, many kebabs: smoky mushrooms, shawarma-style (page 206) or spiced minced (ground) lamb, shaped into logs and rolled through a pool of hot sauce and yoghurt as a nod to local late-night haunts (page 203). There will be fluffy flatbreads smeared with butter and wild garlic I foraged from a patch of woodland and there will be courgettes (zucchini) cooked right in the coals, mashed and served on top of cold yoghurt. I want sardines grilled fast and dipped into a pool of olive oil and salt so that I can mash the flesh to a golden paste and spread it on toast with lemon juice. I might follow them with jammy peaches, cooked gently over the dying coals while my ice cream softens on the worktop indoors and I try not to forget about it.

In winter, the barbecue is the best place to cook meals that will properly warm you through. I'll use richer flavours and hardier veg, like leeks, which can be cooked until 'blackened' and are a great way of fooling someone their dinner is completely ruined, until you split them to reveal tender insides. I like to grill fat steaks seasoned with a shining crust of salt, medium rare and carved into slices to share between two or three people, and I make bubbling pots of rich chilli, thick with flavour and finished with grated dark chocolate. I want coal-baked beetroots (beets), sweet charred onions and a pile of sticky figs with salty, pungent cheese.

I think of the barbecue as an extension of my kitchen, and while I might use it nearly every day during warmer months, I'm still using it at least twice a week during winter to bring the extra dimension of flavour to my food that only live fire cooking can. However, I realise this might be a hard sell for some of you when the weather isn't great, and particularly during the autumn and winter, so in many cases here I've provided instructions to cook indoors, too – just in case.

Different Barbecues, Accessories and Techniques

Lots of people I know are scared of barbecue because they think it's something best left to professionals; they're put off by the fact that there are fewer rules around how to do it than there are for indoor cooking. To cook something in an oven, for example, you'd set the temperature, shut the door and wait for 'X' number of minutes; barbecuing can be a little more instinctive. 'Instinctive' cooking sounds like an innate skill bestowed upon a lucky few, but it's actually something you get a feel for quite quickly with practice. Despite what the backyard warriors may want you to think, barbecue cooking is simple. Not everyone needs (or indeed wants) to cook the perfect competition-worthy brisket; most of us just want to have fun and a nice dinner at the end of it. I can teach you how to make that happen.

Barbecues

As the popularity of barbecue cooking increases, so does the range of barbecues available. It can be overwhelming. I have lots of different barbecues at home because it's my job to play around with them, but for day-to-day cooking I regularly use two: a standard lidded kettle and a more 'serious' ceramic barbecue.

— Kettle barbecues: The lidded kettle is the style that most people will be familiar with, and it's the one I'd recommend to anyone who is looking to buy their first barbecue. Get a decent-sized one if you can afford it, as you'll have more space to cook and to try out different techniques. The lid is essential if you want to cook larger pieces of meat, for example, using the barbecue more as an outdoor oven. The lid brings more versatility and I'd say it's essential for some recipes.

Every recipe in this book was tested on a large kettle barbecue because it's the most common type of grill out there, and I wanted to make sure the recipes worked on one. For the sake of transparency, I will say that it was a Weber Mastertouch Premium. You don't need to buy this model, but I thought it might be useful to know what I use.

— Ceramic barbecues: These are brilliant, but expensive. They hold heat consistently over a long period of time, which makes them great for smoking ribs or whole vegetables like celeriac (celery root), but they can also be used for grilling or 'direct cooking' (more on this shortly). Thanks to their ceramic insulation they also use far less charcoal. They come with a number of fancy accessories, too, such as ceramic pizza stones and rotisseries. This is all good fun but they're really not necessary: it's best to find out how much you like barbecuing using a standard kettle grill first.

— Gas barbecues: There's a huge amount of snobbery around gas grills in the barbecue world as they are, essentially, outdoor hobs (stovetops). If you want to use one, then rock on – I can't stand food snobbery of any variety. They're easy to use and many people appreciate their convenience. You won't get the same flavour as you do from charcoal or wood smoke, and it's hard to get any decent char on anything, but that is your choice.

Accessories

As I said, there's no need to go out and spend thousands of pounds on barbecue equipment, but a few basic accessories are useful as you begin to experiment.

— Chimney starter: This piece of kit – like a big metal mug to light your charcoal in – makes lighting a barbecue much faster and easier.

— Long-handled barbecue tongs: You'll need these to move food around without getting too close to the fire.

— Heatproof gloves: These are helpful if you need to get closer to the grill to manoeuvre something around (like the grill itself). They're also great for moving hot plates of food, picking up skewers and so on. If you want to use a frying pan in the barbecue then you will really need them. They'll give you confidence; burns are not fun.

— Metal skewers: You'll often see recipes that call for soaking wooden skewers but to be honest, I find them pretty useless. They're generally small and spindly and tend to catch fire anyway. Invest in some decent-sized metal skewers and ditch those oversized toothpicks for good.

— A fish cage: Mostly these aren't necessary, but they can be handy when you have a lot of small fish like sardines (as it will help to stop them falling through the grill) or a big piece of fish like the skate wing on page 30 (the cage will make it easier to turn the fish over).

— Grill basket: These can be really useful for cooking smaller vegetables, which have a tendency to slip through the grill. It's not absolutely necessary, but if you're going to regularly cook green beans or other skinny veg on the barbecue then it might be something worth investing in.

— Wire rack: Useful if you want to smoke fish or elevate something above the grill bars slightly.

— A probe thermometer: This isn't vital for every recipe, but if you're going to cook large pieces of meat like the pork shoulder on page 110 or the rib of beef on page 229, then it's useful to invest in a thermometer (not least because those cuts are more expensive, so you'll want to know what's going on). Barbecue cooking is dependent on lots of factors that vary, such as the temperature outside and the fuel you're using, so it's often better to cook your food to temperature rather than relying on a specified amount of time.

— A cast-iron frying pan with a lid: This is a really useful piece of kit for the barbecue because cast iron will withstand high temperatures, which opens up cooking possibilities, such as the Pull-apart Garlic Bread on page 134. It's a great tool for indoor cooking, too, so well worth the (very reasonable) investment.

— A bristly wire brush: This is for cleaning your barbecue. The best way to clean the grill is to light a fire underneath and let everything on the grill heat up and burn off. You can then give it a quick brush and… ta-da! It's ready. I never wash my barbecue grill indoors.

— A smaller brush: An easy to clean brush is useful for applying marinades and glazes to food while it's on the barbecue.

Barbecue Techniques

There are two main barbecue cooking techniques you need to know about: *direct* and *indirect* cooking. When setting up a barbecue, I nearly always set it up for what is known as 'two-zone cooking'. This simply means there is one area with lit coals in it, and one area without. There are various ways to arrange the coals to achieve this, but I often do mine in the simplest way possible, which is to place the hot coals on one side and leave the other side empty. Occasionally I prefer to place the coals in the middle and leave the edges clear, e.g. when I'm cooking chicken wings.

The reasons behind this are that two-zone cooking enables you to: sear food for colour and flavour before moving it to the cooler side to finish cooking more slowly; move food to the cooler area if the fire starts to flare up; keep food warm on the cooler side while you finish cooking something else; or slow cook something on the cooler side with the lid on. I'll explain this in recipes where it's relevant.

Just so you know, there are other ways of arranging charcoal – particularly for slow cooking – but for the purposes of this book I wanted to keep things as simple as possible.

Just think of your barbecue as having a range of temperature zones that work horizontally: the closer to the coals, the hotter it's going to be. Simple!

The Best
Things
to Burn

Charcoal

We're nearly through all the boring 'how to' stuff now, I promise. First, a few important notes about charcoal and wood and how to light your barbecue. It's easy to think 'charcoal is charcoal' (why wouldn't you?), but this is not the case. The mass-produced stuff (the kind you find on garage forecourts) is often made from illegally felled rainforest and pumped full of chemicals that taint your food. These chemicals take ages to burn off, which is why you'll often see recipes saying, 'wait until the coals are covered in a layer of grey ash before cooking'. I've written this myself in recipes back when I knew less about charcoal than I do now.

The best option – if you can – is to buy good-quality lumpwood charcoal, ideally one that's made with wood harvested from ecologically sound resources and produced in a sustainable way. You'll find that lumpwood behaves very differently to briquettes or other cheap charcoal: it lights faster, burns 'cleaner', with less smoke and you'll be able to add pieces to your fire while it's lit (e.g., if you need to refuel during cooking) which you can't do with cheaper briquettes as they take an age to light and become viable for cooking.

Charcoal production is an ancient woodland skill and there are producers reviving old practices and pioneering new ones using British wood. Done properly, charcoal production works with natural woodland ecosystems, harvesting in cycles to minimise impact. Since the UK is no longer covered in woodland as it once was, the remaining pockets need to be managed in order to preserve them and charcoal production can help do this by mimicking natural processes. Some of my favourite producers of lumpwood charcoal are listed at the end of this book. All charcoals are different and you will get used to the one you choose and the way it burns.

Wood

It's not necessary to add chunks of wood or chips when barbecuing, but it can be a fun way to add extra flavour. When wood burns it releases flavour compounds, which differ depending on type and composition. Without getting into too much detail, the differences lie in the fact that some woods contain glucose molecules which produce sweet flavours such as peach, coconut and green apple, whereas others – known as phenolics – are more pungent and spicier.

That said, I don't find a huge amount of difference between as many types of wood as others do. Honestly, once you're smoking something, it's going to taste ... smoky. The main difference is in whether a smoke is heavy or light. Perhaps you will find the differences listed opposite more pronounced than I do. It is fun to choose different types of wood though, no denying that, so here are some suggestions. I think of the woods more as having personalities than 'flavours' as such.

— English oak: This is one of the most popular woods for barbecue cooking because it burns at a steady rate and produces a fairly heavy smoke. When used carefully it's a good all-rounder but do take care by adding just a chunk or two.

— Beech: Beech is often considered a better multipurpose wood than oak as it's a little lighter in flavour and therefore a bit 'safer' to use, as you don't run the risk of over smoking. It also works with pretty much any food.

— Sweet chestnut: Slow burning, toasty and nutty, this wood is good with most meats.

— Alder: A very sweet smoking wood that is great for smoking fish and adding a 'honeyed smoke' characteristic to foods.

— Silver birch: A milder, sweet wood that works well with pork and poultry.

— Apple: A lovely light, fruity and sweet wood that is fun to use with pork in particular.

— Pear: A little cleaner and less sweet than apple. One for when you want to keep things mellow.

Chunks vs. chips

For everyday barbecuing and hot smoking, 2.5–5 cm (1–2 in) chunks of wood are my go-to choice. Bags of chips are also available, and generally the packaging will instruct you to soak them first, but I've found that this isn't necessary. They'll burn faster but produce a nicer-tasting smoke if you just add them dry.

A quick word of warning: don't just pick up a piece of fallen oak or other tree wood and use it on the barbecue; wood for smoking must be 'seasoned', which basically means 'dried out', and that can take anything from six months to two years. I buy mine online (see stockists on page 17).

Firelighters

Just as all charcoal is not made equal, neither are firelighters. There's no longer any need to use those nasty white bricks that are soaked with petroleum. Natural firelighters are made from wood 'wool' dipped in paraffin wax and are widely available. They're also just as effective.

The easiest way to light a barbecue

The simplest way to light a barbecue is by using a chimney starter. This is basically a cylindrical piece of metal with a heatproof handle that will get your coals going in 5–10 minutes.

To use it, shove some scrunched up paper in the bottom, stack the coals on top, then light the paper from underneath. Wait for 10 minutes or so, don your heatproof gloves if you like, then tip the coals into the barbecue.

Obviously, cooking on a barbecue is not like cooking in an oven; it's not possible to turn the temperature dial and set it to exactly 120°C/250°F (or, let's face it, 180°C/350°F, because that's just the temperature for cooking nearly everything, right?). There are ways to control the temperature on your barbecue, however. The first is down to the amount of coals you add (see below), and the second is how you control the fire using the air vents at the top and bottom of the barbecue. The more open the vents are, the more air flows through to fuel the fire and raise the temperature. If all the vents are fully shut, the fire will go out. Close the vents every time you finish cooking to 'turn your barbecue off' and preserve any remaining fuel for next time.

You'll want around a third of a chimney-full for low heat, half for a general-purpose temperature of 180°C (350°F), and a full starter for something that requires high heat, such as steaks. Longer cooks may require a top-up, and I'll indicate this in recipes where appropriate.

You want to be cooking over hot embers, not flames. Flames that come from fat dripping onto the coals are fine, but flames that have not properly died down will just taint the flavour of the food.

Some Notes on Cooking and Ingredients

Indoor Cooking

As much as I want you to cook every recipe in this book over live fire, I appreciate that sometimes it's not going to happen, and I don't want anyone to miss out because it's raining. One of the best investments you can make for indoor cooking is a cast-iron griddle pan – they're reasonably priced, will last forever, and will allow you to cook flatbreads and griddle meat, seafood and vegetables over a high heat. I suggest using one in nearly all of the alternative cooking instructions in this book.

Timing

With every recipe, you'll need to factor in time for lighting your barbecue and making sure the coals are ready for cooking, just as you would preheating an oven. This time isn't included in the prep time listed for each recipe because the time it takes to light a barbecue varies, primarily according to the quality of the charcoal but also other factors such as arrangement of coals and the weather. I've provided some rough guidelines below.
— Lighting good-quality charcoal in a chimney starter: 5–10 minutes.
— Lighting average to poor-quality charcoal in a chimney starter: anything from 15 minutes onwards.
— Lighting without a chimney starter: a little longer – about 15 minutes, to be on the safe side.

Measurements

It may seem as if I've been a little slapdash in specifying the amount of ingredients in some recipes, which call for a 'handful' of this, or a 'dash' of that. This is deliberate. I like to be bold with my flavours and barbecue is not a style of cooking that generally lends itself to very precise measurements – a part of why it's so fun in the first place.

Herbs and spices

I use herbs and spices liberally and in generous quantities, and my recipes are powerfully flavoured as a result. Life is too short for adding minuscule quantities of anything, to my mind. I also recommend that you buy whole spices, toast them briefly in a dry pan and grind them at home – the flavour is approximately 100 per cent better than that of the ready-ground versions, because they're fresher.

Salt

I use a good-quality, flaky sea salt for cooking, so this is what's called for in all the recipes that follow. It has a better flavour, is less aggressively 'salty' than fine salt and has a beautiful appearance and texture when eaten. Crunching down on a piece of flaky sea salt – on a piece of butter-drenched garlic bread, for example, has to be one of my all-time favourite edible pleasures. Occasionally fine sea salt is required, however, and I'll specify this where necessary.

Oils

When I mention 'neutral' oil, I mean an oil with a neutral flavour and a high smoking point, such as vegetable or groundnut (peanut) oil. I usually reserve olive oil for sides, sauces and dressings.

Butter

Butter is always unsalted unless specified otherwise; this allows you to have complete control of the seasoning.

Pepper

I use freshly ground black and white pepper most often in my cooking (although my cupboards are stuffed with varieties from around the world). White pepper may have fallen out of fashion in the UK but I use it regularly when I want its bright, citrus notes and clean heat. It's used a lot in South East Asian cooking (so you'll find it in recipes like the bánh mì on page 119) and of course, it's at home with British flavours too.

Rubs

Applying dry rubs onto meat before cooking is 'a barbecue thing' and you'll notice that I use the technique occasionally. This is why you'll see ingredients such as onion powder and garlic powder in recipes. Don't be alarmed by them – they're readily available in supermarkets and they work much better in rubs than fresh onion and garlic, which are (obviously) wet.

Brining and seasoning

I don't do tons of brining, but I will occasionally brine chicken, more often than not brine pork chops and absolutely always brine turkey for the barbecue. I don't want to get technical in this book, but the purpose of brining is to prevent dry meat. Salt denatures some of the meat proteins, which unwind and get tangled with one another creating a mesh that traps more moisture. There are pros and cons and other techniques for large cuts of meat, such as injecting brine, but as I said, this isn't that kind of book.

With dry-aged meat such as good steak, I season as close to the cooking time as possible, because the meat has far less moisture than 'fresh meat' to start off with and I don't want to draw any more of it out.

A Few Words about Meat

Anyone who takes even the briefest look at my Instagram feed will deduce that I like to eat meat – it's a festival of steak tacos, crispy chicken thighs and lamb sandwiches over there. However, don't take it at face value, as my approach to buying and consuming meat has changed in recent years in line with concerns about health and the environment. Perhaps yours has too. Through my work I've met lots of people who are wading upstream against a strong current of harmful farming practices, trying to replace them with more regenerative ones and restore some harmony in our environment. I know, then, that it is not sustainable or healthy to regularly consume industrially farmed meat and, if possible, we should be aiming to rebalance our diets a little more in favour of vegetables and planet-friendly seafood. However, I am not here to preach. I'll give a little nod to some of my favourite, ethically sound producers later on, so you can look them up if you'd like to (page 17). My main point is that barbecue is about more than large hunks of protein, as lovely as they are.

Some of My Favourite Ingredients

Pul biber and Urfa chilli

Pul biber, or Aleppo pepper, is a chilli flake used in Mediterranean and Middle Eastern cuisine and I use it liberally, pretty much every day. It has a sun-roasted flavour and mild heat that makes it versatile and it can be used easily in large quantities or as more of a table seasoning, like salt and pepper. Korean chilli flakes (gochugaru) have a similar flavour and heat level.

Urfa is a darker flake from Turkey made by salting and drying the chillies then wrapping them up so they sweat. The flavour is richer and smokier than pul biber.

Other Chillies

The world of chillies is vast and exciting. You will notice that (other than pul biber and Urfa) I use scotch bonnet chilli an awful lot. It's a very hot chilli, so care should be taken when preparing it (wash your hands well and try not to touch the inside too much) but I love it for its fruity, tropical flavour.

I also use lots of dried Mexican chillies, which have complex flavours of smoke, fruit, leather and tobacco. They add extraordinary depth.

Yoghurt

I go through huge tubs of thick natural yoghurt, using it as a cool base for hot charred vegetables, as a 'condiment' for kebabs, a base for cold sauces, in salad dressings and more. I tend to buy mine from the local Turkish Food Centre, but any good, thick, natural (and preferably full-fat) yoghurt will do.

Fresh Herbs

Herbs come in handfuls in my kitchen, and I really don't see the point in using tiny amounts unless they are particularly strong e.g., rosemary, thyme or sage. I like a lot of freshness and fragrance in my cooking and often eat herbs as salad leaves, particularly tarragon and basil. So, be generous and don't fret over the amounts too much unless I've specified them.

Masa Harina

Masa harina is ground corn 'flour' that has been specially prepared for making tortillas (tacos). While corn tortillas are now available to buy in shops, making your own is a lot more cost effective, very easy and the flavour and texture is miles better. A tortilla press is very handy: they are inexpensive and worth it if you're going to make tacos regularly, as I do. However, it is perfectly possible to roll them out by hand.

Stockists and Suppliers

In London I have access to lots of shops serving different communities. I buy my pul biber, Urfa and sumac from The Turkish Food Centre; shrimp paste, galangal, banana leaves and Chinese chilli oil from the Asian supermarket; fresh turmeric and spices from Indian grocers; and so on. If you have food shops like this near you then I urge you to patronise them because the produce is often much better quality and value than what you'll find in the supermarkets. Plus, you are supporting local businesses and there is the potential for discovering new ingredients.

For Mexican ingredients
(masa, dried chillies, tortilla press, achiote/annatto)
— Mex Grocer
mexgrocer.co.uk
— Cool Chile Co
coolchile.co.uk

For Middle Eastern and Mediterranean ingredients
(pul biber, Urfa chilli, sumac, pomegranate molasses)
— Turkish Food Centre
online.tfcsupermarkets.com/index
— Sous Chef
souschef.co.uk

For Chinese, Vietnamese and other Asian ingredients
(Chinese chilli oils, kimchi, galangal, Sichuan peppercorns, shrimp paste, banana leaves, daikon, miso, seaweed. Also MSG, which is by no means just an Asian ingredient but it is available in Asian grocery shops)
— Wai Yee Hong
waiyeehong.com
— See Woo
seewoo.com
— Longdan (particularly for Vietnamese ingredients)
longdan.co.uk
— Thai Food Online
thai-food-online.co.uk

For African ingredients
(grains of sclim, tesmi, mekelesha)
— Steenbergs
steenbergs.co.uk
— The Ethiopian Foodie
ethiopianfoodie.co.uk
— Cubeb Pepper, kampot pepper and Kashmiri chilli powder

Raw honey
— Holland and Barrett
hollandandbarrett.com
— The Raw Honey Shop
therawhoneyshop.com

Meat
I buy all my meat (except goat) from Flock and Herd in Peckham. Support your local butcher!
flockandherd.com
— Goat
cabrito.co.uk
— HG Walter
hgwalter.com
— Swaledale
swaledale.co.uk
— The Ethical Butcher
ethicalbutcher.co.uk

Wood/charcoal
— Whittle & Flame
whittleandflame.co.uk/kiln
— Birchwood Forestry
birchwoodforestry.co.uk
— Stag Charcoal
stagbritishcharcoal.co.uk

Sugar Snap Peas
with Mint

Setup: Direct cooking
Equipment: Tongs, 1 long
metal skewer or several
short ones
Prep time: 5 minutes
Cook time: 5 minutes
Serves: 4

good handful of mint leaves,
chopped
2 tablespoons malt vinegar
2 teaspoons caster
(superfine) sugar
1 tablespoon olive oil
400 g (14 oz) sugar snap peas
neutral oil, for tossing
sea salt

Yep, she's opening the book with a plate of grilled peas.
No traffic-light veg kebabs here, friends (unless you really,
honestly, like them). Let's hear it for more single-vegetable
grilled dishes like this one, where the sweet pods char and
suck up the bright, herbal dressing.

Skewering the peas is a neat trick to stop them falling
through the bars – a game changer. And yes, that dressing is
based on the kind of mint sauce you'd serve with roast lamb
(so naturally, this dish goes very well with the lamb on page 47).

— Prepare a barbecue for direct cooking over medium heat.
— Combine the mint, malt vinegar, sugar, olive oil and
a generous pinch of salt in a clean jar or bowl and shake or
whisk to combine. Set aside.
— Toss the sugar snap peas in a little neutral oil, then thread
them onto the metal skewer or several short ones and grill
over direct heat for a few minutes on each side, or until charred
on both sides.
— Combine with the mint sauce and serve.

To Cook Indoors: Preheat a cast-iron griddle pan over a high
heat for at least 5 minutes. Char the sugar snap peas for a few
minutes, turning occasionally.

Baby Artichokes
with an Anchovy Dip and Herb Crumb

Setup: Direct cooking
Equipment: Tongs
Prep time: 10 minutes
Cook time: 25 minutes
Serves: 2–4, depending
on appetite

1 × 50 g (1¾ oz) tin of anchovy
fillets in olive oil
150 g (5½ oz) breadcrumbs
from stale crusty bread,
such as sourdough
small handful of mint leaves,
finely chopped
small handful of parsley
leaves, finely chopped,
plus extra to serve
2 garlic cloves, peeled
3 tablespoons lemon juice,
plus ½ lemon for rubbing
4 tablespoons olive oil
12 baby artichokes
neutral oil, for cooking
sea salt and freshly ground
black pepper

Baby artichokes are a spring barbecue highlight for me; nowhere near as offensively thistly as their mature relatives, they can be easily whittled down and grilled until tender. The fact they have a much better leaf-to-heart ratio than the large plants means it's so satisfying to pile into a big plate of them. A word of warning though: they really do need to be small, otherwise you'll be choking on a spray of prickles. There are two ways you can serve these: either dip them into the anchovy sauce then swipe them through the crumb, or serve them on a plate with dip and crumb on top. Which is better? You decide.

— Heat a frying pan over a medium heat and add the oil from the anchovy tin. Add the breadcrumbs and fry for about 15 minutes until crisp and golden, stirring regularly. Remove from the heat, add the herbs and set aside.
— Put the anchovies, garlic and lemon juice into a small food processor and blend, adding the olive oil in a slow trickle until it's all used up (you could also smush the anchovies and garlic together first, then use a hand whisk to incorporate the oil). Season with black pepper and set aside.
— Prepare a barbecue for direct cooking over medium heat.
— Slice off the tips of the leaves from the artichokes (take off a good few centimetres) and peel off the outer purple leaves until you are left with only those that are bright yellow/green. Trim off the stalks and any outer tough layers surrounding them. Halve each lengthways and rub with the edge of a cut lemon.
— Toss the artichokes with a splash of oil and a little salt. Cook them, cut side down first, over direct heat for about 10 minutes, turning them occasionally, until the base is tender (it's worth giving one an exploratory nibble, as they tend to feel hard even when they're ready).
— Serve with the dip in a shallow bowl and the crumb alongside, or dress on the plate.

To Cook Indoors: Preheat a cast-iron griddle pan over high heat for at least 5 minutes and add the oiled artichokes. Cook for about 5 minutes per side until charred on both sides, then add a decent splash of water to the pan and cover. Allow the artichokes to steam for a couple of minutes, or until cooked through.

Monkfish Cheek Kebabs
with Peas and Preserved Lemon

Setup: Direct cooking
Equipment: Metal skewers,
tongs, heatproof gloves
Prep time: 10 minutes
Cook time: 5 minutes
Serves: 4

3 tablespoons olive oil
4 garlic cloves, crushed or
finely grated
100 g (3½ oz) frozen peas
the rind from ½ preserved
lemon (about 10 g/⅓ oz),
finely chopped
1 teaspoon caster
(superfine) sugar
juice of 1–2 lemons
handful of mint leaves,
finely chopped
handful of basil leaves,
shredded
700 g (1 lb 9 oz) monkfish
cheeks (or a regular cut
of monkfish, or another
firm white fish), cut into
bite-sized chunks
neutral oil, for cooking
sea salt and freshly ground
black pepper
lemon wedges, to serve

These are really quite elegant little kebabs, which look fancy
when you pour the dressing over them. Of course, you could
use another firm white fish or the regular body/tail part
of a monkfish, although the cheeks seem to hold together
particularly well. I love to serve these with flatbreads, couscous,
freekeh or a potato salad. The dressing is fresh and lively, with
the curious perfume of preserved lemons mingling with basil
and sweet pops of pea.

— Prepare a barbecue for direct cooking over high heat.
— To make the dressing, heat 2 tablespoons of the olive oil
in a frying pan over a low heat, add the garlic and let it sizzle
gently for a minute or so. Add the peas and preserved lemon
and season with the sugar and some salt. Allow to warm
through and dissolve before turning off the heat and adding
the fresh lemon juice, mint and basil, reserving a little of each
for serving.
— Toss the monkfish pieces with a splash of neutral oil
and some salt and pepper. Thread onto skewers.
— Grill over direct heat for about 5 minutes, turning once.
Check the fish is cooked through before serving.
— Pour the dressing over the skewers, scatter with the
remaining herbs and serve with an extra wedge of lemon.

To Cook Indoors: Cook the monkfish skewers under a hot grill
(broiler) for a couple of minutes on each side.

Smoked Salmon and Craster Kippers

Smokehouses have peppered the UK's coastline for hundreds of years; racked fish dangling in foggy chimneys fed by gently smouldering sawdust. Now considerably reduced in number, traditional operations pride themselves on unchanged methods, while new, modern businesses find their own style and market.

In his book, *Salmon* (2020), Mark Kurlansky describes the significance of the fish to these shores, noting that the 8th century monk, The Venerable Bede, observed that Britain boasted, 'the greatest plenty of salmon and eels' and that in Anglo Saxon times,' salmon had monetary value: there are a number of records of rent being paid in salmon'. Salmon has historically been a lucrative commodity.

Enthusiastically consumed, it was poached, boiled or preserved for later consumption through pickling, salting or, of course, smoking. Jewish people introduced this technique from Eastern Europe, where they'd smoked salmon to preserve it due to 'a constant fear of scarcity' writes Claudia Roden in *The Book of Jewish Food* (1996). People from Russia then introduced the method to New York, and to London's East End in the late 1800s, settling mainly in Whitechapel and Spitalfields, close to the docks. The first East End smokehouses were soon established.

In contrast to the 'old-style Brooklyn' smoked salmon ('lox after the Yiddish word *lachs* for salmon,' writes Roden), which was 'pickled in brine days before refrigeration, then desalted and lightly smoked', the East End style was dry-salted, rinsed and dried before smoking. One of the first London smokehouses was in Spitalfields' Frying Pan Alley, owned by the Barnett family. Jo and Maurice Barnett took over from their grandfather, and a story reported in the *Dundee Chronicle* (1948) describes how Maurice – returned from RAF service as a bomb disposal officer – was surprised to find an unexploded British cannon shell inside a 23lb fresh salmon. I'll bet. Unperturbed – presumably due to his training – he simply took it outside and detonated it. The company continued smoking salmon until the mid-90s.

Some London-produced smoked salmon has PGI status (Protected Geographical Indication), but only if it is produced using a 'London cure' and adheres to rules surrounding production, processing and preparation. The protected status for 'salmon cured and smoked using only a combination of rock salt and oak smoke' was awarded to just two smokehouses at the same time: industry goliath H. Forman & Son, and East London's Secret Smokehouse, a smaller, artisanal operation founded in Scotsman Max Bergius's back garden in 2015.

Max is passionate about the PGI status, seeing the value in protecting standards, and in making the cure available to everyone. 'The PGI status should be philanthropic; you should be able to stand naked in front of the mirror every morning thinking, I'm gonna leave a brilliant legacy because I've created this PGI,' he says. Max is currently working with DEFRA (Department for Environment, Food and Rural Affairs) on an amendment to the criteria, 'It should be simple: fish from the south of Scotland, oak smoked and a dry salt cure, happy days.'

The Secret Smokehouse (a tongue-in-cheek reference to the secrecy surrounding industry methods) is located under an East London archway, and, while it uses modern equipment, it focuses on traditional methods. Space is tight, and while they deliver nationwide, they also have a refrigerated cabinet at the front of the shop, serving customers oak-smoked salmon, haddock, trout and kippers.

Those glorious, burnt umber kippers are actually smoked herrings – small oily fish that have been gutted, butterflied and cold-smoked, usually over oak (a bloater, mentioned on page 152, is an ungutted cold-smoked herring).

Neil Robson owns L Robson & Sons Ltd. in Craster, a fishing village situated on the coast of Northumberland, England's northernmost county. A fourth-generation smoker, it was his great grandfather who started the business in 1906. 'The smokehouse was built in 1856,' he says. 'The herring were traditionally caught locally and landed in the village. My grandfather used to take them by horse and cart to the nearest train station to get them down to London for the next day.'

Once an important dietary component for much of the population of the British Isles, they were packed into barrels. 'The methods haven't changed much,' says Neil, 'except that before you had 10 or 15 herring girls splitting them by hand but now we have a machine. It was backbreaking work, salting them and packing them. The girls would follow the fleet, which landed first up in the North in Peterhead, Aberdeen and even the Shetlands, then they would follow them all the way down to finish the season off at Lowestoft.'

'There aren't many of us left [using traditional methods],' explains Neil. 'It's more work because they've got to be put up into the smokehouse, and it's a gradual process with small fires to start with, then a bit more heat as the process goes on – to give them the golden sheen. It takes about 15–16 hours before they're fully smoked.'

One of the main skills in danger of being lost, Neil tells me, is knowing how to adapt to the weather. 'On a nice sunny day with a bit of wind blowing the smoke goes through the fish okay, but on a damp, muggy evening you've got to give them more air. We are only about 50 yards from the North Sea, so we have some weather!'

As the climate has changed, the herrings have started shoaling further north, where the water is colder, so these days Neil uses herrings landed in Norway. Kippers are more popular than ever, he says, thanks to a surge of interest in healthy eating and the benefits of oily fish.

'The only thing that puts people off is the smell,' he says, referring to the downside of cooking smoked fish indoors. 'We advise people to jug them – put them in a jug of boiling water until you see the flesh start to cook.' It won't surprise you to learn that I have another idea, however, and yes, it is that they are best warmed through slowly on the barbecue. Place the kippers inside a fish cage (if you have one) and cook them slowly over low embers until just warmed through. Top with a hefty pat of butter and eat with a poached egg and toast for one of the best breakfasts of your life (lingering kitchen odour not included).

Hot-smoked Salmon
with Horseradish Labneh and Pickled Radishes

Setup: Indirect cooking
Wood: Oak
Equipment: Tongs, small wire rack (useful but not essential). You will also need a clean piece of muslin (cheesecloth) or a brand-new cloth for straining the yoghurt
Prep time: 15 minutes, plus minimum 2 hours straining time (overnight if possible)
Cook time: 10 minutes
Serves: 4

4 skin-on salmon fillets
neutral oil, for cooking
sea salt
3 tablespoons horseradish from a jar
2 tablespoons finely chopped dill
4 bagels, toasted, to serve
2 spring onions (scallions), thinly sliced

Labneh
good pinch of sea salt
250 g (9 oz/1 cup) natural full-fat yoghurt

Pickled radishes
100 ml (3½ fl oz/scant ½ cup) rice vinegar
1 teaspoon sea salt
3 tablespoons caster (superfine) sugar
100 ml (3½ fl oz/scant ½ cup) hot tap water
80 g (2¾ oz) radishes, thinly sliced

While cold-smoking salmon is perfectly possible at home with a small cold smoker, hot-smoked salmon is much quicker and doesn't need any special equipment. I think it's a fun introduction to smoking fish if you've never done it before, and fresh hot smoked salmon tastes amazing – the key is not to overcook it. I like to serve it with labneh (strained yoghurt), which has the richness of sour cream, but a fresher flavour.

— First, strain the yoghurt. A couple of hours before you want to eat – or even the night before – mix the salt into the yoghurt then place it in a brand-new cloth or a clean piece of muslin (cheesecloth). Gather it up at the sides and secure with string or an elastic band. Suspend the pouch of yoghurt over a bowl using string, to allow the liquid to drain out. You will have a lovely result after a couple of hours, but leaving it overnight will give you a really thick and lovely yoghurt reminiscent of cream cheese. If leaving it overnight, it's best to hang it in the fridge (particularly if it's in warm weather).

— To pickle the radishes, combine the vinegar, salt, sugar and hot tap water in a bowl, mix until the sugar and salt have dissolved, then add the sliced radishes. Leave at room temperature for at least 30 minutes or up to 24 hours.
— Prepare a barbecue for indirect cooking, with just a few lit coals. Place a small piece of wood on top of the coals and let it smoulder.
— Rub the salmon lightly with neutral oil and place on the wire rack (if using). Season with salt, place on the cooler side of the barbecue and put the lid on. Close the vents until they are about a quarter open and smoke the salmon for about 10 minutes, or until just cooked (the exact cooking time will depend on the shape and size of your salmon fillets).
— Stir the horseradish and dill into the strained yoghurt and serve with the toasted bagels, sliced spring onions (scallions) and pickled radishes.

Skate Wing
in Super-green Garlic, Caper and Olive Sauce

Setup: Direct cooking
Equipment: Fish cage, heatproof gloves
Prep time: 10 minutes
Cook time: 10–16 minutes
Serves: 2

650 g (1 lb 7 oz) skate wing
neutral oil, for cooking
sea salt

Super-green garlic, caper and olive sauce
150 g (5½ oz/10½ tablespoons) butter
4 garlic cloves, crushed or finely grated
20 g (¾ oz/2 tablespoons) capers, rinsed
50 g (1¾ oz) green olives, pitted and roughly chopped
small handful each of mint leaves, flat-leaf parsley, dill and chives, finely chopped
juice of 1 lemon

I admit skate should be eaten rarely, since it has been so over-fished. I will also admit that it is incredibly delicious and I am not yet perfect. A richly fleshed fish, it has a robust structure that makes it ideal for grilling. Here, I've given it one of my favourite treatments, which is to put a lot of great-tasting things into a pool of melted butter, then pour it over the fish (or whatever I've grilled), claiming it's 'a sauce'. Trust me, you won't look back.

A fish cage makes things easier here, but don't be put off if you don't have one. It'll be fine cooked straight on the grill. The key is to let the fish release itself naturally from the grill before turning; force it, and it will stick.

— Prepare a barbecue for direct cooking over medium heat.
— To make the sauce, melt the butter in a saucepan over a low-medium heat, add the garlic and let it sizzle gently for a couple of minutes, taking care not to burn it. Add the capers, olives, herbs and lemon juice, remove from the heat and set aside.
— Lightly oil the skin of the skate wing and season with salt. Place inside the fish cage and secure it.
— Grill over direct heat for 5–8 minutes on each side (depending on the thickness of the wing) or until the fish is cooked through. Transfer to a plate and pour over the green sauce. Serve immediately.

To Cook Indoors: Preheat the oven to 200°C (400°F/gas 6) and the grill (broiler) to medium heat. Grill the oiled skate wing until golden (about 7 minutes), then transfer to the oven for 5 minutes or so, or until cooked through.

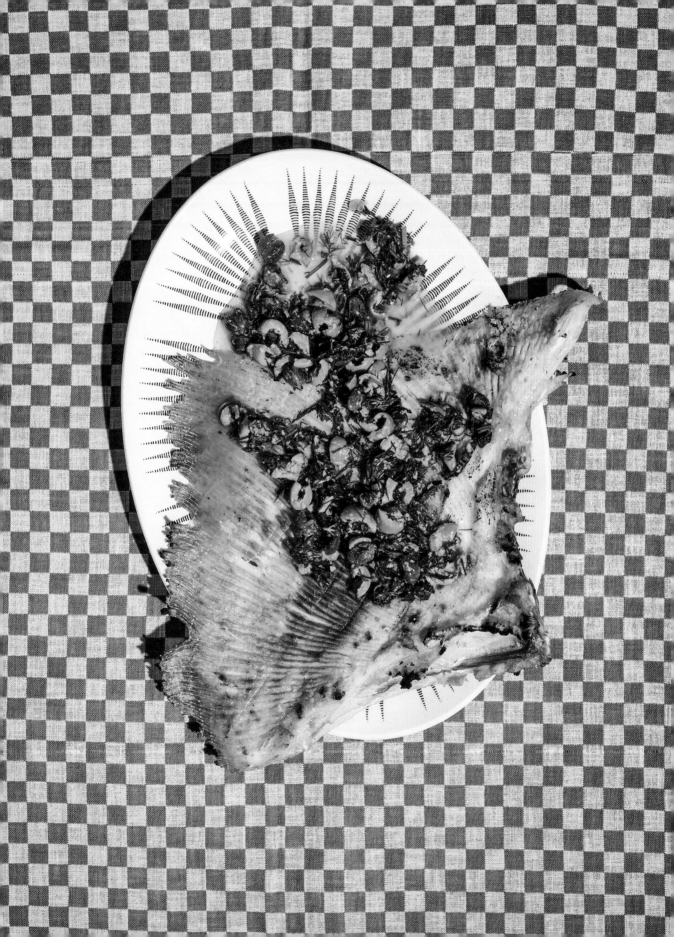

Sweetheart Cabbage
with Brown Shrimp Butter

Setup: Direct cooking
Equipment: Tongs
Prep time: 5 minutes
Cook time: 20 minutes
Serves: 2 as a main dish,
4 with other dishes

2 sweetheart cabbages, flappy
outer leaves discarded and
cabbages cut into quarters
60 g (2¼ oz/4 tablespoons)
butter
100 g (3½ oz) brown shrimp
1 tablespoon lemon juice
sea salt and freshly ground
black or white pepper

Also known by its far trendier moniker, 'hispi cabbage', the
sweetheart cabbage was made for grilling. Halved and on the
grill, the frilly leaves burn a little, while the centre softens and
steams. I love it with a lemon-laced butter and lots of tiny brown
shrimp, which are soft and buttery themselves.

— Prepare a barbecue for direct cooking over medium heat.
— Cook the cabbage quarters in a pan of boiling salted water
for 2 minutes, then drain.
— Melt the butter in a small saucepan. Once the cabbage
quarters are drained, brush each with just a little of the
melted butter.
— Grill over direct heat for 6–8 minutes on each side,
until charred.
— Add the brown shrimp, lemon juice and some salt and pepper
to the melted butter and cook to warm the shrimp through.
— Arrange the cabbage quarters cut side up on a plate and pour
the shrimp butter over.

To Cook Indoors: Preheat a cast-iron griddle pan over a high
heat for at least 5 minutes. Once the cabbage has been blanched,
char on the griddle pan on high heat until well charred and
cooked through.

Pork Cheek Tacos
with Wild Garlic Crema

Setup: Indirect cooking
Wood: Oak, beech or apple
Equipment: Tongs, drip tray,
tortilla press
Prep time: 1 hour
Cook time: 4–5 hours
Serves: 4–6

Pork cheeks

1 tablespoon chipotle powder
1 tablespoon light brown sugar
1 tablespoon dried oregano
1 tablespoon ground cumin
2 teaspoons onion powder
2 teaspoons garlic powder
2 generous pinches of salt
1 kg (2 lb 4 oz) pork cheeks,
trimmed of fat or sinew
300 ml (10 fl oz/1¼ cups)
orange juice
500 ml (17 fl oz/generous
2 cups) chicken stock (broth)

Wild garlic crema

2 avocados, stoned and peeled
1 tablespoon lime juice
good handful of wild garlic
(ramson) leaves, washed
thoroughly

Pink pickled onions

1 red onion, thinly sliced
4 tablespoons lime juice
1 teaspoon salt
2 teaspoons caster sugar

To serve

corn tortillas (page 244)
hot sauce
handful of coriander (cilantro),
chopped

Pork cheeks must be cooked very slowly in order to become soft and melting, and while this is possible on a kettle barbecue, it's going to take ages and use a fair bit of fuel for such small pieces of meat. What I like to do instead is get some wood smoke into them for a couple of hours, then braise the meat to finish it off. This way you can get the best of both worlds.

Although the pig cheeks are rich, these tacos still feel fresh and seasonal thanks to the wild garlic crema and bright pink pickled onions.

— Combine the chipotle powder, light brown sugar, dried oregano, ground cumin, onion powder, garlic powder and salt in a bowl. Rub the spice mixture all over the trimmed pork cheeks.
— Prepare a barbecue for indirect cooking over medium heat, with the coals banked to one side. Position the drip tray in the base of the barbecue on the side without any coals and fill it with about 1 litre (34fl oz/4 ¼ cups) of water. Place the pork cheeks on the grill above the tray and add a chunk of wood to the coals and let it smoulder. Close the lid and the vents until they are a quarter open and smoke on low heat for 2 hours, topping up the charcoal when necessary.
— After this time, remove the cheeks from the barbecue and place them in a casserole dish (Dutch oven). Add the orange juice, stock and a generous pinch of salt and set over low heat on the hob (stovetop). Put the lid on and braise for 2–3 hours more, or until tender.
— To make the pink pickled onions, put the onions in a heatproof bowl, cover with boiling water and let sit for 10 minutes, then drain and return to the bowl. Combine the lime juice, salt and sugar and mix well. Pour the mixture over the onions and set aside while you make the remaining components.
— Make the avocado and wild garlic crema by combining the avocado flesh, lime juice and wild garlic in a blender with a generous pinch of salt and blending to a puree.
— Once the cheeks are ready, shred the meat and combine it with a little of the juice from the dish. Serve with the pickled onions, crema, tortillas, hot sauce and coriander (cilantro).

Langoustines
with a Spicy, Sour and Herbal Dip

Setup: Direct cooking
Equipment: Tongs
Prep time: 10 minutes
Cook time: 2–3 minutes
Serves: 4

---

12 live langoustines

Spicy, sour and herbal dip
3 tablespoons fish sauce
3–4 tablespoons lime juice
1 spring onion (scallion),
thinly sliced
1 teaspoon palm sugar
(or light brown sugar)
2 bird's eye chillies, thinly
sliced (add more if you like
it spicier!)
2 tablespoons finely chopped
coriander (cilantro) leaves
and stalks

Langoustines fall very much into the celebration and show-off categories for me – they're not cheap so I only buy them for special occasions or when I just fancy a blow-out. I save their spiny shells afterwards and put them in the freezer for making shellfish stock (broth), to really get my money's worth. If langoustines aren't available, you could serve the hot and herbal dip with some plump prawns (shrimp) instead.

— Prepare a barbecue for direct cooking over medium heat.
— Combine all the dip ingredients in a bowl and set aside.
— Dispatch the langoustines by cutting through them lengthways from the tip of the head, through the body using a large, sharp knife. This will also butterfly them so that you can open them out – gently press down on them with the heel of your hand.
— Grill the langoustines flesh side down over direct heat for 2 minutes, then turn them over and continue cooking them very briefly – just 20–30 seconds. Remove and serve immediately with the dip.

To Cook Indoors: Cook the langoustines in heavily salted boiling water for 3–4 minutes, then drain.

Herby Spatchcock Street Chicken
with Chicken-fat New Potatoes

Setup: Indirect cooking
Equipment: Drip tray, tongs,
heatproof gloves (optional)
Prep time: 15 minutes
Cook time: 1 hour
Serves: 4

1 chicken
(around 2.5 kg/5 lb 8 oz)
grated zest of 3 lemons and
juice of 1 lemon
8 dried bay leaves
2 teaspoons dried rosemary
2 tablespoons dried thyme
1 teaspoon dried oregano
½ teaspoon ground white
pepper
1 kg (2 lb 4 oz) small new
potatoes such as Jersey
Royals, halved if large
(all the potatoes should be
roughly the same size)
500 ml (17 fl oz/generous
2 cups) chicken stock
sea salt

I came up with this recipe purely because my friend Chris
wouldn't stop going on about the street rotisserie chickens he
used to eat in Spain as a kid. Like, seriously: would, not, stop.
They were, apparently, rubbed with a dry herb mixture and
almost certainly quite dry themselves, but nostalgia is a funny
thing – he has been searching for a similar chicken experience
for the last 30 years. I fed him this chicken and he said it was
'very close' to the original, so there we go: make it and get your
own dose of Spanish street life.

The idea is that the potatoes catch the chicken drippings, so
make sure you get a good-quality chicken with plenty of fat on it
and keep the potatoes small, otherwise they won't cook in time.

— Spatchcock the chicken by placing it breast side down on
a board and cutting up either side of the backbone with sharp
kitchen scissors. Remove the bone, turn the bird over and press
down firmly with the heel of your hand.
— Squeeze the lemon juice over the bird. In a bowl, mix the
lemon zest with a few pinches of salt and the herbs and pepper.
Rub the mixture all over the bird.
— Prepare a barbecue for indirect cooking over medium heat,
with the coals banked to one side. Position the drip tray in the
base of the barbecue, on the side without any coals. Place the
potatoes in the tray and add the stock.
— Position the spatchcocked chicken breast side up, legs facing
towards the coals, on the grill above the potato tray and cook
for about 1 hour, with the lid closed and the vents around
a quarter open, until cooked through. If you have a probe
thermometer, it should register 74°C (165°F) when inserted
into the thickest part of a thigh. Allow the chicken to rest for
15 minutes before serving with the potatoes, which will have
collected all the chicken drippings and soaked up the stock.

To Cook Indoors: Preheat the oven to 180°C (375°F/gas 4).
Pour the stock into a roasting tray and put the potatoes in it,
then the chicken, breast side up, on top. Cook for 1 hour 10
minutes to 1 hour 30 minutes, or until the chicken is cooked
through. The chicken skin can be crisped under a hot grill for
5–10 minutes.

Chicken Wings
with Tahini and Za'atar

Setup: Indirect cooking
Equipment: Tongs
Prep time: 25 minutes, plus
minimum 3 hours marinating
time (or overnight if possible)
Cook time: 30 minutes
Serves: 6–8

1 tablespoon Turkish red
pepper paste (biber salçasi)
75 ml (2½ fl oz/5 tablespoons)
sunflower oil
juice of 1 lemon
4 garlic cloves, crushed
or finely grated
1 heaped tablespoon pul biber
20 chicken wings (separated
into flats and drums if you like
(discard the tips or put them
in the freezer as I do, to use
for making chicken stock)
sea salt

Za'atar
150 g (5½ oz) sesame seeds
4 teaspoons sea salt
2 tablespoons sumac
2 tablespoons dried chilli
flakes
2 tablespoons dried thyme
1 tablespoon dried oregano
1 teaspoon ras el hanout
½ teaspoon rose petals

Tahini sauce
8 garlic cloves, crushed
6 tablespoons tahini
juice of 4 lemons
2 tablespoons olive oil

These wings went down a storm when I cooked them for
a Lebanese-themed supper club in collaboration with Château
Ka – a winery based out in the Beqaa Valley. The wings at that
supper club were oven-cooked not grilled but trust me, they
absolutely would've been had I had access to a barbecue.

Could you use shop-bought za'atar for this? Absolutely,
although it won't be the same dish, so please bear that in mind.
The recipe below makes a large batch, tastes about 1,000 times
nicer and is good for throwing on anything from your eggs in the
morning to flatbreads, salads and grilled fish. Both the tahini
sauce and za'atar can be made the day before.

— Combine the red pepper paste, sunflower oil, lemon juice,
garlic and pul biber to make the marinade. Place the wings in
a non-reactive dish and add the marinade, mixing well to make
sure they're well coated. Cover and refrigerate overnight,
or for at least 3 hours.
— To make the za'atar, first toast the sesame seeds in a dry
frying pan over a medium heat until golden, keeping a careful
eye on them to make sure they don't burn, and stirring
regularly. Allow them to cool, then mix with all the other
ingredients. Store in an airtight container away from bright
light. The za'atar will stay fresh for a few weeks.
— To make the tahini sauce, mix the crushed garlic in a bowl
with the tahini. Slowly whisk in the lemon juice and loosen with
a splash of cold water and some salt. Finally, whisk in the olive
oil. It should be nice and sharp, and well-seasoned.
— Prepare a barbecue for indirect cooking over medium heat,
with the coals arranged in the centre of the barbecue and space
around the edge.
— Once the barbecue is ready, arrange the marinated wings in
a circle around the coals, but not directly over them. Cook the
wings for about 30 minutes, turning them every so often, until
cooked through and caramelised. You can move the wings
further into the centre of the barbecue as the coals burn down.
— Serve the wings drizzled with the tahini sauce and sprinkled
with the za'atar.

To Cook Indoors: Preheat the oven to 200°C (400°F/gas 6).
Bake the wings in the oven on a roasting tray for about
45 minutes, or until crispy and cooked through.

Crisp Quails
with Garlic Mayonnaise and Watercress Salad

Setup: Direct cooking
Equipment: Tongs
Prep time: 15 minutes
Cook time: 8–10 minutes
Serves: 4

8 quails
neutral oil, for cooking

Garlic mayonnaise
2 egg yolks
½ teaspoon Dijon mustard
100 ml (3½ fl oz/scant ½ cup)
neutral oil
50 ml (1¾ fl oz/3½ tablespoons)
light olive oil
1 really fat garlic clove,
crushed or finely grated
1 teaspoon lemon juice
sea salt and freshly ground
black or white pepper

Watercress salad
1 teaspoon Dijon mustard
2 tablespoons lemon juice
4 tablespoons extra virgin
olive oil
pinch of sugar
160 g (5½ oz) watercress

Little quails are a joy to cook on the grill: they take minutes and their skin goes lovely and crisp. I like to nibble every last piece of meat off them, dunking them regularly into thick, wobbly garlic mayo. Some charred sourdough would be great with this if you wanted bulk it out because, let's face it, it's another vehicle for garlic mayonnaise and that should always be encouraged.

— First, make the garlic mayonnaise. Combine the egg yolks and mustard in the bowl of a stand mixer fitted with the whisk attachment, or in a large, clean bowl if using a hand whisk, and whisk briefly to combine. With the motor running (or the hand whisking), very slowly begin adding the neutral oil, a drop at a time, making sure each drop is incorporated before adding the next. As the mayonnaise begins to thicken, you can start adding the oil in a thin, steady stream, whisking constantly. Once it's all used up, add the olive oil in the same way. Whisk in the lemon juice and garlic and season really well with salt and pepper.
— Make the dressing for the watercress salad by combining all the ingredients except the watercress with some salt and pepper in a clean lidded jar or bowl and shake or whisk to combine.
— Prepare a barbecue for direct cooking over medium heat.
— Trim the wing tips off the quails using kitchen scissors, then use the scissors to cut out their backbones before turning them over and gently pressing them flat.
— Rub the quails with a little neutral oil and grill for 8–10 minutes over direct heat, until cooked through, moving them to the cooler edges if they start to burn. You want the skin to be crisp!
— Combine the watercress with the dressing and serve at once with the quails and the garlic mayonnaise.

To Cook Indoors: Preheat the oven to 200°C (400°F/gas 6). Don't spatchcock the quails but rub them with oil, season and roast in the oven for about 20 minutes, or until cooked through.

Brined and Grilled Chicken Salad
with a Buttermilk Dressing

Setup: Indirect cooking
Equipment: Large container
for brining, tongs
Prep time: 15 minutes,
plus overnight brining time
Cook time: 45 minutes
Serves: 4

Chicken
1 chicken (2.5 kg/5 lb 8 oz)
5 tablespoons sea salt
5 tablespoons caster sugar
1 head of garlic, cloves
smashed and peeled
zest of 2 lemons in strips
2 onions, halved
a few bay leaves
1 sprig of rosemary
a few sprigs of thyme
2 litres (68 fl oz/8½ cups) water

Buttermilk dressing
150 ml (5 fl oz/⅔ cup)
buttermilk
2 tablespoons mayonnaise
1 garlic clove, crushed
2 tablespoons lemon juice
freshly ground black pepper

Toasted seed mix
40 g (1½ oz) mixed seeds
1 tablespoon onion flakes
or onion granules
1 teaspoon sea salt

Salad
1 soft (butterhead) lettuce
4 spring onions (scallions),
thinly sliced at an angle
5 radishes, thinly sliced
1 fennel bulb, thinly sliced

Brining a chicken can be fun; basically you submerge the bird in a salt solution overnight and enjoy juicier meat the next day. The brine seasons the chicken and also provides another opportunity to add flavour, such as bay leaves, garlic and so on.

It's not a problem if you don't have time or don't fancy doing it, however: the dish will still be a keeper. The words 'chicken salad' might conjure memories of limp pre-packed sandwiches or layered supermarket lunches, but this couldn't be more different. The plumpest bird and its burnished skin; soft lettuce and crisp fennel; a light buttermilk dressing; and a topping of toasted seeds and onion flakes. Dare I say it would make a very good sandwich?

— First, spatchcock the chicken by placing it breast side down on a board and cutting up either side of the backbone with sharp kitchen scissors. Remove the backbone, turn the bird over and press down firmly with the heel of your hand.
— Combine the salt, sugar, garlic, lemon zest strips, onion halves, bay leaves, rosemary and thyme with the water, whisking until the salt and sugar have dissolved. Pour this into a plastic tub or other large container, submerge the chicken, cover and refrigerate overnight.
— When you're ready to cook, remove the spatchcocked chicken from the brine and pat the chicken dry.
— Prepare a barbecue for indirect cooking over medium heat, with the coals banked to one side. Crisp the chicken first over direct heat, then move to indirect heat with the legs facing towards the coals, and cook slowly with the lid closed and vents around a quarter open for about 45 minutes, until cooked through. If you have a probe thermometer, it should register 74°C/165°F when inserted into the thickest part of a thigh.
— Make the buttermilk dressing by whisking all the ingredients together with a good grind of black pepper.
— Lightly toast the seeds in a dry frying pan, then transfer to a bowl and stir in the onion flakes and sea salt.
— Combine the salad ingredients and coat with half the buttermilk dressing. Divide among four plates.
— Allow the chicken to rest for 15 minutes, then carve and put on top of the salad, finally scattering with the seed mixture.

To Cook Indoors: Preheat the oven to 180°C (350°F/gas 4). Roast the chicken breast side up in a roasting tray for 1 hour 10 minutes–1 hour 30 minutes, or until cooked through, then pop under a hot grill for 5–10 minutes to crisp up the skin.

Foraging, Pickling and Preserving

What do foraging, pickling and preserving have to do with barbecue? This was the (perfectly reasonable) question posed to me by my editor over Zoom one morning. The fact is that pickling and preserving are so much a part of my kitchen routines and recipes that it hadn't occurred to me that they might not fit with a certain style of cooking. We might think of pickles and 'cue as an American 'thing' and it is (dill pickles with white bread and onions alongside Texas barbecue, for example), but for me, any seasonal pickle is game for biting through the richness of a fatty piece of meat, and I love a quick pickled onion with oleaginous fish. I love the feral funk of kimchi with a beef taco, and the lighter sting of pickled fennel with a slow-grilled chicken.

Pickling and preserving is often about tricking time; making a stockpile of good things to enjoy when they're out of season. I love the last of the season's nectarines pickled for pork in the few weeks where the morning air is noticeably cooler, rosemary-pickled green beans with autumn lamb, and fermented tomatoes in a winter salad. Pickled Brussels Sprouts and Brussels Sprout Kimchi are two of my winter non-negotiables, the kimchi an essential sidekick to a smoked ham (and a really good addition to a Stilton and leftovers toastie).

Pickles cut richness, they add interest and I've always been a sucker for anything lip puckering. That said, pickles need more sugar than you think, which is why my basic brine is on the sweet side. It's just more food friendly, and they quickly become something you'll want to chuck on everything rather than just looking good on the shelf.

If pickles are an essential barbecue side, then hot sauce is an essential condiment. I have never been interested in heat for heat's sake – the flavour combined with heat is what makes a chilli special, and it's why I've become so obsessed with the scotch bonnet over the years. That crackling electric burn combined with lingering tropical perfume is very hard to beat. It is by far the queen of chillies in my eyes, and I love to combine it with equally fragrant fruits such as quince, mango or pineapple.

Would I smoke chillies on the barbecue? Absolutely, and I know a man who does. Ben Farey makes a sauce called Peckham Smoker, using scotch bonnets that he ferments for three months at a time, then preserves using a churning method, which allows the vinegar to break down the chilli naturally and prevent separation. He combines this mixture with smoked jalapeños, which he began smoking in his back garden in an old filing cabinet (methods have since been upgraded, not least because his neighbours started complaining about the smoke). The end result is a 'keep it in your handbag', everyday hot sauce, which is quite an achievement when you think about how many hot sauces miss that mark.

While I've yet to experiment with a smoked chilli hot sauce, I absolutely love fermenting them, and the results are perfect for serving with pretty much anything that comes off your grill. A good place to start is my Quince and Scotch Bonnet Hot Sauce (page 217) and perhaps you'd like to move onto Scotch Bonnet Pickled Pineapple (page 251) or Jerk-spiced Pineapple Relish (page 251). I told you I really love chilli...

But what about foraging? Well, it's something that, at first, just added another layer of fun to preserving. I mainly forage in springtime, when three-cornered leek, wild garlic and nettles are abundant. Three-cornered leek is a triangular-stemmed allium with small white flowers, each sporting a green central stripe. I use them in pickles and ferments, to garnish tacos or chop finely into mayonnaise or a salsa. Wild garlic is the urban forager's gateway drug; a few leaves picked in a graveyard leads to one jar of pesto leads to at least 10 wild garlic posts on Instagram. I know, I've been there. Now, I mostly ferment it into kraut (page 67) where it brings a real donkey kick of pungency. Go funky or go home.

Nettles are the real steal of the season, however. Truly a weed that everyone avoids, for obvious reasons, they are fantastic when young, with a strong, iron-rich flavour that's like a grassier version of spinach. Use gloves to pick the young tips, and make sure to wash them well before blanching to remove the sting. They can then be handled and eaten. We use them in a stuffing for lamb like the Leg of Lamb Stuffed with Nettles, Wild Garlic and Seaweed overleaf. I suppose I have a penchant for foraging 'green things', then, rather than berries, fruits and the like, and I think it's because I am most enthusiastic about the idea of bothering to go out and find food rather than just buying it in the spring time. Green is hopeful.

Foraging is as much about slowing down and taking time to appreciate your immediate surroundings in a different way as it is about finding something edible. As John Rensten points out in his book, *The Edible City*, this is particularly true of urban foraging. 'Putting on your foraging goggles will transform your city surroundings, from somewhere to be hurried through, to a place to be lingered over.' For me, this also sums up the transformative power of the words, 'Let's have a barbecue?' which are like a catalyst for the loosening of boundaries and easing of formalities surrounding what should and shouldn't happen at mealtimes. The mere suggestion of a barbecue is a euphemism for 'let's just chill' - at least it is in this house.

Leg of Lamb
Stuffed
with Nettles,
Wild Garlic
and Seaweed

Setup: Indirect cooking
Equipment: Drip tray, tongs,
heatproof gloves
Prep time: 10 minutes
Cook time: 1 hour
Serves: 8

100 g (3½ oz) nettles, washed
(wear gloves!)
100 g (3½ oz) pine nuts
10 g (¼ oz) dried seaweed, such
as nori, blitzed to a powder
grated zest of 1 lemon
150 g (5½ oz) wild garlic
(ramsons), washed
2 tablespoons olive oil
1 tablespoon sea salt,
plus extra for the lamb
1 lamb leg (shank end),
deboned and butterflied
(a butcher will do this for you)

This is a fun stuffing for lamb; nettles have such an iron-rich twang to them, which is enhanced by the iodine character of the seaweed. There had to be wild garlic (ramsons) here, too – spring's must-have ingredient for the on-trend griller. It's available to buy if you can't forage it yourself, or you can just use regular garlic. I won't tell anyone.

Nettles are much easier to come by than wild garlic – just make sure you pick the tender spring tips and, obviously, wear gloves. Once blanched, the sting will disappear and they're safe to handle and eat. I'd serve this with the New Potato Salad with Onion and Herbs (page 68), or with some Easy Barbecue Flatbreads (page 60), salad and natural yoghurt, for making wraps.

— Blanch the nettles in boiling water for 1 minute. Drain and squeeze out excess water (they will have lost their sting now).
— Put the nettles in a blender with the pine nuts, dried seaweed powder, lemon zest, wild garlic, olive oil and salt, and pulse to a coarse paste.
— Open out the lamb leg and rub the paste all over it, getting into every corner of the meat. Roll it back up and secure with string – there are fancy ways of doing this with butcher's knots but honestly, I usually just tie several loops of string tightly around it in each direction.

— Prepare a barbecue for indirect cooking over medium heat, with the coals banked to either side and a drip tray positioned between them to catch the fat. Once the drip tray is in position, pour 1 litre (34 fl oz/4¼ cups) water into it (this will stop the fat burning on the bottom and create some lovely steam).
— Season the outside of the lamb with salt, then place it on the grill, over the drip tray. Cook for about 1 hour (turning halfway through), or until a probe thermometer registers 66°C (150°F) for medium-cooked meat (you don't want the meat too rare for this recipe, as the stuffing needs to warm through).
— Allow the lamb to rest for 10 minutes before serving.

To Cook Indoors: Preheat the oven to 170°C (340°F/gas 3). Roast the lamb in a roasting tray with a glass of white wine or stock in the bottom for about 1 hour 45 minutes.

Xinjiang-style Cumin and Chilli Lamb Skewers

Setup: Direct cooking
Equipment: Tongs,
4 long metal skewers
Prep time: 5 minutes
Cook time: 10 minutes
Serves: 4

2 tablespoons ground cumin
1 tablespoon dried chilli flakes
2 teaspoons sea salt
800 g (1 lb 12 oz) lamb rump,
meat diced and fat trimmed
and diced separately

Anyone who lives in South East London knows a restaurant called Silk Road, which serves food from the Xinjiang autonomous territory of China. This North Western region is situated at the convergence of the 'stans (Pakistan, Afghanistan, Kazakhstan, Kyrgyzstan, Tajikstan), and flavours are influenced by the Middle East, which explains the use of cumin in this dish. They're usually cooked on the street, where the scent of hot fat hitting coals effortlessly lures customers.

Smoke is so important to the flavour of this dish, which is why there are cubes of fat on the skewers as well as meat: for the all-important sizzles. Those chunks can be eaten too, of course, but do it fast as they are much less appealing once cool. To be honest, I tend to see them as an aid to cooking rather than a large part of the eating experience, although you (and I'm sure many others) may feel differently. The amount of spicing is generous, and deliberately so.

Eat the skewers with rice, noodles or flatbreads (the Uyghur people of Xinjiang would have *nang*, similar to an Indian naan). If you're eating them with breads, lay those on top of the skewers as they finish cooking, to soak up some of that aforementioned fat.

— Prepare a barbecue for direct cooking over medium-low heat.
— Combine the cumin, chilli flakes and salt in a bowl.
— Combine the diced lamb and a little of the diced fat with two-thirds of the spice mix. Rub the spice mix all over the meat, reserving the extra spice mix for cooking and sprinkling.
— Thread the meat onto skewers, alternating every so often with a piece of the fat. Grill the skewers over low-medium direct heat for about 5 minutes on each side, sprinkling them with some of the remaining spice mix now and then.
— The skewers are ready when the meat is cooked through and caramelised. Sprinkle with the remaining spice mix.
— Eat immediately!

To Cook Indoors: Cook under a hot grill for 5 minutes on each side and sprinkle with the remaining spice mix before serving.

Lamb Chops
with Charred Chilli Sauce

Setup: Indirect cooking
Equipment: Tongs
Prep time: 10 minutes, plus
minimum 1 hour marinating
time (a few hours if possible)
Cook time: 5–10 minutes
Serves: 2 as a main dish,
4 with other dishes

8 lamb chops

Charred chilli sauce
5 red chillies
2 teaspoons cumin seeds
2 teaspoons coriander seeds
1 teaspoon caraway seeds
1 garlic clove, peeled
6 tablespoons olive oil
4 tablespoons red wine
vinegar
1 tablespoon lemon juice
large handful of coriander
(cilantro) stalks and leaves
small handful of mint leaves
sea salt

We eat a lot of lamb chops in this house; in fact, they're probably our number-one speedy dinner option, with a big salad on the side. If there's no time to marinate them, then we rub them with loads of big flavours - crackling spices and lip-jolting acidity - then cook them hot and fast until their fat drips and frizzles. There's a lot of fun to be had in nibbling around the bones. I love the drama of taking a big plate of chops and a stack of napkins to the table and watching the carnage unfold.

— I like to use half of this sauce to marinate the lamb chops, so tend to char the chillies indoors (as I'm probably not going to light the barbecue just to char some chillies). There are several ways to do this - either in a dry pan over a high heat, under a hot grill or directly over a gas flame. Char them until blackened, then put into a bowl and cover for a minute. Remove and slip off the skins (it's up to you whether or not you keep the seeds).
— Lightly toast the cumin, coriander and caraway seeds in a dry pan over medium-low heat until fragrant, giving the pan a shake every now and then to ensure they don't burn.
— Place the charred chillies in a blender with the toasted spices and all the other ingredients except the lamb chops, plus a generous pinch of salt, and blend until you have a smooth-ish sauce.
— Use half the sauce to marinate the lamb chops for at least 1 hour (leave them for a few hours in the fridge, covered, if you can).
— When you're ready to eat, prepare a barbecue for indirect cooking over medium heat.
— Grill the lamb chops over direct heat, moving them a little offset to cook if they start to burn. The cooking time will depend on the thickness of the chops, but a few minutes on each side for small chops should do it.
— Serve with the remaining sauce.

To Cook Indoors: Cook the marinated chops under a hot grill for about 5 minutes on each side.

Onglet
with Scotch Bonnet and Grapefruit

Setup: Direct cooking
Equipment: Tongs
Prep time: 10 minutes
Cook time: 10 minutes
Serves: 2

350 g (12 oz) onglet
200 g (7 oz) vermicelli rice
noodles
2 spring onions (scallions),
very thinly sliced
1 teaspoon toasted sesame oil
2 little gem (bibb) lettuces,
leaves separated
flaky sea salt

Scotch bonnet and grapefruit
dipping sauce
100 ml (3½ fl oz/scant ½ cup)
grapefruit juice
grated zest of ½ grapefruit
2 tablespoons lime juice
1 scotch bonnet chilli,
deseeded and finely chopped
2 tablespoons fish sauce
1 tablespoon honey
2 garlic cloves, crushed or
finely grated
1 tablespoon rice vinegar
1 teaspoon cornflour
(cornstarch)
small handful of mint leaves,
finely shredded

Onglet is so different to other steaks in both flavour and texture. Cut from the lower belly, it has an offaly character that stands up incredibly well to char and smoke. You must cook this cut rare and rest it very well, otherwise it will be too tough to eat. Do it right however (it's actually very easy to get right) and you will be richly rewarded. I love to dunk it into this dipping sauce perfumed with grapefruit and scotch bonnet chilli, and I've added lettuce cups and noodles to make the dish more substantial. This is a messy meal and all the better for it – eat with someone who couldn't care less about the sauce on your chin and stray noodle in your hair.

— Prepare a barbecue for direct cooking over high heat.
— Once the barbecue is ready, season the steak heavily with flaky sea salt on both sides.
— Grill the onglet over direct heat for a few minutes on each side, then rest the steak for 10 minutes.
— Combine all the dipping sauce ingredients except the mint in a small saucepan. Whisk to combine and bring to the boil, whisking all the time, until thickened – a minute or two. Remove from the heat and stir in the mint. Set aside.
— Put the rice noodles in a heatproof bowl, cover with boiling water and soak for 5 minutes, or until tender, then drain. Refresh in a colander under cold running water to cool, then transfer to a bowl and add the spring onions (scallions) and sesame oil. Toss to combine.
— Slice the steak thinly across the grain and serve with the noodles, lettuce leaves and the dipping sauce. Eat by wrapping some rice noodles and steak in a lettuce leaf and dipping it into the sauce.

To Cook Indoors: Preheat a cast-iron griddle pan over a high heat for at least 5 minutes, add the steak and cook for a few minutes on each side, before resting.

Grilling Goat

I first met the UK's most famous 'goat guy' on a freezing day in South London; he'd come to my mate Holly's house* to set up a 3-foot-long spit at the end of her garden, on which he would cook a giant goat shawarma. In a blizzard.

It was a shoot for our magazine, *Pit*, and we'd invited 30 people round to help us eat what was, essentially, a whole goat. The snow turned the garden into a mud bath very quickly, but James was a trooper, dutifully tending the rotating kebab as a bunch of raucous Londoners sunk multiple beers around him in an effort to keep warm. He still tells me it was his favourite ever 'cook'.

This gives you some idea of the kind of guy James is: generous, hardworking, and always up for a laugh. He's also very handy on the barbecue, as it happens, not to mention a James Beard Award-winning author (some people are just annoying like that). He won that award for his book *Goat*, which is a collection of recipes and a record of his work towards solving a big problem within the UK dairy-goat industry: unwanted male kid goats. Unable to produce dairy, the goats were being euthanised at birth.

James was working as a chef at the time his company, Cabrito, was conceived and (to cut a much longer story short) he tried putting goat on his menu. It sold out and he realised he was onto something. James now sells around 30 per cent of all the male kid goats in the UK under the name Cabrito Goat Meat.

Goats arrived in Britain at around 6000BC, having already proved themselves useful as far away as western Iran in 11,000BC (again, I must thank James, because I have just gleefully lifted this information from the introduction to *Goat*). As a food (and by extension a travel) writer, I've visited a lot of goat farms around the world, to the point where it became a running joke: rarely would an itinerary be thrust into my hands that was absent of a visit to local goat farmers, and every single visit was a pleasure. Goats are the most incredible animals in that they're good natured, resilient and produce both fantastic dairy and meat. It's no wonder they were the first animals to be domesticated and continue to be farmed prolifically.

On a trip to the Swiss Alps I met a goat-farming couple called Catarina Strassl and Johannes Pobitzer, who lived in a small wooden house on the mountainside, 1000 m (3,300 ft) above sea level. It was summer, and a cut-glass mountain breeze tempered powerful sunshine; absolutely perfect weather. All around us skinny meadow flowers

bobbed and swayed, the scent of nearby pines drifting down through a cloudless sky. The goats were free to roam the slopes, their heads dipping and nimble hooves picking a path slowly across the mountain. It was here that I learned lots about their temperament from Catarina, who described their tolerant nature and preference for a varied diet: 'they would rather die' than eat the same meal every day, she told me. At the back of the house, behind a wooden door, Johannes had a giant copper pot set over a crackling wood fire. Here he carefully heats the goat milk for cheese; it's hard work and technically challenging – too much or too little heat and the cheese will be ruined. Even when done correctly, 'there are always some surprises with cheesemaking'.

Goat farming is important not just in Switzerland, but all across Europe. However, it never really took off in the UK thanks to the high demand for English wool. Goat meat remained peasant food and therefore our records of how it was eaten and farmed are practically non-existent. Even now, many in the UK will turn their nose up at the cheese found on every supermarket shelf, complaining that it smells 'goaty' (well, duh), and by extension they can't imagine eating the meat, which they would probably discover is fabulous and tastes a lot like lamb.

Goat meat works particularly well on the barbecue thanks to that robust flavour. I was once lucky enough to share a whole barbecued goat grilled high up in the Andes in Chile's Coquimbo region; the animal was slow-roasted for 3 hours over glowing embers, the skin rubbed periodically with onion and sprayed with beer through a hole poked in the can. This isn't so practical for the back garden at home, though. I often cook the chops, which are tender and can take aggressive, crackling spice (see opposite), while the shoulder responds incredibly well to slow cooking until the connective tissues break down and the meat can be pulled apart – try the Slow-smoked Shoulder of Goat with Bay and English Mustard Barbecue Sauce on page 58.

I hope these recipes will give you a taste of this fabulous meat. If we are going to farm goats for dairy, then we should make use of the males: a whole animal should not be considered a 'by-product'. I promise you that once you taste goat meat cooked over fire, you will need no further persuasion.

*Holly also designed this book!

Page 55: James' gigantic goat shawarma, being sliced.
Above top: James seasons the shawarma.
Above: James with his masterpiece, ready to cook.

Spiced
Goat Chops

Setup: Direct cooking
Equipment: Tongs
Prep time: 5 minutes
Cook time: 8–10 minutes
Serves: 4

2 tablespoons cumin seeds
4 teaspoons coriander seeds
2 teaspoons fennel seeds
10 garlic cloves, crushed
or finely grated
2 tablespoons pul biber
2 tablespoons Urfa chilli
2 tablespoons sumac
2 really generous pinches
of sea salt
6 tablespoons neutral oil
1 kg (2 lb 4 oz) kid goat chops

Goat chops are begging to be barbecued. I never bother marinating them for this recipe as there's so much flavour going on, but of course you could if you have time (or are more organised). The idea is that the chops get blackened and charred and the result is a big, hot, delicious mess. Serve them on top of flatbreads, with cold yoghurt straight from the fridge, and a big salad. If you can't get hold of goat chops, lamb chops will work well.

— Toast the cumin seeds, coriander seeds and fennel seeds in a dry frying pan over a medium-low heat until fragrant (moving them around so they don't burn). Add to a spice grinder or pestle and mortar and grind or crush to a coarse powder.
— Mix the toasted spices with all the other ingredients in a bowl and smother the mixture all over the goat chops.
— Prepare a barbecue for indirect cooking over medium heat, with the coals banked to one side and sloping into the middle.
— Cook the goat chops in the central section of the barbecue for 4–5 minutes each side, moving them towards the heat if you want to crisp them up, and away from the heat if they start to flare up. Personally, I like them still a little pink in the middle.

To Cook Indoors: Cook the chops under a hot grill for about 5 minutes on each side.

Slow-smoked Shoulder of Goat *with Bay and English Mustard Barbecue Sauce*

Setup: Indirect cooking
Wood: Oak
Equipment: Roasting tray, heatproof gloves
Prep time: 5 minutes
Cook time: 6 hours
Serves: 8

2.5 kg (5 lb 8 oz) kid goat shoulder

Bay rub
1 tablespoon garlic powder
2 teaspoons paprika
1 teaspoon English mustard powder
20 dried bay leaves
2 teaspoons salt

English mustard barbecue sauce
100 g (3½ oz) English mustard
100 g (3½ oz/½ cup) light brown sugar
50 ml (1¾ fl oz/3¼ tablespoons) cider vinegar
2 tablespoons ketchup
1 tablespoon Worcestershire sauce
½ teaspoon celery salt
½ teaspoon ground white pepper

This is a British riff on the whole 'pulled slow-cooked meat and tangy barbecue sauce' genre. Kid goat is what you want here; rubbed with blitzed bay leaves, it's cooked for hours then teased apart in tender chunks with pockets of glistening fat.

The quantity of English mustard in the sauce is not a typo; this is a deliberately powerful barbecue sauce. I love it. Serve the goat with something like the Grilled Sugar Snap Peas with Mint on page 21, and perhaps some Grilled Jersey Royals with Rosemary (page 71) or buttery boiled new potatoes.

— Put all the rub ingredients into a spice grinder or small food processor and blitz to a fine powder. Rub the powder all over the meat.

— Prepare a barbecue for indirect cooking over medium heat, with the coals banked to one side. Place the goat shoulder in the roasting tray and add a cupful of water. Add a chunk of wood to the coals and let it smoulder. Place the goat on the cooler side of the barbecue. Shut the lid, leave the vents around a quarter open and cook for about 6 hours, or until the goat is tender. Top up the charcoal as necessary, adding a few chunks of wood throughout the cooking time.

— Combine all the sauce ingredients in a small saucepan and heat gently. Simmer for 5 minutes, remove from the heat, cover and allow to cool.

— Rest the meat for 30 minutes before pulling it apart and serving it with the mustard barbecue sauce.

To Cook Indoors: Preheat the oven to 130°C (260°F/gas 2) and cook the goat shoulder in a roasting tray with a cupful of water for 5 hours, or until very tender.

Easy Barbecue Flatbreads

Setup: Direct cooking
Equipment: Tongs
Prep time: 10 minutes, plus 30
minutes–1 hour rising time
Cook time: 5 minutes
Makes: 4 large or 8 small
flatbreads

Dough
500 g (1 lb 2 oz/3 cups plus
2 tablespoons) '00' flour,
plus extra for dusting
2 teaspoons instant yeast
300 ml (10 fl oz/1¼ cups)
hand-hot water
2 tablespoons olive oil
10 g (¼ oz) salt

These flatbreads took on a life of their own on the internet. People started referring to me on Instagram as 'the flatbread lady'. There's nothing groundbreaking about my flatbread recipe but I think it appeals to people because it's really easy and works every time. There's nothing quite as satisfying as puffy, steaming bread hot off the grill. Use them to wrap the various kebabs in this book like the Adana Kebabs on page 203; swipe them through dips like those on the smoky aubergine (eggplant) spectrum on pages 113–115; and top them with pretty much anything you fancy, like a sort-of pizza. It is possible to make pizzas on the barbecue but you really need a pizza stone or, ideally, a pizza oven – this is a simple idea that works when you don't have either.

— Combine the ingredients in a bowl and mix to combine. Knead for 5 minutes until smooth and elastic (you can do this either by hand or in a stand mixer fitted with the dough hook attachment).
— Place in a lightly oiled bowl, cover and let it rise until doubled in size – this will take anything from 30 minutes to 1 hour.
— Just before you roll out the dough, prepare a barbecue for direct cooking over medium heat.
— Divide the dough into 4 equal pieces (or 8 smaller pieces) and roll them out on a lightly floured surface to roughly 23 cm/9 in (or 15 cm/6 in) in diameter.
— Cook the flatbreads on a hot barbecue over direct heat for a minute or so, turning once, until puffy and charred in places.
— Repeat with the remaining flatbreads, although keep the raw dough well away from the barbecue, where it will melt!

To Cook Indoors: Preheat a cast-iron griddle pan over a high heat for at least 5 minutes. Cook the flatbreads one by one in the dry pan for a minute or so on each side, or until puffed and slightly charred.

4 garlic cloves, crushed,
plus 1 finely chopped
300 g (10½ oz) crème fraîche
4 tablespoons chopped
parsley
grated zest of 1 lemon
150 g (5½ oz) shelled cockles
2 tablespoons chilli flakes
4 tablespoons grated Pecorino
extra virgin olive oil,
for drizzling
sea salt and freshly ground
black pepper

Garlic Crème Fraîche, Cockles and Gremolata Topping

— Combine the 4 cloves of crushed garlic with the crème fraîche
in a bowl and season with salt and pepper. Set aside.
— Combine the clove of finely chopped garlic with the parsley
and lemon zest in a bowl to make a gremolata. Set aside.
— Once you've rolled out your flatbread dough, put one on the
barbecue and wait until it's cooked on one side, then flip it over
and quickly top it with a spoon of the crème fraîche, some
cockles and chilli flakes, then continue to cook until the base is
crisp. Once this happens, move the flatbread to the indirect side
of the barbecue and cook for a minute or two more with the lid
on, to make sure the topping is warmed through.
— Finish with the gremolata, a swirl of olive oil and
grated Pecorino.
— Repeat with the remaining flatbreads.

250 g (9 oz) asparagus,
woody ends trimmed
4 garlic cloves, crushed
300 g (10½ oz) crème fraîche
4 handfuls of grated Parmesan
extra virgin olive oil,
for drizzling
dried chilli flakes, to taste
sea salt and freshly ground
black pepper

Garlic Crème Fraîche, Asparagus and Parmesan Topping

— Blanch the asparagus in boiling water for 2 minutes,
then drain well and cut into short lengths.
— Combine the crushed garlic with the crème fraîche in a bowl
and season with salt and pepper. Set aside.
— Once you've rolled out your flatbread dough, put one on the
barbecue and wait until it's cooked on one side, then flip it over
and quickly top it with a spoon of the crème fraîche, some
asparagus and grated Parmesan, then continue to cook until
the base is crisp. Once this happens, move the flatbread to the
indirect side of the barbecue and cook for a minute or two more
with the lid on, to make sure the topping is warmed through.
— Finish with a swirl of olive oil and some chilli flakes.
— Repeat with the remaining flatbreads, although keep the raw
dough well away from the barbecue.

150 g (5½ oz) washed and
roughly chopped wild garlic
(ramsons), plus a handful
for the butter
generous amounts of butter
sea salt and freshly ground
black pepper

Wild Garlic Flatbreads with Wild Garlic Butter

— Mix 150 g (5¼ oz) washed and roughly chopped wild garlic into
the flatbread dough before leaving it to rise. Blanch a handful of
wild garlic leaves briefly in boiling water, drain well, then chop
and mash into softened, seasoned butter, for spreading on top
of the hot flatbreads. I could eat these forever, to be honest.
— Repeat with the remaining flatbreads, although keep the raw
dough well away from the barbecue.

Stuffed Barbecue Flatbreads

Setup: Indirect cooking
Equipment: Tongs, pizza peel or baking tray
Prep time: 10 minutes, plus 1 hour rising time
Cook time: 10 minutes
Makes: 4 large flatbreads

Dough for Stuffed Barbecue Flatbreads
500 g (1 lb 2 oz/3 cups plus 2 tablespoons) '00' flour, plus extra for rolling out
2 teaspoons instant yeast
300 ml (10 fl oz/1¼ cups) hand-hot water
2 tablespoons olive oil
10 g (¼ oz) salt
fine cornmeal polenta, for dusting

What's better than a flatbread? A stuffed flatbread, of course. These are like a fun hot pocket that you can fill with whatever you fancy, as long as it heats up well – cheese is obviously an excellent choice. Here you will find some of my favourite combinations, including spinach and artichoke (based on the great American dip) and… Boursin. As a full-time Boursin enthusiast, I have been asked many times why I think it's so good and the answer is: if you have to ask, you're never going to understand. That one is for you, Boursin Friends (other garlic and herb cream cheeses are available, I guess).

— Combine the flour, yeast, water, olive oil and salt, and mix to combine. Knead for about 5 minutes until smooth and elastic (you can do this either by hand or in a stand mixer fitted with the dough hook attachment). Place in a lightly oiled bowl, cover with a tea towel or cling film (plastic wrap) and set aside in a warm place to rise until doubled in size (30 minutes–1 hour).
— Just before you roll out the dough, prepare a barbecue for indirect cooking over medium heat, with most of the coals banked to one side and just a few in the centre.
— Divide the dough into 4 equal pieces and roll one out on a lightly floured surface. You are looking for a roughly circular shape around 23 cm (9 in) in diameter. Coat the pizza peel or baking tray with polenta and place the dough on top.
— Place a quarter of the filling (your chosen filling, see overleaf) on the bottom half of the dough and fold the top half of the dough over, crimping at the edges like a pasty. Try not to press down too firmly on the peel.
— Cook each flatbread on the barbecue, close to the coals but not directly over them. Once golden and crisp all over, move to the cooler side for a few minutes, to finish cooking through. You will need to turn the flatbreads once using tongs.
— Repeat with the remaining flatbreads, although keep the raw dough well away from the barbecue, where it will melt!

To Cook Indoors: Preheat a cast-iron griddle pan over a high heat for at least 5 minutes and cook the flatbreads one at a time over medium heat for a few minutes on each side. Ensure the filling is hot before serving.

250 g (9 oz) block low-moisture mozzarella, grated
300 g (10½ oz) feta, crumbled
50 g (1¾ oz) chives, finely chopped
25 g (1 oz) tarragon, leaves picked and chopped
1 tablespoon nigella seeds
3 tablespoons honey
2 teaspoons dried chilli flakes
sea salt

Cheese and Herb Flatbread Stuffing with Chilli Honey

You could use the fermented hot garlic honey on page 249 for this instead of the honey and chilli flakes, if you like.

— Make the stuffing mixture by combining the mozzarella, feta, chives, tarragon and nigella seeds in a bowl and mixing well. Taste and add a pinch of salt, if necessary.
— Make the chilli honey by warming the honey and chilli flakes gently in a pan. Serve the honey with the flatbreads.

300 g (10½ oz) Boursin cheese
2 fresh jalapeños (or other green chillies), finely chopped

Jalapeño Popper Flatbread Stuffing

— Combine the Boursin and chopped jalapeños in a bowl and mix well.

150 g (5½ oz) frozen spinach, thawed and excess water squeezed out (or, just warm it through in a pan, and the excess water will evaporate)
280 g (10 oz) jar artichoke hearts in oil, drained and chopped
200 g (7 oz) Rollright, Stinking Bishop or taleggio cheese, diced
100 g (3½ oz) low-moisture mozzarella, grated
bunch of basil, leaves chopped
2 garlic cloves, crushed or finely grated
sea salt and freshly ground black pepper

Spinach, Artichoke and Cheese Flatbread Stuffing

— Mix all the ingredients together in a bowl and season with salt and pepper.

Lamb Neck Fillet
with Artichoke Mayonnaise

Setup: Direct cooking
Equipment: Tongs
Prep time: 10 minutes
Cook time: 15 minutes
Serves: 4

2 lamb neck fillets
neutral oil, for cooking

Artichoke mayonnaise
125 g (4¼ oz) mayonnaise
280 g (10 oz) jar artichoke
hearts in oil, drained well
1 small garlic clove, crushed
small handful of mint leaves,
thinly sliced, plus extra
to garnish
1 teaspoon lemon juice
sea salt and freshly ground
black pepper

Artichoke mayonnaise! It's gorgeous: nutty, rich and so lovely with lamb (and in leftovers sandwiches, of course). You want the yellower varieties of shop-bought mayonnaise for this, rather than Hellman's (I have nothing at all against Hellman's, except the fact that it plain doesn't work in this recipe). Homemade mayonnaise would be lovely, but I never bother making it just for this.

I might serve the lamb and artichoke mayo with the Jersey Royals with Rosemary on page 71 and Spring Coleslaw with Sugar Snaps, Almonds and Miso (page 68).

— Prepare a barbecue for direct cooking over medium heat.
— Put all the ingredients for the mayonnaise in a blender with a pinch of salt and some pepper and blend until smooth-ish (the artichokes will give it some texture).
— Season the lamb neck fillets and rub lightly with oil. Grill over medium-high direct heat for about 8 minutes on each side, for pink lamb. Rest for 10 minutes, then slice and serve with the artichoke mayonnaise.

To Cook Indoors: Preheat a cast-iron griddle pan over a high heat for at least 5 minutes. Cook the lamb neck fillets on the pan for 8–10 minutes on each side for pink lamb.

Charred Spring Onion Salsa Verde

Setup: Direct cooking
Prep time: 5 minutes
Cook time: 5 minutes
Serves: 8 as a condiment

3 bunches of spring onions
(scallions) (about 18)
a small splash of neutral oil,
for cooking the spring onions
handful of mint leaves, finely
chopped
large bunch of basil
leaves, finely chopped
(about 50 g /1¾ oz)
1 tablespoon capers,
finely chopped
about 5 cornichons,
finely chopped
2 garlic cloves, crushed
or finely grated
4 anchovy fillets in oil,
finely chopped
1 tablespoon Dijon mustard
4 tablespoons good-quality red
wine vinegar
6 tablespoons extra virgin
olive oil
sea salt

Salsa verde is a great sauce to have knocking about at
a barbecue because it goes well with so many things: grilled
chicken, fish, vegetables, potatoes and – one of my personal
favourites – steak. This is my standard recipe, beefed up with
some grilled spring onions, which bring body and a sweeter,
gentler version of themselves. The sauce as a whole is electric
though, and a splosh on the plate will make pretty much
anything taste better.

— Prepare a barbecue for direct cooking over medium heat.
— Remove any straggly leaves from the spring onions (scallions)
and toss them with a small splash of neutral oil. Grill over direct
heat, turning regularly, for 5–10 minutes until they're charred
in most places.
— Finely chop the spring onions and combine them with all the
remaining ingredients and a pinch of salt.

To Cook Indoors: Preheat a cast-iron griddle pan for 5 minutes
over high heat.

Fermented Wild Garlic 'Kraut'

Setup: Indoors
Prep time: 20 minutes, plus
fermenting time (about 10
days)
Makes: 1 litre (34 fl oz/4¼ cups)

2 leeks, washed really well
and fairly thinly sliced
6 large spring onions
(scallions), thinly sliced
2 bunches of Swiss chard,
sliced
1 Chinese leaf cabbage, tough
bottom core removed and
tender leaves sliced
6 heads of garlic, cloves peeled
1 tablespoon white miso
100 ml (3½ fl oz/scant ½ cup)
cold water
200 g (7 oz) wild garlic,
sliced into ribbons
fine sea salt

The first thing I do with a batch of wild garlic is preserve it in some way. It's great in kimchi, and also in this 'kraut' which is a bit like a sauerkraut but with more clout. Krautclout. It's really good with barbecued sausages and pork chops and is just generally fun to have around: I like it with eggs in the morning, which is probably quite hardcore (it's worth noting that I do always work from home and therefore rarely bother anyone other than the cats with my garlic breath).

— Weigh the leeks, spring onions (scallions), chard and Chinese leaf, then work out 5% of that weight – this will be the amount of salt you need to use (total weight of vegetables × 0.05).
— Combine the salt with the vegetables in a bowl, mix well and leave in the bowl, covered with a large plate or clean tea towel, at room temperature for 24 hours.
— Rinse the vegetables a couple of times with fresh water and drain well.
— Combine the garlic cloves and white miso with the water in a blender and blend to a paste.
— Mix the miso-garlic paste with the vegetables and wild garlic and transfer to a sterilised jar, pushing everything down really firmly. Weigh the mixture down with something like a small round dish, a plastic bag filled with water (very effective, if not the most environmentally friendly method), or a made-for-purpose weight (widely available online). All the vegetables should be fully immersed in the liquid.
— Seal the jar with a lid and leave at room temperature to ferment – this should start to happen within a few days. After this time you will need to open the jar every few days to 'burp' it (let the gas out that will have built up during fermentation). The kraut should be ready to eat in about 2 weeks. Once you're happy with the flavour, transfer to the fridge, where it will keep for months.

Setup: Indoors
Prep time: 5 minutes
Cook time: 15 minutes
Serves: 4–6

---

1 kg (2 lb 4 oz) waxy
new potatoes
2 tablespoons crème fraîche
1 tablespoon white
wine vinegar
1 small red onion,
finely chopped
1 tablespoon olive oil
handful each of basil, tarragon
and chives (dill and mint
would also work well),
chopped
sea salt and freshly ground
black pepper

New Potato Salad
with Onion and Herbs

There isn't a potato salad for every season in this book and
that's just something I have to live with. We will make do with
two. This one falls into the 'fairly traditional' camp with its
lightly creamy dressing. I like to keep a freshness to my potato
salads in general, which is why this one has generous quantities
of herbs and nibs of sweet red onion.

— Cook the potatoes in salted boiling water for 10–15 minutes,
until tender, then drain. It's actually good if they're a little
overcooked, as they break up and mingle with the salad
ingredients better.
— Combine the crème fraîche, white wine vinegar, red onion
and olive oil in a bowl with some salt and pepper. Tip the warm
potatoes on top and mix well.
— Stir through the herbs and serve.

Setup: Indoors
Prep time: 10 minutes
Cook time: 5 minutes
Serves: 4

---

30 g (1 oz) blanched almonds
1 teaspoon white miso
150 ml (5 fl oz/⅔ cup)
buttermilk
¼ teaspoon ground
white pepper
150 g (5½ oz) sugar snap peas,
thinly sliced lengthways
3 spring onions (scallions),
thinly sliced lengthways
1 kohlrabi (about 350 g/12 oz),
peeled and thinly sliced
(a mandoline is useful here)
2 tablespoons finely
chopped dill
sea salt (optional)

Spring Coleslaw
with Sugar Snaps, Almonds and Miso

As soon as I started thinking about this book, I knew I had to
write a coleslaw recipe for every season. Coleslaw may be the
greatest barbecue side dish of all time and should therefore get
the attention it deserves. This spring iteration is light, fresh and
crunchy, with enough savoury intensity in the dressing to keep
you coming back for another spoonful or three.

— Lightly toast the almonds in a dry pan over medium heat
moving them around regularly until they are golden in places
(this will take 5 minutes or so). Remove from the heat and
roughly chop.
— Combine the white miso, buttermilk and white pepper
in a bowl and whisk until well combined.
— Combine the sugar snaps, spring onions (scallions) and
kohlrabi in a bowl. Pour over the buttermilk dressing and mix
well, then check for seasoning – you may want to add a small
pinch of salt, although the miso is already salty. Once you're
happy, add the toasted almonds and serve.

Jersey Royals
with Rosemary

Setup: Direct cooking
Equipment: Tongs
Prep time: 5 minutes
Cook time: 20 minutes
Serves: 4, I suppose

several sprigs of rosemary
splash of neutral oil
1 kg (2 lb 4 oz) new potatoes,
such as Jersey Royals, cut into
5 cm (2 in) chunks, if large
2 tablespoons olive oil
2 garlic cloves, crushed
or finely grated
sea salt and freshly ground
black pepper

I wanted to call these 'wrinkly, crusty, salty, oily' potatoes but wasn't sure if that would sell them so well (even though it definitely should). This is my absolute favourite way to cook new potatoes and my all-time favourite potato recipe. A bold claim. Grilling the potatoes means they turn crisp on the outside, creamy on the inside, and once their nutty skins are coated in flaky salt crystals, rosemary and oil ... well, it's just an incredible experience. I am uncontrollable around them and I will fight you for the last one.

— Prepare a barbecue for direct cooking over medium heat.
— Bash the rosemary and a generous pinch of sea salt together a bit in a pestle and mortar. Add the splash of neutral oil and combine, then rub all over the potatoes.
— Grill the potatoes over direct heat for about 20 minutes, moving them around regularly, until crusty and cooked through. Transfer to a serving plate.
— Combine the olive oil, crushed garlic and another small rosemary sprig in a small frying or saucepan pan over a medium-low heat. Sizzle gently for a minute or so, then pour the oil over the potatoes. Add some more salt and pepper, and serve.

To Cook Indoors: Sorry, but I really want you to cook these on the barbecue.

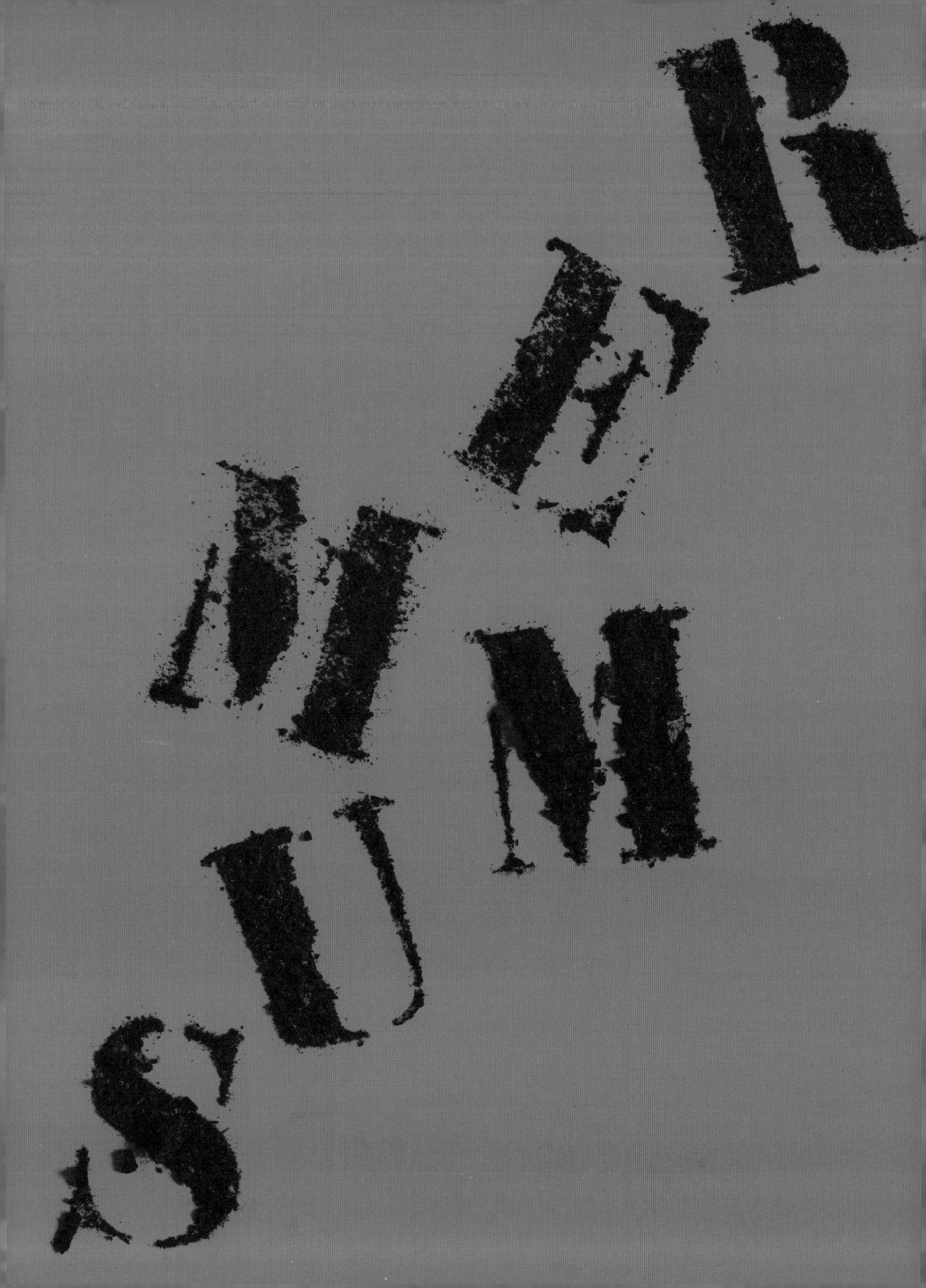

Charred Tomatoes
with Cool Yoghurt, Pomegranate Molasses and Herbs

Setup: Direct cooking
Equipment: Tongs
Prep time: 10 minutes
Cook time: 5 minutes
Serves: 4

1 garlic clove, crushed
300 g (10½ oz/scant 1¼ cups) natural full-fat yoghurt
1 kg (2 lb 4 oz) cherry tomatoes on the vine
handful of mint leaves, chopped
large handful of basil leaves, torn
handful of pomegranate seeds

Dressing
2 tablespoons pomegranate molasses
2 teaspoons za'atar (see my recipe on page 41 if you'd like to make your own)
4 tablespoons extra virgin olive oil, plus extra for drizzling
3 tablespoons lemon juice
sea salt

I have made, and will continue to make, many iterations of this tomato and yoghurt arrangement. It's so, so good. Hot, charred tomatoes in a pomegranate molasses dressing are tumbled on top of cool yoghurt, straight from the fridge. A plate of glorious contrasts. You may not want to use all the dressing, but personally I love the way it pools into the yoghurt. Obviously, you will want fresh flatbreads or toasted sourdough to really make the most of this.

— Prepare a barbecue for direct cooking over medium heat.
— Combine the dressing ingredients with a pinch of salt in a clean lidded jar or bowl and shake or whisk to combine. Set aside.
— Combine the crushed garlic, yoghurt and a pinch of salt in a bowl and mix well. Set aside.
— Grill the tomatoes over direct heat for about 5 minutes until charred and soft.
— To serve, spread the garlic yoghurt on a plate. Remove the grilled tomatoes from the vine and combine with the herbs in a bowl. Add two-thirds of the dressing and mix gently.
— Top the yoghurt with the tomato mixture and pour the remaining dressing on top. Add another drizzle of olive oil, a scattering of pomegranate seeds and some more salt, if you like.

To Cook Indoors: Preheat a cast-iron griddle pan over a high heat for at least 5 minutes and use it to char the tomatoes. You could also cook them under the grill – just make sure they get nice and black in places.

Charred Green Salad
with Burrata

Setup: Direct cooking
Equipment: Tongs, metal
skewer
Prep time: 5 minutes
Cook time: 10 minutes
Serves: 2

1 heaped tablespoon
pumpkin seeds
200 g (7 oz) Tenderstem
broccoli
150 g (5½ oz) sugar snap peas
2 baby gem (bibb) lettuce,
quartered lengthways
small handful of basil leaves
(optional)
1 burrata (optional)
neutral oil, for cooking
the vegetables

Dressing
2 tablespoons lemon juice
2 teaspoons honey
1 garlic clove, crushed
or finely grated
2 tablespoons extra virgin
olive oil
sea salt and freshly ground
black pepper

This was one of the biggest surprises for me during recipe testing for this book; as a germ of an idea, I thought it probably wouldn't be as fun as it sounded, but it's actually far better. The natural sweetness of the sugar snaps and broccoli contrasts so well with their bitter charred edges, and the gem lettuce catches all the dressing within its various frills and gills.

The salad really doesn't need the cheese, to be honest. People sure do love burrata though.

— Prepare a barbecue for direct cooking over medium heat.
— Combine the dressing ingredients and some salt and pepper in a clean lidded jar or bowl and shake or whisk to combine. Set aside.
— Lightly toast the pumpkin seeds in a dry frying pan over a medium heat, then set aside. Move them around in the pan to make sure they don't burn.
— Toss the broccoli, sugar snaps and little gems in a little neutral oil and season with salt. Thread the sugar snaps onto a skewer, then grill all the vegetables over direct heat until nicely charred. Don't be afraid to really get some charred bits on that broccoli – it really comes alive in the dressing.
— Combine all the warm, grilled vegetables with the dressing and arrange on a plate. Mix through the pumpkin seeds and the basil, if using. Top with the burrata, if you like.

To Cook Indoors: Preheat a cast-iron griddle pan over a high heat for at least 5 minutes, then use it to char the vegetables.

Suya and the Power of Yaji

My first taste of suya comes from a local high street joint, where I order beef suya with jollof rice and eat it on a park bench, marvelling at how ignorant it is possible to be about the food right on my doorstep. The restaurant had been there for years, serving the local Nigerian community, and others who had taken far less time than I to step through the door. The strips of meat are thin and smoky, obviously skewered and cooked over live fire, smothered in a paste of spices and peanuts, and served with a spice mixture that is both hot and very savoury. I later learn this is called yaji. Raw tomato and onions bring bite and acidity between mouthfuls. I fall in love. Trying to recreate the dish at home, I do a poor job even with the yaji I am gifted by a friend's boyfriend, carried back from Nigeria wrapped in someone's bank statement.

Years later, at the start of the pandemic, a van starts serving suya in Greenwich, South West London. Food circles whisper about Alhaji Suya: 'This guy really knows his stuff' and 'You have to try the tozo'. I was interested. The man behind the operation was Aliyu Dantsoho who moved to the UK from Nigeria 20 years ago and decided to dedicate his time to perfecting the art of this West African street food.

Fast forward two difficult years and I meet Aliyu at his shop in Peckham, just off the Old Kent Road. He has recently reopened after a fire devastated his first attempt at expansion. 'There was nothing like the authentic suya in London, no one doing it properly' he tells me. 'There was no one giving the energy. It's like Scottish haggis – only the Scottish people get it. With suya, only the Hausas (an ethnic group living across northern Nigeria, Chad, Niger and Ghana) make the best suya. And I am Hausa.'

I ask Aliyu to explain suya, expecting him to describe the process of mixing crushed peanuts with yaji, but he replies, 'suya is the act of grilling meat, without getting it burnt. You don't want to char it – it's more like roasting on the grill.' Aliyu uses fish cages to cook his meat in an even layer, angling them so that it doesn't touch the grill. 'It needs experience; there isn't a perfect temperature to set, and while any meat will taste good grilled once, with suya you have to cook it twice. Cook it, cool it, and cook it. That's why it's suya.'

In Northern Nigeria 'the average man will eat suya once or twice a week,' says Fatima Usman (who oversees Alhaji Suya's production). The yaji is the defining characteristic of suya: a spice blend of dried red chillies, peppercorns including grains of Selim, ginger, garlic and other ingredients according to the cook's preference. Often, it includes bouillon powder. 'People will make their own yaji and have their own secrets,' says Fatima. There is a muskiness and floral, aromatic dimension to the flavour, alongside chilli heat.

A memorable article in *The New Yorker* by Ghanaian-born

Below: suya is cooked in cages so it doesn't come into direct contact with the grill.
Right: Yaji is suya's superpower.

writer Mohammed Naseehu Ali tells a story of the powers of yaji on some African men. Recalling his childhood in the Hausa Muslim community of Kumasi, Ghana, he remembers a special yaji kept high up, out of the reach of children. 'There's this idea that it has this almost mystical power to it, and different households and mothers and different people have their yaji and it ignites the soul – it's like a West African Viagra.' He later recalls the server at a suya joint asking him, 'What yaji does your uncle want? The one for men with three wives or the one for men with two wives?' Perhaps this is a reference to burantashi, a powdered tree bark additive used as a sexual enhancement supplement and added to some yaji blends...

Aliyu's yaji boasts a short, sharp rush of intense heat that burns out quickly, necessitating the need for another mouthful. 'The yaji mixed with crushed peanuts is what makes suya unique,' says Fatima. 'Peanuts are crushed to almost a fine powder, then mixed with the spices before going on the meat.' The super-savouriness of peanuts also helps to increase umami, thanks to their high concentration of glutamates, an important neurotransmitter that has an excitatory effect on nerve cells. 'I tried to mimic what is back home and replicate it,' says Aliyu. 'That's why I had to learn how to cook it in Nigeria. I cooked with different people, learned their differences and their techniques.'

But it was not just the Aliyu's yaji that took years to perfect. 'Every meat, the chicken, the tozo [fatty beef], the lamb, every one has gone through about 4 years of research,' he says. 'It's the meat, the temperature, the spice, it's a combination of cooking slowly, the temperature control. I don't know why people think it's easy. We don't use the same breed of cows here as in Nigeria, so the meat is different; it was trial and error.'

The work has paid off. 'Originally we just had a lot of Nigerians but the funny thing is, the Africans, the Hausa, they make the suya but it's more accepted by the Westerners. The Europeans love it. We like it, but they LOVE it,' says Aliyu. Fatima agrees: 'We have a lot of people from different cultures coming in here to buy suya: Chinese, Indians, it's really amazing.' 'That was the whole idea behind the business', says Aliyu, 'to get lots of people to try suya. Lots of people who are not African.'

I eat Aliyu's tozo every other week, and snack on his kilishi, a beef jerky brushed with a paste made from yaji, with alarming frequency. Mission accomplished. How did he end up here, on a quest to introduce people to one of the world's greatest barbecued dishes? I ask. He looks at me with a twinkle in his eye before replying, 'I dunno ... I think it was the weather.'

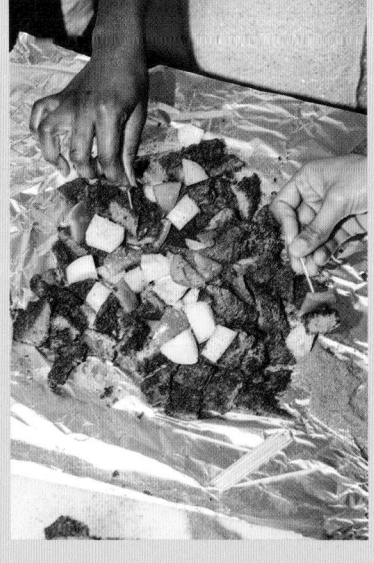

Above: pieces of suya are picked up with cocktail sticks and dipped into yaji. Below: Aliyu Dantsoho seasons the suya with yaji.

Suya
with Tomato and Onion Salad

Setup: Direct cooking
Equipment: Tongs,
4 metal skewers
Prep time: 30 minutes
Cook time: 20 minutes
Serves: 4

---

600 g (1 lb 5 oz) sirloin steak
sea salt

Yaji
1 teaspoon grains of Selim
(see Stockists)
1 tablespoon hot chilli powder
1 tablespoon vegetable
bouillon powder
2 teaspoons ground ginger
1 teaspoon garlic powder
50 g (1¾ oz) unsalted
skinned peanuts

Salad
½ white onion, thinly sliced
2 tomatoes, thinly sliced

There is no point in pretending I am expert in cooking suya like Aliyu Dantsoho, a man who has spent years researching and practising his craft. This is my version of the classic Nigerian street food, adapted for cooking at home on a simple kettle barbecue. For me, the grains of Selim and bouillon powder are both crucial to the final flavour of the yaji, so do try to include them if you can.

You will notice I haven't cooked my suya twice like Aliyu, and this is largely because I don't want to leave the barbecue to go out only to relight it a little while later. This is just a more practical method for the home cook. I also use skewers, rather than a fish cage, as I find this simpler for a small amount of suya.

— Place the steak in the freezer for 15 minutes or so, until it's firm enough to slice thinly (but not beginning to freeze). Slice the steak into 1 cm (½ in)- thick slices across the grain and set aside.
— Prepare a barbecue for direct cooking over low heat.
— Make the yaji by toasting the grains of Selim in a dry frying pan over a medium heat for a minute or two until fragrant (moving them around so they don't burn). Grind to a fine powder using a pestle and mortar or spice grinder and mix with the chilli powder, bouillon powder, garlic powder, ground ginger and ½ teaspoon salt.

— Crush or blitz the peanuts to a coarse powder, taking care not to over-blend as they will turn into peanut butter.
— Reserve 1 tablespoon of the yaji for serving and set aside. Mix the remaining yaji with the peanuts in a bowl and add the beef. Stir to coat the beef evenly, then thread onto skewers.
— To prepare the onion for the salad, soak it in very cold or iced water while you cook the beef.
— Once the coals are ready, cook the beef skewers over direct heat for 10 minutes on each side – this may seem like a long time but the idea is to cook the beef gently.
— Drain the onions and mix them with the tomatoes. Sprinkle with a small pinch of sea salt.
— Serve the suya with the tomato and onion salad.

Halloumi
with Nectarines, Tarragon and Basil

Setup: Direct cooking
Equipment: Tongs
Prep time: 5 minutes
Cook time: 5-10 minutes
Serves: 2

---

4 ripe nectarines, stoned
and quartered
a little neutral oil,
for cooking the nectarines
handful of tarragon,
leaves picked
small handful of basil
leaves, torn
½ teaspoon dried chilli flakes
2 tablespoons lemon juice
1 tablespoon lime juice
500 g (1 lb 2 oz) halloumi,
cut into roughly 1 cm (½ in)
thick slices
sea salt

Barbecued halloumi has fallen out of fashion, which is just a horrible mistake. I love to serve it with perfumed summer fruits like nectarines, and lots of soft herbs. Brushing the halloumi with oil before grilling it stops it sticking to the barbecue, which I think (I hope) is what puts a lot of people off cooking it. It's an intense, salty cheese, which in my opinion is a selling point.

— Prepare a barbecue for direct cooking over medium heat.
— Brush the cut sides of the nectarines with a little neutral oil, then grill cut side down over direct heat, turning occasionally with tongs, for about 5 minutes, or until charred and softened.
— Once cool enough to handle, dice the grilled nectarines and combine in a bowl with the tarragon, basil, chilli flakes, lemon and lime juices and a little salt.
— Rub the halloumi slices with a little neutral oil to stop them sticking, and grill quickly over direct heat for a minute or so on each side, or until charred. Serve immediately, with the nectarine mixture.

To Cook Indoors: Preheat a cast-iron griddle pan over a high heat for at least 5 minutes, then rub the nectarines with a little neutral oil and cook, cut side down, for about 5 minutes, turning occasionally, until charred and softened. Rub the halloumi with oil and cook for a minute or so on each side, or until charred.

Setup: Direct cooking
Equipment: Tongs
Prep time: 10 minutes
Cook time: 35 minutes
Serves: 2

1 garlic clove
5 anchovy fillets in olive oil
1 tablespoon capers, rinsed
2 tablespoons red wine
vinegar
2 tablespoons extra virgin
olive oil
3 courgettes (zucchini)
2 slices of stale sourdough
or other sturdy bread
1 red onion, very thinly sliced
small handful of mint leaves,
thinly sliced
generous handful of basil
leaves, torn

Blackened Courgette Panzanella

This is a fun and fiery spin on the classic Tuscan bread salad. Courgettes are completely charred on the outside then lopped into large chunks; once combined with the other ingredients they leak all their juice into the bowl and onto the bread. At first it seems a bit odd to add all that blackened skin into the salad but it mingles and adds flavour. You could happily bung a torn buffalo mozzarella into this, too.

— Smush the garlic clove, anchovies and a pinch of salt in a pestle and mortar or with the side of a knife.
— Combine with the capers, red wine vinegar, extra virgin olive oil and some black pepper in a lidded jar or bowl and shake or whisk to combine.
— Prepare the barbecue for direct cooking over medium heat. Cook the courgettes (zucchini), whole, over direct heat until soft and blackened, around 25 minutes with the lid closed.
— Quickly char the bread on the barbecue, then tear into chunks. Chop the courgettes into large chunks and combine with the dressing, red onion and the herbs. This is great eaten immediately but will increase in juiciness as it sits.

Setup: Direct cooking
Equipment: Tongs
Prep time: 5 minutes
Cook time: 10 minutes
Serves: 4

$\frac{1}{4}$ red onion, thinly sliced
2 tablespoons neutral oil
1 teaspoon dried chilli flakes
2 pitta breads, split in half
4 ripe peaches, quartered
2 large tomatoes, in wedges
handful of basil leaves, torn
handful of mint leaves,
chopped
sea salt

Dressing
2 tablespoons lemon juice
1 teaspoon honey
3 tablespoons olive oil
1 tablespoon sumac

Grilled Peach and Tomato 'Fattoush'

I have always loved fattoush: a Levantine salad of fresh, crunchy vegetables such as lettuce, tomatoes and radishes, combined with golden, deep fried shards of bread and lots of sumac.

So yes, this steers quite a way away from a classic fattoush, but those juicy tomatoes and sweet peaches will work their own kind of magic.

— Prepare a barbecue for direct cooking over medium heat.
— Put the sliced onion in a bowl of iced water.
— Combine 1 tablespoon of the neutral oil with some salt and the chilli flakes and rub over the pittas on both sides. Toast the pitta on the barbecue until crisp. Chop into 'chips' and set aside.
— Brush the cut sides of the peaches with the remaining oil and grill cut sides down for a few minutes, turning occasionally, until all cut sides are charred.
— Combine the dressing ingredients and whisk to combine.
— Cut the peaches into thick wedges and combine in a bowl with the tomatoes. Drain the onions and add those too, then add the herbs, dressing and finally the pitta chips. Toss to combine and serve immediately.

Corn, Comal
and Carne Asada

I am standing in a small, meticulously organised kitchen in Belize, Central America. Its roof is corrugated metal and its sides are open to the thick, humid air, which hangs heavy over dusty earth, dense jungle visible in the near distance. Chickens scratch outside, one fewer in number since I turned up for lunch. I am sweating profusely, mesmerised by the shaping of a tortilla – *pat pat* goes a hand on top of masa, which is in turn on top of a carefully cut circle of plastic, a barrier between the dough and work surface.

This is San Isidro, a tiny village a couple of hours' drive west of the tourist destination Placencia. Sisters Rosa Bulum and Ana Salam have invited me into their home where they are cooking a lunch of caldo – a traditional chicken soup – which will be served with corn tortillas cooked fresh on the comal, a multipurpose cooking surface that is essentially a large, flat piece of metal (traditionally clay) set over fire. Cooking over live fire is an everyday occurrence here in rural Belize, where a fire is lit in a small, well-ventilated annex. The sisters' hands are a blur, their speed and dexterity something that comes only with daily repetition. I feel a little sheepish about the tortilla press I have at a home, which makes my crude efforts look 100 times smoother (Ana, in a kind effort to make me feel better, jokes that her first tortilla 'looked like the map of Belize'). The smoke-laced caldo is oddly refreshing in the heat but a substantial chicken broth nonetheless, plumped with waxy nubs of cassava. I scoop up the pieces with the still-warm corn and let the ends slip into the broth where they swell with the chicken's fat and flavour.

As Rosa and Ana finish the tortillas they pad them onto the comal with the heels of their palms, flipping and spinning them to check they're cooked. They puff proudly as steam expands inside, and are deemed ready for eating. I return home and boast about my new tortilla-making technique, but find I am still some way off the perfect circles I saw in Ana and Rosa's kitchen, their versions superlatively soft and springy.

It's hard to overstate the significance of corn to the people of central America and Mexico. The Maya Empire – which evolved in Belize around 350BC – worshipped maize gods, an example of how the development of agriculture changed the way civilisations ideated their deities. In Mayan mythology, the god of maize was decapitated at the end of the growing season, and reborn at the start of the next, an explanation for the natural cycle of the seasons. The Mayans believed that the gods modelled the first human from maize dough.

The Aztec Empire was born around 1100-1200BC in present-day Central Mexico, falling in the 16th century when the Spanish colonised. While these Mesoamerican cultures had figured out how to nixtamalize corn (cook it with lime) to make it edible, the

Spanish rejected it and introduced wheat, which they used to make bread. Corn became a symbol of poverty, and wheat, status and wealth.

After the Second World War, major irrigation systems were developed in the north, which supported the growth of wheat, and while the central Bajío region was once known as Mexico's 'bread basket', the north west is now the country's primary wheat-producing region. Here, wheat rather than corn tortillas are celebrated, particularly in Sonora. In *The Essential Cuisines of Mexico*, Diana Kennedy explains, 'tortillas of wheat flour (tortillas de carina de trigo) are common all over the north of Mexico, but they come into their own in Sonora.'

Back in London, I had been following the journey of a taqueria named after the north west state, adjacent to the Baja California peninsula, separated by the Gulf of California. Sonora (the restaurant) was founded by Michelle Salazar de la Rocha and Sam Napier just before the pandemic hit, and when I speak to them, we have had three lockdowns and they have been reimagining their business.

Michelle, a Sonoran native, is explaining the regional tacos over the phone to me from Holland, where she and Sam are quarantining after returning from a research trip to Mexico. 'The most traditional Sonoran tortillas are the ones that are made with pork fat, but vegetable shortening is popular too,' she says. 'I think the fat adds more flavour but also at the beginning of the tortilla process it is almost like making a shortbread, so shortening the flour with the fat to incorporate the flour really well means that in its final form it will create a pocket and feel like a layered flatbread with a rich flavour.'

When she and Sam reopen their restaurant, it will be reborn as a carne asada spot, 'which is the most Sonoran thing that there is, grilling beef over coal. Technically it's just grilled beef but obviously, it's also much more than that. In Northern Mexico especially, it's more of a family union, so it's a big cook-out, there are lots of traditions around it, and there's something of a personal ritual about it too: everyone has their own way of doing it. There are many tiny little elements that are specific to each cook.'

'In the taqueria, they will chop up the meat really finely,' says Sam, 'as it's usually done with a more affordable cut of beef that tends to be tougher; it's hot-held in a pot over the grill, mixed with the juices.'

'Home grilling is more of a family event on the weekend,' says Michelle. 'We all get together (like gathering for a Sunday roast) and divide tasks. Some make the salsas, some light up the charcoal, some just sit around and drink a cold beer and wait for the meat to be done. It's an event, so you buy your favourite cuts – in my family's case it's arrachera (hanger steak) or cabrería (top loin).

Every family has their special tricks on how to grill, what to cook as sides, how spicy they like their salsa, who gets to eat first, and so on.'

So, Sonoran barbecue is all about the beef. 'The cow is on the state flag, so it's important to their culture,' explains Sam. 'They say the beef tastes better because the cows are so hot they don't move around lots, so they build up fat!' He laughs: 'Imagine standing in front of a barbecue in 45-degree heat, but that's what they do. It might be a family occasion, a special event, or perhaps they just feel like grilling some beef.'

As with any regional speciality, there are plenty of disagreements about how it should be done. 'You'd think everyone would know how to grill steak,' says Sam, 'but everyone disagrees, and everyone thinks their method is the right one. For example, they don't salt the steak until it is right on the grill and it must be coarse salt, but then some people will be like, it should just be salted on one side, another will say two sides.'

As a recipe writer keen to have a go at making carne asada at home, it is quite comforting to find that methods vary. At least I know that the steak must not be salted in advance, and I decide to adopt the finely chopped method of the taqueria when it comes to serving. Sam tells me that meat must also never be marinated – in fact, 'it is a sin' to do so. Nervously, I decide to grill it and serve it with a smoky chilli salsa. Find my recipe on page 88.

Carne Asada with Flour and Fat Tortillas and a Smoky Chilli Salsa

Setup: Direct cooking
Equipment: Tongs
Prep time: 30 minutes,
plus 2 hours resting time
Cook time: 30 minutes
Serves: 4

Tortillas
450 g (1 lb) plain flour
200 g (7 oz) vegetable
shortening
250 ml (8 fl oz/1 cup)
warm water
1 teaspoon fine sea salt

Smoky chilli salsa
2 dried ancho chillies
2 dried guajillo chillies
2 chipotle chillies in adobo
3 tablespoons orange juice
2 tablespoons lime juice
2 garlic cloves
1 tablespoon light
brown sugar
1 teaspoon cumin seeds,
toasted
1 tablespoon olive oil

Onions
1 white onion, finely chopped
handful of coriander (cilantro)
stalks, finely chopped
about 1 tablespoon lime juice

Carne asada
800 g (1 lb 12 oz) onglet
sea salt
lime wedges and sour cream,
to serve

Michelle Salazar de la Rocha (page 87) tells me that 'lots of practice' is the best tip for making flour and fat tortillas. I can't pretend I've been making them for years, but I did go through quite a few different versions during testing; I think these make perfectly good tortillas, even if a Sonoran might think otherwise.

Michelle also told me that marinating the steak for carne asada is 'a sin', so I have cooked it very simply with salt; there is so much flavour from the smoky salsa, that it feels right to let the flavour of the beef stand out. It is all about the meat, after all.

— First, make the tortilla dough. Place the flour in a mixing bowl and rub the fat in with your finger tips, as if you are making pastry. Dissolve the salt into the water then gradually add it until the dough comes together. Knead until smooth on a lightly floured surface for about 5 minutes. Divide into 10 balls, around 80 g (2 ¾ oz) each. Place on a well-greased surface. Cover and rest for 2 hours.

— Dry toast the ancho and guajillo chillies in a dry frying pan until fragrant, to wake them up. They will become softer and smell amazing after 5 minutes or so. Remove the stalks and transfer them to a blender with the other salsa ingredients and some salt. Blend to a salsa and set aside.
— Combine the onion, coriander (cilantro) stalks and leaves, a squeeze of lime juice and some salt in a bowl. Set aside.
— Roll out the tortillas on a lightly floured surface to around 18 cm (7 in) diameter. Cook over a medium heat in a preheated frying pan for around 30 seconds on each side, until browned in patches. Stack the tortillas inside a tea towel (dish towel), to keep them warm and soft.
— Prepare the barbecue for direct cooking over high heat.
— Season the steak heavily with salt on both sides. Cook for about 3 minutes on each side, then rest for 10 minutes.
— Slice the steak as thinly as you can, until you have lots of very thin pieces of meat (give it all another chop if necessary). Serve with the tortillas, onions, the salsa, sour cream and lime wedges.

Summer Coleslaw

Setup: Indoors
Prep time: 20 minutes
Serves: 4

1 cucumber, halved
lengthways, seeds removed
and thinly sliced
2 celery stalks, thinly sliced
4 spring onions (scallions), cut
into short sections, then thinly
sliced lengthways
1 fennel bulb, thinly sliced
lengthways
100 g (3½ oz) dried apricots
handful blanched hazelnuts
handful of small, yellow
celery leaves (if your celery
has them!)
very generous handful of mint
leaves, roughly chopped
very generous handful of basil
leaves, roughly chopped
2 tablespoons red wine
vinegar
2 tablespoons olive oil
1 teaspoon honey
⅓ teaspoon chilli flakes
sea salt and freshly ground
black pepper

Welcome to the summer instalment of The Coleslaw Diaries. This is an incredibly light, crunchy, perfect-for-summer side dish. Don't skip soaking the vegetables in cold water – it's necessary to crisp them up and is essential to the character of the coleslaw, which is so refreshing. I have served this in a bowl rested on top of another bowl filled with ice when the heat was particularly punishing.

— Place the cucumber into a colander over a bowl. Sprinkle with 1 teaspoon of salt, toss and allow to drain for 20 minutes.
— Meanwhile, soak the celery, spring onions (scallions) and fennel in iced water for 10 minutes.
— In a separate bowl, soak the apricots in cold water for 10 minutes, then slice.
— Lightly toast the hazelnuts in a dry pan (moving them around so they toast evenly and don't burn) then roughly chop.
— Briefly rinse the cucumber. Drain the vegetables and combine them in a bowl with the cucumber, the celery leaves (if using) and herbs. Add the toasted, chopped hazelnuts and drained apricots.
— In a clean, lidded jar (or a bowl if you don't have one), combine the red wine vinegar, olive oil, honey and chilli flakes along with a small pinch of salt and a good amount of black pepper. Shake or whisk to combine.
— Pour the dressing over the salad and serve immediately.

Grilled Corn
with Whipped Beer Butter

Setup: Direct cooking
Equipment: Tongs
Prep time: 5 minutes
Cook time: 10 minutes
Serves: 3 (everyone wants
2 corn cobs, right?)

25 g (1 oz/2 tablespoons)
butter, softened
3 tablespoons IPA beer
dash of hot sauce, plus extra
to serve
6 corn cobs
neutral oil, for cooking
sea salt and freshly ground
black pepper

Grilled corn is so good at the end of summer I find it hard not to have it with every meal (don't be tempted to buy cobs out of season – they are always dry and disappointing). If you can find corn in-husk, then use that. It stays much juicier on the grill than ready prepared cobs (I've given instructions for both below). Beer butter is even better than it sounds, the faint bitterness a great counterpoint to the rich butter and sweet niblets of corn (I'm so happy I got to use the word 'niblets').

— Prepare a barbecue for direct cooking over medium heat.
— Put the butter into a stand mixer fitted with the whisk attachment (or a high-sided bowl if you are using a hand-held electric whisk) and whip for a couple of minutes until light and fluffy. Add the beer and hot sauce and whip for a couple of minutes more. Put into the fridge to firm up a bit while the corn cooks.
— If using in-husk corn, snip off any long silky parts using kitchen scissors then place the cobs over direct medium heat for 15 minutes, or until the husks are black and the corn inside is soft and yellow (you can peel a little husk back to check). If you want to char the corn, now is the time to peel off the husks and do that, taking care not to leave it on the grill for more than a few minutes longer.
— If using pre-prepared corn cobs, rub them with a little neutral oil. Grill over direct heat medium heat, turning occasionally with tongs, for about 10 minutes until soft, golden and charred.
— Serve with the beer butter and extra hot sauce. Season well with salt (and pepper, if you like).

To Cook Indoors: Either wrap the corn in foil with some of the butter inside and bake at 180°C (350°F/gas 4) for 30–35 minutes, boil the cobs for 5 minutes, then drain and top with the butter, or cook them in a preheated cast-iron griddle pan for 10 minutes, turning occasionally with tongs, before serving with the butter. Season well with salt (and pepper, if you like).

Prawns
with Gooseberry Salsa

Setup: Direct cooking
Equipment: Tongs
Prep time: 10 minutes
Cook time: 20–25 minutes
Serves: 2–4, depending on
other dishes and appetite
for prawns

Prawns
16 shell-on king prawns
neutral oil, for cooking
sea salt
tortillas, to serve (optional)

Gooseberry salsa
300 g (10½ oz) gooseberries
2 garlic cloves
2 green chillies, 1 finely
chopped and 1 left whole
(stalk removed)
¼ teaspoon ground coriander
seeds from 2 green cardamom
pods
juice of ½ lime
½ small onion, finely chopped
handful of coriander (cilantro)
leaves, chopped
small handful of mint leaves,
chopped
1–2 teaspoons caster
(superfine) sugar

I first developed a version of this recipe for a magazine but have
continued to make and tweak it ever since. The inspiration was
a tomatillo salsa, but since tomatillos are quite hard to find in
the UK, I've replaced them with a bristly back-garden classic:
gooseberries. They have the same tartness and 'green' flavour,
and roasting them first before dressing allows them to develop
some charred notes. Here, I've served them as a taco filling,
but they are just as good on their own.

— Preheat the oven to 180°C (350°F/gas 4).
— Place the gooseberries in a roasting dish and roast in the
oven for 20 minutes, until they are totally collapsed and a little
charred.
— Place the roasted gooseberries in a blender with the garlic,
1 whole green chilli, ground coriander, cardamom and lime juice
and blend until smooth. Transfer to a bowl and combine with
the onion, coriander (cilantro), mint leaves, the finely chopped
green chilli and a generous pinch of salt, then add half a
teaspoon of sugar at a time, tasting as you go, until the salsa
is pleasantly sour.
— Prepare a barbecue for direct cooking over medium heat.
— Lightly coat the prawns with a splash of neutral oil and
season with salt. Grill over direct heat for 1–2 minutes on each
side, or until completely pink. Serve immediately with the salsa.

To Cook Indoors: Preheat a cast-iron griddle pan over a high
heat for at least 5 minutes. Cook the lightly oiled prawns for
1–2 minutes on each side, or until completely pink.

Prawns
with Fennel Seed Butter

Setup: Direct cooking
Equipment: Tongs
Prep time: 5 minutes
Cook time: 5 minutes
Serves: 2–4, depending
on sides

12 shell-on king prawns
1 tablespoon fennel seeds
50 g (1¾ oz/3½ tablespoons)
butter
1 teaspoon dried chilli flakes,
or to taste
1 tablespoon lemon juice,
plus wedges to serve
neutral oil, for cooking
sea salt and freshly ground
black pepper

Sometimes simple is best. Make sure to melt the butter at the last minute so it sizzles when it's poured over the prawns, and follow it with a squeeze of lemon. I would serve this with a glass of cold white wine.

— Prepare a barbecue for direct cooking over medium heat.
— Lightly oil the prawns, season with salt and grill them over direct heat for 1–2 minutes on each side, until completely pink.
— Lightly crush the fennel seeds (either in a pestle and mortar or with something heavy), then combine them with the butter, chilli flakes, lemon juice and some salt and pepper in a small saucepan. Sizzle gently for a minute, then pour the butter over the hot prawns.
— Serve immediately, with lemon wedges.

To Cook Indoors: Preheat a cast-iron griddle pan over a high heat for at least 5 minutes and cook the prawns for 1–2 minutes on each side, or until completely pink.

Beach Barbecue

Setting up a beach barbecue can feel idyllic: what could be better than cooking seafood right next to the sea (maybe you even caught it!), the sun on your face and salt on your lips? It's a really special and memorable place to cook. However, it's important to do things properly. You can't just set up a barbecue in any public space, and there's the small matter of safety to consider. Here are my tips for a gloriously uneventful beach barbecue.

Permission

There are restrictions on where we can barbecue in public spaces, and some beaches don't allow it. Don't assume that just because you can barbecue on one beach, it'll be fine at the next one just down the road. Check signage, by-laws and your local authority's website before you lug everything down there.

The tide

Find out exactly what the tide is doing before you set up; a bowl of hot coals or a fire pit and sea water won't mix well. Tide times are predicted well in advance and are available online. Pitching camp above the high-tide water mark on the sand is a great strategy if you forget.

Lighting fires

Take the usual precautions for lighting a fire, including setting up well away from any vegetation that might catch a spark, or any other people close by – no one wants a face full of smoke every 30 seconds. Of course, it goes without saying that a fire should be properly extinguished when you leave the beach. Use sand or water to do this, and always make sure the barbecue is properly cooled down before moving it. Never bury hot coals in the sand.

Barbecues

Avoid disposable barbecues – they are nasty, chemical-soaked polluters that ruin your food, if they even manage to cook it through. A small, portable barbecue is great (although you will need to wait a few hours for it to cool before moving).

Building a fire pit

If you don't have a barbecue but you do have a grill (i.e., a grate that you can use over a fire), then building a pit in the sand is an option. Dig your hole around a foot deep and make sure you have some dry wood for fuel. Wet wood will either not light, or will make a very smoky fire. Keep rocks from the beach out of your fire – any moisture and air in them will quickly expand and they could explode. You could use them around the outside, however. Personally, I would totally avoid lighting fires on rocky beaches.

Making a Swedish Candle

I was taught about Swedish candles by Craig Evans, who runs coastal foraging courses in Wales. An expert in coastal marine life and beach cooking, he showed me that a self-feeding fire can be made from a log, although it does require some preparation. You can also buy ready-cut logs online.

If you do decide to make the candle yourself, you will need a seasoned log (that means wood that has been thoroughly dried out over time, like the wood you use for smoking on the barbecue) and a chainsaw. Use a chainsaw to make several large cuts into the end of the log (as if you are cutting a cake) but don't cut all the way through to the base – three-quarters of the way down is perfect. Make sure the base of the log is stable before you begin! Stuff some kindling such as wood shavings, tree bark or a firelighter into the centre of the log and light it. Hot embers will drop down inside the log, igniting it from the inside.

A pot can now rest on top of the log and be used to cook foraged shellfish such as mussels, prawns and clams.

Clean up

Take all your litter home with you. Littering is juvenile, inconsiderate and incredibly damaging to the environment and wildlife that you have spent time enjoying. It's also illegal.

Foraging

Coastal foraging can be very fun, particularly when looking for mussels, prawns and clams. These can be boiled in a pot with wild fennel or other herbs and sea vegetables (or cooked directly on the grill), and it goes without saying you'll want to bring some basic aromatics and ingredients like herbs, lemons, bread and butter with you. Make sure you always forage from clean, unpolluted water, and that you know what you're eating. Shellfish can be cooked in seawater and will take just a few minutes to steam open or cook through.

Equipment

What you need to take to the beach will depend on your cooking method, but as a general rule, other than your barbecue, fuel and firelighter (plus matches/a lighter!) you will want to make sure you have some of the following:
— Tongs, spatula, fork, skewers
— A cooking pot with a lid, if you want to prepare shellfish or boil anything
— Cutlery, plates, cups or other non-glass vessels, bottle opener, scissors
— Chopping board and knife
— Cooler bag or box
— Bin bags, napkins, paper towels, wet wipes
— Heatproof gloves can be really useful (and a mini first-aid kit is never a bad idea)
— Water for drinking
— Don't forget the salt and pepper!

Crabs Steamed in Seaweed

Setup: Direct cooking
Equipment: Tongs, foil,
a screwdriver, sharp knife
or other long implement for
dispatching the crabs
Prep time: 15 minutes
Cook time: 45 minutes–1 hour
Serves: 2

2 live brown crabs, packed
in ice in a chill box
a few generous handfuls large
seaweed, such as serrated
wrack, for wrapping the
crabs (the seaweed should be
as fresh as possible)
1 fennel bulb, sliced
50 g (1¾ oz/3½ tablespoons)
butter
a few generous pinches of
chilli flakes (I prefer pul biber,
but any will do)

This is the method for
steaming crabs that was
taught to me by Craig Evans,
a coastal forager who runs
guided beach tours in South
Wales. We spent a day
foraging for seafood before
cooking it on the beach on
a Swedish candle, which is
a self-feeding fire lit inside
a seasoned log (see more
about that on the opposite
page). It rained for the entire
day and, while sunshine would
have been preferable, it takes
a lot to dampen the spirits
of this hardcore crab fan.

This recipe involves live
crabs, which must be killed
before cooking. If you don't
want to do this, don't cook
the crabs.

— Prepare a barbecue
for direct cooking over
medium heat.
— To kill the crabs, place
a crab on its back on a flat
surface where it won't slip
around. Lift up the triangular
tail flap and you will see an
indentation. Place your knife
or other long implement over
this and press it down in one
swift motion, pushing it into
the crab. This will instantly
kill the crab and is the
fastest and most humane way
of doing it.
— Lay out a few large sheets
of foil and layer some seaweed
on top followed by the crabs,
side by side. Add the fennel,
plus another layer of seaweed,
then wrap the whole thing
in foil.
— Place on the barbecue over
direct heat and grill for 45
minutes–1 hour, depending
on the size of the crabs.
The crab's shell will be bright
orange when fully cooked.
— Melt the butter gently in
a small pan with the chilli and
use it as a dip for the crab
meat. I find that a small rock
comes in handy for cracking
those claws.

Scallops
with Sorrel and Chilli Butter

Setup: Direct cooking
Equipment: Tongs, oyster
shucker or small knife with
a flexible blade
Prep time: 20 minutes
Cook time: 5 minutes
Serves: 4

12 live scallops
150 g (5½ oz/10½ tablespoons)
butter, softened
1–2 red chillies, finely chopped
8–9 sorrel leaves, thinly sliced
bread, to serve

Sorrel is the most extraordinary leaf, with an electric lemon flavour; a little goes a long way. It's in season in the UK through late spring and summertime but if you can't find it then lemon juice and zest obviously make a good substitute. The in-shell cooking method for scallops of course works well with any flavoured butter: try adding 'nduja, small brown shrimp, garlic and herbs, capers or anchovies to butter before grilling. The sight and smell of scallops sputtering away in their pools of butter is irresistible. Make sure you have enough bread to hand to make the most of the situation.

— First, remove the scallops from their shells. Insert an oyster shucker or other small knife at the hinge of the scallop and twist it to prise the shell apart slightly. Ensure the scallop is flat side down, then insert another flexible knife (such as a flexible butter knife) into the shell and use it to release the scallop from the base of the shell. The shell will now come open. Remove and discard all parts of the scallop except the white meat and the coral.
— You can give the shell a wash at this point, if you like – make sure to dry it thoroughly before you put the scallop back inside. Refrigerate the scallops while you prepare a barbecue for direct cooking over medium heat.
— Mash together the butter, some of the chopped chilli and some of the sorrel in a bowl and dot it onto the scallops in the shells.
— Grill the scallops in their shells over direct heat for about 5 minutes until just cooked through.
— Garnish with the remaining sorrel and chilli and serve at once with bread for dipping into the butter.

To Cook Indoors: Cook the scallops and their shells, with the butter, under a hot grill for a few minutes, or until just cooked through.

Piri Piri Chicken Thighs
with Tomato and Onion Salad

Setup: Indirect cooking
Equipment: Tongs
Prep time: 15 minutes,
plus 1 hour marinating time
Cook time: 25 minutes
Serves: 4

Chicken
juice of 1 lemon
5 garlic cloves, crushed or
finely grated
2 teaspoons salt
8 bone-in, skin-on chicken
thighs (about 1.3 kg/3 lb)

Piri piri sauce
5 mild red chillies
2 bird's eye chillies
2 teaspoons smoked
hot paprika
10 garlic cloves
6 tablespoons red
wine vinegar
2 tablespoons dried oregano
4 tablespoons olive oil
2 teaspoons caster
(superfine) sugar

Tomato and onion salad
4 large or a large handful of
cherry tomatoes, thickly sliced
1 onion, thinly sliced
a generous squeeze
of lemon juice
1 teaspoon dried oregano
extra virgin olive oil,
for drizzling
sea salt and freshly ground
black pepper

A few years back I went on a piri piri pilgrimage to Portugal with a group of journalists and Marco Mendes, founder of London's Casa do Frango restaurants. Marco grew up eating at traditional piri piri restaurants ('frangarias') around the Algarve and he took us around some of his favourites, the kind with multiple rotisseries spinning chickens over charcoal and lazy Susans on every table, for whizzing chips to your mates.

Piri piri originated with the first chilli plants in South and Central America, which were spread around the world by Portuguese explorers. The piri piri chicken dish, reckons Marco, was a product of immigration back to Portugal from Africa in the '70's, and the fact that chicken was abundant and affordable around the same time.

I think we can all agree that piri piri did pretty darn well for itself. Here's my version, which falls somewhere between the traditional Portuguese recipes and modern takes popularised by the high-street chain.

— Combine the lemon juice, garlic and salt to make a marinade. Spread all over the chicken thighs and set aside (room temperature is fine) for 1 hour.
— Prepare a barbecue for indirect cooking over medium heat, with the coals banked to one side.
— Make the piri piri sauce by combining all the ingredients with a generous pinch of salt in a blender and blending to a coarse paste. Reserve half the paste for brushing the chicken as it cooks (the other half is to serve).
— Cook the marinated chicken thighs on the side without any coals with the lid closed for about 30 minutes and vents half open, brushing them regularly with the piri piri sauce and turning with tongs to ensure even cooking. Crisp up the skin over direct heat, if necessary.
— Make the tomato salad by combining the tomatoes and onion on a serving plate. Sprinkle over the oregano. Add the lemon juice and a big swirl of olive oil. Season with salt and pepper.
— Serve the chicken with the tomato salad and the remaining piri piri sauce. This is also great with chips (obviously).

To Cook Indoors: Preheat the oven to 180°C (350°F/gas 4). Cook the chicken in a roasting tray in the oven for 40–45 minutes, brushing regularly with the marinade.

Jamaican Jerk Chicken

A person minding their own business while walking down the northern end of Peckham High Street, South East London, will smell JB's Soul Food before they can see it. The scent of allspice and scotch bonnet flurries on the air, hooking customers by their noses and away from their intended path. They might turn down the squat side street and walk through the door of a small yellow shop. To one side is a passageway, open to the skies, and in it an old but still-sturdy jerk drum – the same drum that has chugged alluring smoke from its chimney every day since JB's opened, sometime back in 2014. At the grill stands Bill (real name Fitzroy) Hawes, long barbecue fork in hand, while in the kitchen his wife Jennifer cleaves chicken through the bones, piling meat into takeaway containers with the customers' choice of rice and peas, coleslaw, salad, and, sometimes, macaroni cheese. By midday there is a queue around the block.

Jerk – a method of seasoning native to Jamaica in which meat is rubbed with pimento (allspice) and scotch bonnet peppers – is the culinary legacy of the fusion of indigenous Arawak Indian, Taino (an Arawak sub group) and African cultures. The Spanish had brought enslaved African people to the Caribbean, and when the British forced them out in the 17th century, those people fled to the mountains and became known as Maroons, a Spanish word derived from *cimarrones*, meaning mountaineers. They mixed with the remaining Taino people (most of whom had been killed by disease introduced by the Europeans) and adopted their culinary traditions, one of which was jerking meat, specifically the boar that lived wild in the mountains.

At this time, jerk was a cured meat; salt and spices preserved the pigs, preventing them from rotting in the tropical humidity. In his snappily titled *A Voyage to the Islands Madera, Barbados, Nieves, St Christophers and Jamaica: with the Natural History of the Herbs and Trees, Four Footed Beasts, Fishes, Birds, Insects, Reptiles, &c of the Last of those Islands* (phew), Hans Sloane (an Anglo-Irish physician) writes in 1725 that the wild pigs in Jamaica were, 'cut open, the bones taken out, and the flesh is gash'd on the inside into the skin, fill'd with salt and expos'd to the sun, which is call'd jirking ... it eats much as bacon, if broil'd on coals'. This coal cooking, however, took place underground, where the meat was wrapped and steamed over low embers. The Maroons, hiding in the mountains around the plantations where they had originally been enslaved, used this method to avoid generating smoke, which might alert someone to their presence.

It was after the abolition of slavery that meat was jerked and grilled outside, the fires fuelled with aromatic wood and leaves. In his book *Untrodden Jamaica* (1890), Herbert T. Thomas, an Inspector with the Jamaican constabulary, writes that cooks, 'constructed a gridiron of green sticks about two feet from the ground. This is called about the Blue Mountain Valley a "patta", while among the Maroons, and in the Cuna-Cuna district it is known as a "caban" – a word that has a distinctly Spanish flavour'. He goes on to rather gruesomely describe the cooking: 'Underneath this a fire is kindled, into which the carcase is first thrust in order to singe the hair, which is then easily scraped off with a knife. This done, the animal is disembowelled, split open down the back, the bones extracted, and the carcase laid skin downwards upon the sticks and subjected to a slow grilling during which it is plentifully sprinkled with black pepper and salt. This process lasts from six to eight or nine hours, according to the size of the animal. The adding of pimento leaves, or those of the pepper elder to the fire imparts an improved flavour to the meat, which, when properly done, is as gamey and toothsome a dish as a hungry man can desire.'

The flavour of pimento leaves and/or wood is what many claim is missing from jerk cooked outside of Jamaica, and although pimento wood is available to buy online here in the UK, it would be prohibitively expensive and impractical for a restaurant to buy it (if they even wanted to). Some home cooks now use bay leaves and wood, which is said to partially replicate the flavour of pimento wood (see my recipe on page 109).

Nowadays, of course, it's just not jerk unless it's cooked on a jerk drum – a barbecue made from an old oil drum, cut in half, hinged, and mounted sideways on metal legs, with a two-level grill inserted inside. Riaz Phillips, author of *Belly Full: Caribbean Food in the UK* (2016) writes in an article for *Vice* that, 'Jamaica has limited sources of natural gas and by the 1950s, its dependency on oil imports had grown. Empty oil barrels began littering yards and street corners, and enterprising cooks found an opportunity to transfer the pit-cooking techniques of the Maroons onto these disused canisters, using cinnamon, cloves, and thyme to mimic the flavours of the original allspice wood. The iconic jerk drum was born.'

Page 105: Bill with his trusty drum.
Below top: jerk chicken on the grill.
Below bottom: Jennifer chops the jerk chicken into pieces before serving.
Page 107: Jennifer and Bill, the J and B of JB's Soul Food.

Bill, the 'B' of JB's Soul Food – a former welder – made his own drum, which sits right outside the shop. 'Most people are not fortunate enough to have a back area where there's no neighbours. We have such a good spot here, because it's so hard to find somewhere that can handle the smoke without complaints. When the chicken is cooking on the drum, we knock it so the seasoning drops in there and the smoke comes up and goes over the chicken. It's all about the smoke.' The chicken cooks for a long time on the grill to pick up lots of flavour and become very tender, almost falling off the bone. 'What I do is cook it just enough – not cooked through – then I put it at the top to smoke more.' Bill points to a shelf at the top of the drum where it's cooler. 'The longer it smokes, the better it tastes. The tenderness from slow cooking is also key, says Jennifer, as she brings down her shiny cleaver on a cooked chicken leg, holding a fork in the other hand to steady the meat. 'Jerk chicken is always cut right through the bone into pieces before it's served because it's easier to eat and you know for a fact that it's properly cooked.'

Bill's recipe is closely guarded. 'I cut my own seasoning: scotch bonnet, allspice, a lot of garlic, thyme – but not the dry one, the fresh one ... I think I've gone far enough! I prep everything fresh, everything. And the rest is secret!' he laughs. 'He loves it though,' says Jennifer. 'Yes, we are doing it to pay the bills but also we are not. He puts everything into it. You can tell if someone enjoys it. It's love.'

The jerk is the best in the area, by some distance. The skin is burnished pimento-brown and evenly charred to a thin, crisp layer; the fizzing fruit of scotch bonnet chilli powers through the marinade, over a growling bass of pimento. Rather than offering a red, obviously chilli-based hot sauce as many jerk shops do, Jennifer and Bill serve a sweet and spicy shiny brown sauce; an addictive slick of flavour itself laced powerfully with the buzzing heat of scotch bonnet and pimento, its presence a rumbling warmth.

Wherever Jamaican people settle, they bring jerk with them, but for Bill and Jennifer, the transition from living in Jamaica to the UK was not an easy one. 'We've been in Peckham 30 years or so,' says Bill. 'I was in my twenties when I first came here. It was the motherland, you know, and my nan – my mum's mum – used to be here and she made sure we all thought that the motherland is gonna be better, but when I first came over here I didn't like it – I cry innit. Because it's not what you know. I was living in a high block and I looked down and I was thinking, how could I come here? It was winter and all the trees didn't have leaves

and I'm thinking what have I done! The tears started running down. So, I did go home, but then I came back. It was less than a year and I came back and said I'd give it a proper go.'

At first, Jennifer wasn't keen to open a Caribbean food business in Peckham. 'She wasn't interested because this place, honestly speaking, it had a reputation,' Bill says, referring to the fact that Peckham hit headlines through the 70s, 80s and 90s for gang violence and racially motivated crimes. 'I always wanted to do it but not here!' says Jennifer. Peckham looks very different today. JB's stands firm. When I first started chatting to Jennifer and Bill back in 2019, they were selling around 40 kg (88 lb) of chicken a day. When I ask them again in 2021, it is more than 100 kg (220 lb). This is due to the success of Bill's recipe and his faithfulness to Jamaican traditions. 'I thought if I'm gonna do food like this then I'm going to make sure it tastes like home,' he says. 'I want it to taste like your mum's cooking. Now, when I go back home, I have jerk chicken some places and I think nah, it's not right because now it's commercial – they're not doing it with the love, they're doing it for the money. That's why we kept our prices low for a long long time because it's not about the money – it's about running your own thing and making people happy at the same time.'

As we chat by the drum, he drops a leg of chicken on the floor and smiles: 'Back home, we said when it drop, it's all gonna go. It's all gonna sell! If it falls on the floor we're gonna have a good day today. It's funny how it goes, you know. You can never tell what's going to happen. Yesterday I didn't want to turn up here, even when I got here I didn't want to do it, and it was the best day. We were so busy it was mad! Proper!'

Helen tears into a portion of Bill's jerk chicken with rice and peas, and coleslaw.

Jamaican Jerk Chicken

Setup: Indirect cooking
Wood: Bay leaves and allspice
berries (pimento wood
is also available online)
Equipment: Tongs
Prep time: 10 minutes, plus
overnight marinating time
Cook time: 45 minutes
Serves: 6–8

a few good handfuls of
dried bay leaves
large handful of
allspice berries
16 pieces of skin-on, bone-in
chicken, such as thighs and
legs (I never cook breast on
the barbecue unless it's part
of a whole chicken)

Jerk marinade
3 tablespoons ground allspice
100 g (3½ oz/½ cup) dark
brown sugar
1 head of garlic, cloves
separated and peeled
2 tablespoons thyme leaves
12 spring onions (scallions)
1 teaspoon ground cinnamon
½ teaspoon grated nutmeg
1 teaspoon ground ginger
1 teaspoon ground cloves
4 scotch bonnet chillies,
deseeded
juice of 4 limes
2 teaspoons salt
2 teaspoons ground
black pepper
1 tablespoon light soy sauce
1 tablespoon rum
1 tablespoon vegetable oil

This is one of my most
requested recipes, and I'm
happy to finally release her
into the world. I became
fascinated by jerk chicken
around 10 years ago, and the
buzzing combo of allspice,
fruity scotch bonnet and
thyme remains a favourite.
Nothing smells better on the
grill than a slowly
caramelising jerk marinade.

I can't remember who
taught me the trick of using
a bay leaf 'mat' under the
chicken but it's something I've
been doing for many years now
– the flavour is apparently
similar to that of pimento
wood (the wood of the allspice
tree), which isn't readily
available here. I also add some
soaked allspice berries and
chuck them onto the hot
coals when cooking, for lots
of extra smoke and flavour.
Jamaican jerk chicken is all
about the smoke.

Serve this with rice and
peas, if you like, and the
Plantains with Honey Butter,
Chilli and Lime on page 137.

— Place all the marinade
ingredients into a blender
and blend until smooth.
— Reserve around 100 ml
(3½ fl oz/scant ½ cup) of the
marinade for basting
the chicken as it cooks.
Use the remaining marinade
to coat the chicken and
refrigerate overnight.
— Cover the bay leaves and
allspice berries with water
and leave to soak overnight.
— The next day, prepare
a barbecue for indirect
cooking over medium heat,
with the coals banked to
one side.
— Throw a handful of the
drained bay leaves onto the
grill directly over the coals
and cook the marinated
chicken pieces directly on top
of the bay leaves for 5–10
minutes until beginning to
crisp up. After this time, move
the chicken pieces over to the
cooler side of the grill and
throw some of the drained
allspice berries and remaining
bay leaves into the coals to
create smoke. Put the lid on
and close the vents so that
they are about a quarter open
at the top and bottom. You
want to get as much smoke
into the chicken as you can.
— Leave the chicken to cook,
turning the pieces
occasionally, for about
30 minutes or until cooked
through, brushing them
a couple of times with the
reserved marinade.

To Cook Indoors: Not really
an option: jerk chicken really
does need smoke – that's what
it's all about.

Slow-cooked Shoulder of Pork
with Peach Salsa, Peach Barbecue Sauce and Tortilla Chips

Setup: Indirect cooking
Wood: Oak, beech or apple
Equipment: butcher's paper
(or baking paper or foil),
temperature probe,
heatproof gloves
Prep time: 30 minutes,
plus 1 hour marinating time
Cook time: 6 hours minimum,
plus resting time
Serves: 8

Pork shoulder and rub
1 half pork shoulder (bone-in),
around 2.5 kg (5 lb 8 oz)
2 tablespoons light
brown sugar
2 tablespoons paprika
4 teaspoons fennel
seeds, ground
4 teaspoons coriander
seeds, ground
2 teaspoons garlic powder
2 teaspoons onion powder
1 teaspoon English
mustard powder
2 tablespoons sea salt

This is one of my favourite ways to cook pork shoulder –
properly pulled pork is nothing like the cotton-wool-mush-and-
sauce that was everywhere a few years back. The shoulder
should be pulled with some restraint, leaving large chunks of
tender meat, and there's no need for a cloying sauce that
annihilates everything. I like to serve mine with a fresh peach
salsa and a barbecue sauce made with tinned peaches – trust me
on the tinned part, it's sweet, sour and all kinds of fun.
Tortilla chips are a slightly silly addition but c'mon, who doesn't
want crisps in their sandwich?

A couple of notes about the cooking on this one: while
good-quality lumpwood charcoal is a beautiful thing, you are
going to go through a lot of it doing a long cook like this one in
a kettle barbecue, no doubt about it. This is one situation where
I might use good-quality briquettes and something called the
'snake' method, which involves lining up the briquettes in a row
around the inside of your kettle and lighting one end; the even
size of the briquettes means that they slowly burn around the
outside without causing big temperatures spikes and dips.
I promised this book wouldn't be too technical, so go ahead and
look this technique up online if you want to (it's not difficult).

One thing you will need for this recipe is a temperature
probe, so that you know what's going on with the temperature
of the pork – it's likely to 'stall' at some point (the meat stops
rising in temperature due to evaporative cooling) and you'll
want to know when that happens so that you can wrap it to
speed things up, otherwise it can take hours and hours to get
going again. Some purists don't like to wrap, as it stops the
formation of 'bark' around the outside. I am in favour of
wrapping it and enjoying my dinner.

— Trim the fat on the pork shoulder to about 1 cm ($\frac{1}{2}$ in)
thickness and remove any fibrous silverskin from the underside
of the shoulder.
— Combine the sugar, spices, garlic powder, onion powder,
mustard powder and salt in a bowl and mix well, then rub half
of the mixture all over the shoulder and set aside for 1 hour
at room temperature. Reserve the remaining rub for later.

Peach barbecue sauce
150 ml (5 fl oz/⅔ cup)
cider vinegar
50 ml (1¾ fl oz/3½ tablespoons)
water
2 tablespoons light
brown sugar
2 teaspoons paprika
1 teaspoon English mustard
1 teaspoon garlic powder
dash of hot sauce (e.g.,
Tabasco)
200 g (7 oz) tinned peaches,
drained
pinch of salt

Peach salsa
4 ripe peaches, peeled,
stoned and diced
handful of mint leaves,
chopped
handful of coriander (cilantro)
leaves, chopped
2 green chillies, finely chopped
1 tablespoon rice vinegar
pinch of sugar (if the peaches
are a touch sour)

To serve
sour cream
salted tortilla chips
white buns
hot sauce

— Prepare a barbecue for indirect cooking with half a starter of chimney coals and bank them to one side. Place the pork on the grill on the other side, fat side up. Add a chunk of wood to the hot coals and let it smoulder. Put the lid on and leave the vents about a quarter open. You'll need to check the coals every hour or so and top up as necessary, but there's no point adding more wood after the first few hours.

— The total cooking time is likely to be about 6 hours. As I've said, the meat will most likely 'stall', probably at 65–75°C (150–167°F). Cook the pork to about 70°C (158°F), or whenever it stalls. At this point, wrap it fairly snugly in butcher's paper, baking paper or foil to kickstart things again and cook the wrapped pork for another few hours until it reaches 90°C (194°F) on the probe thermometer before removing it from the heat, to ensure the connective tissue has melted down.

— Rest the meat, wrapped in foil, for at least 30 minutes.

— Pull the meat apart, taking care to remove any small, sharp bones. Don't over-pull it, as it will become mushy – you want to leave some nice big chunks. Sprinkle over some of the reserved rub (you might not use it all, the aim is just to add some more seasoning) and mix it gently.

— Make the peach barbecue sauce by combining all the ingredients (except the salt) in a blender and blending until smooth. Transfer to a saucepan, add the salt and bubble gently for 10 minutes, or until everything is thick and glossy. Remove from the heat.

— Make the peach salsa by combining all the ingredients in a bowl and mixing well. Season with salt and set aside.

— Serve the pulled pork with the peach salsa, peach barbecue sauce, sour cream, tortilla chips, buns and hot sauce.

To Cook Indoors: Preheat the oven to 130°C (260°F/gas 2). Place the rubbed pork in a roasting tin and pour in 500 ml (17 fl oz/generous 2 cups) water or apple juice. Cover tightly with foil and cook in the oven for anything between 4 and 8 hours, or until falling apart.

Smoky Aubergines
(and how to serve them)

Setup: Direct cooking
Wood: Oak or beech
Equipment: Tongs
Cook time: 30 minutes

Cook aubergines (eggplants) well and they turn smoky, creamy and complex; cook them badly and you've got something repulsively squeaky. The best way to barbecue them is whole, so that they crumple like witches' hats, their steamy centres sighing and whistling as they puff and heave in the heat. I like to add some wood, too, to pump up that smoke flavour even further. The flesh can be scooped out and used to best effect (I think) in dips. This is why so many cultures have their own version: Lebanese moutabal, Iranian borani, Greek melitzanosalata and many more …

What you see here is something of a spectrum of dishes to make with your smoky aubs, from a simple whipped aubergine butter through to a fully loaded extravaganza. They all work very well with the flatbreads on page 60.

How to make smoky aubergines

This is incredibly easy: just prepare a barbecue for direct cooking over medium heat, place the aubergines on the grill and cook them until they are completely black and starting to collapse. Add a chunk of wood to the coals and let it smoulder, put the lid on and leave the vents a quarter open, for extra smoky aubergines. You will need to turn them a few times with tongs to make sure they're blackened all over – the whole process usually takes about 30 minutes but will depend on the size of the aubergines.

Once they're blackened, carefully lift them onto a baking tray or into a bowl, cover and let them cool a bit – the juice that collects in the bottom is precious and should not be thrown away. Once they're cool enough to handle, split them down the middle and scrape out as much of the flesh from the skins as you can. Leave the skin behind, but don't worry if some of it gets into the mixture. Add the flesh and juice to your recipe.

To Cook Indoors: Char the aubergines either over a naked gas flame on the hob (I like to line my hob with foil before I do this, to make clean up easier), or under a hot grill.

125 g (4¼ oz/9 tablespoons)
salted butter, softened
flesh (and a little juice)
of 1 Smoky Aubergine
2 teaspoons lemon juice

Smoky Aubergine Butter (serves 8-10)

Whipping things into butter is fairly addictive – just to warn
you. This is one of my favourite flavoured butters, and it's
superb melted onto flatbreads or steaks. Honestly, I just like
to have it in the fridge to spread thickly onto a piece of bread
whenever I feel like it. It has great sandwich potential, too.

— Place the softened butter in a blender and blend until light
and fluffy. Add the aubergine flesh and the lemon juice and
process again. Transfer to the fridge to firm up before using.

---

splash of neutral oil
2 large onions, thinly sliced
2 teaspoons paprika
2 teaspoons garam masala
flesh and juice of 4
Smoky Aubergines
1 head of garlic, top sliced off,
drizzled with oil, then wrapped
in foil and roasted with the
aubergines
3 tablespoons lemon juice
3 tablespoons natural yoghurt
½ teaspoon onion seeds
sea salt

A Borani with Caramelised Onions (serves 4)

This dip is warm with paprika and garam masala, and sweet
with caramelised onions and roasted garlic.

— Heat the neutral oil in a frying pan over a low heat, add the
onions and a pinch of salt and cook gently for about 45 minutes,
stirring regularly, until they are caramelised and golden.
Add the paprika and garam masala for the final few minutes
of cooking, stirring to combine them with the onions.
— Chop the aubergine (eggplant) flesh and place it in a blender
with its juice. Squeeze the roasted garlic cloves from their skins
and add them to the blender with the lemon juice. Add half the
onions and some salt and blend to a chunky mixture.
— Transfer the aubergine mixture to a bowl, stir in the yoghurt,
and top with the remaining onions and the onion seeds.

---

2 heads of garlic, cloves peeled
olive oil
flesh and juice of 6
Smoky Aubergines
2 tablespoons lemon juice
handful of parsley, chopped
handful of mint leaves, chopped
50 g (1¾ oz) feta, crumbled
1 tablespoon sesame seeds, toasted
2 teaspoons onion seeds
sea salt and freshly ground
black pepper

Fully Loaded (serves 4)

The topping ingredients here can be swapped and, of course,
completely changed. Sometimes it's just fun to be #extra.

— First, make the confit garlic. Combine the garlic cloves and
olive oil in a small saucepan and place over the lowest heat you
have on your hob. You want the garlic to cook very gently in the
oil for 30 minutes, or until the cloves are soft.
— Chop the aubergine flesh and mix it in a bowl with its juice,
the lemon juice and some salt and pepper. Add the toppings,
including plenty of confit garlic and a swirl of the oil.

---

flesh and juice of 4
Smoky Aubergines
1 garlic clove, crushed or finely
grated
about 3 tablespoons lemon juice
6 tablespoons tahini
sea salt

A Baba Ganoush (serves 2-4)

My basic recipe for this classic Levantine dip, rich with tahini.

— Chop the aubergine flesh and combine it (and its juice)
in a bowl with the remaining ingredients. Season with salt.

Backyard-style
Apricot-glazed Pork Ribs
with Crushed Spices

Setup: Indirect cooking
Equipment: Tongs
Prep time: 15 minutes
Cook time: 1 hour 15 minutes
Serves: 2–4

2 meaty racks of pork ribs
6 tablespoons apricot jam
1 tablespoon Worcestershire sauce
1 tablespoon light soy sauce
1 tablespoon cider vinegar
½ teaspoons ground ginger
dash of Tabasco
1 tablespoon ketchup
½ teaspoon onion powder
½ teaspoon garlic powder
1 tablespoon coriander seeds
1 teaspoon fennel seeds
1 teaspoon dried chilli flakes, or to taste
sea salt

These are 'backyard style' in the sense that they're simmered first, then finished on the grill (I can feel the barbecue crew sneering from here). Yes, fully smoked ribs are wonderful, but this is such as easy method that I turn to it often. The ribs are sticky sweet from the apricot jam and the crushed spices add bold flavour right at the end of cooking. Finishing with toasted, crushed spices like this is one of my favourite tricks for outdoor cooking. Grilled food can take it.

— Bring a large pan of water to the boil and salt it heavily, as if cooking pasta. Add the ribs and simmer for 1 hour, skimming off the scum every so often.
— Combine the apricot jam, Worcestershire sauce, soy sauce, cider vinegar, ground ginger, Tabasco, ketchup, onion powder and garlic powder in a small saucepan. Bring to the boil, stir and simmer gently for 10 minutes.
— Once the ribs are done, remove them from the water and allow to steam dry while you prepare a barbecue for indirect cooking over medium heat, with the coals banked to one side.
— Lightly toast the coriander and fennel seeds and chilli in a dry frying pan, moving them around so they don't burn. Lightly crush with a pestle and mortar or something heavy. Combine with the chilli flakes and set aside.
— Place the ribs on the opposite side of the grill to the coals and brush them with the apricot glaze. Continue brushing and glazing, turning the ribs every so often, for 10–15 minutes, until they're shiny and caramelised in places.
— Slice the ribs and top with the crushed spice mixture.

To Cook Indoors: Preheat the oven to 180°C (350°F/gas 4). Once the ribs are cooked, place them on a baking tray, brush with the apricot glaze and bake in the oven for 10 minutes. Glaze again and cook for a further 10 minutes.

Pork Fillet Souvlaki
with Honeyed Fennel and Olives

Setup: Indirect cooking
Equipment: Tongs
Prep time: 15 minutes, plus
minimum 1 hour marinating
time (overnight if possible)
Cook time: 20 minutes
Serves: 4

1 pork fillet
(around 450 g/1 lb)

Pork marinade
grated zest and juice
of 1 lemon
2 tablespoons dried oregano
1 teaspoon ground cumin
1½ teaspoons paprika
4 garlic cloves, crushed
3 tablespoons neutral oil
sea salt

Honeyed fennel
2 fennel bulbs
2 tablespoons honey
2 tablespoons lemon juice
1 tablespoon neutral oil
sea salt

To serve
flatbreads or pittas (see
flatbread recipe on page 60)
natural full-fat yoghurt
about 16 black olives
(Kalamata are perfect for this)

While souvlaki – a Greek fast-food dish featuring grilled
pork, lamb or chicken – is usually made with skewered meat,
I've taken to using pork fillet, as I find it stays really tender
on the grill. It can then be sliced and served with honeyed
fennel, which is an excellent barbecue side dish for pork
or fish, generally.

— Combine the pork marinade ingredients with a couple of
pinches of salt in a bowl and rub the mixture all over the pork
fillet. Set aside for at least 1 hour at room temperature or up
to overnight (refrigerated).
— When ready to cook, cut the fennel bulbs into fairly thin
slices lengthways through the root (you want it to stay together
on the grill and the root will help with this). Combine the honey,
lemon juice, oil and a generous pinch of salt and rub the mixture
over the fennel, mixing well.
— Prepare a barbecue for indirect cooking over medium heat,
with the coals banked to one side.
— Once it's ready, place the fennel on the grill directly over the
coals to get it lightly charred and caramelised on both sides –
about 10 minutes. Once this is done, move the slices to the
cooler edge of the barbecue so it can continue cooking through
while you cook the pork.
— Place the marinated pork fillet over direct heat and grill,
turning it a few times with tongs for 15–20 minutes, until
cooked through. It's fine for it to remain very slightly pink
in the centre. Remove from the barbecue and rest the meat for
5 minutes, then slice and serve with the honeyed fennel, bread,
yoghurt and olives.

To Cook Indoors: Preheat a cast-iron griddle pan over a high
heat for at least 5 minutes. Cook the pork for about 15 minutes,
or until cooked as above. Rest for 5 minutes before slicing.

Sticky Pork Bánh Mì

Setup: Direct cooking
Equipment: Tongs, skewers
Prep time: 15 minutes,
plus 1–24 hours marinating time
Cook time: 10 minutes
Serves: 4

500 g (1 lb 2 oz) pork shoulder,
cut into 3 cm (1 ¼ in) cubes

Pork marinade
2 lemongrass stalks, outer
removed and thinly sliced
2 tablespoons light brown sugar
½ teaspoon white pepper
3 tablespoons fish sauce
1 tablespoon sesame seeds
½ tablespoon vegetable oil
1 tablespoon dried chilli flakes

Pickles
1 large carrot, peeled and cut
into matchsticks
250 g (9 oz) daikon, peeled
and cut into matchsticks
1 teaspoon sea salt
50 g (1¾ oz/¼ cup) caster
(superfine) sugar
150 ml (5 fl oz/⅔ cup) white
wine vinegar
150 ml (5 fl oz/⅔ cup) hot water

To serve
4 baguettes
4 tablespoons mayonnaise
4 teaspoons sweet chilli sauce
1 cucumber, sliced
handful of mint leaves
large handful of coriander
(cilantro) leaves
1 red chilli, sliced

I think the bánh mì – a product of the French colonial occupation of Vietnam – may just be my favourite sandwich of all time: it's endlessly variable and a lesson in contrasts, thanks to piquant pickles, fragrant herbs, chilli, and in this case, the sticky, caramelised pork.

The smear of sweet chilli sauce is something I got a taste for thanks to a Vietnamese cafe in South East London called Bánh Mì Bay: an oasis of excitement in the middle of the day for me when I worked in an office nearby and was generally miserable. This bánh mì should be generously filled; the pork is sweet, so that needs to be balanced with plenty of aromatic freshness from the other elements.

— Combine all the ingredients for the pork marinade in a bowl and mix well. Combine with the diced pork, cover and marinate in the fridge for at least a few hours, or overnight.
— To make the pickles, sprinkle the carrot and daikon with the salt in a bowl and massage them gently with your hands for about 2 minutes, until the vegetables are soft and pliable. Discard any liquid at the bottom of the bowl.
— Combine the caster (superfine) sugar with the white wine vinegar and hot water in a bowl and stir until the salt and sugar have dissolved. Pour this liquid over the vegetables and set aside for at least 1 hour, if possible (the pickles will keep in a jar in the fridge for a few weeks).
— Prepare a barbecue for direct cooking over medium heat. Thread the marinated pork onto 4 skewers and grill close to the coals for about 10 minutes, until the pork is caramelised and cooked through, turning with tongs to ensure they cook evenly.
— Make the bánh mì by spreading the baguettes with mayo and sweet chilli sauce, adding cucumber and pickles, grilled pork and the herbs and fresh chilli. Go big or go home!

To Cook Indoors: Grill the pork skewers under a medium-hot grill for about 5 minutes on each side, or until cooked through.

Pork Meatball Num Pang

Setup: Direct cooking
Equipment: Tongs
Prep time: 20 minutes, plus
minimum 1 hour pickling time
Cook time: 15 minutes
Serves: 4

Pork
500 g (1 lb 2 oz) minced
(ground) pork

Kroeung paste
1 × 3 cm (1½ in) square thin
slice of dried shrimp paste
2 tablespoons vegetable
or groundnut oil
3 lemongrass stalks, hard
outer layers removed and
tender part thinly sliced
2 banana shallots, peeled
and finely chopped
50 g (1¾ oz) galangal, peeled
and finely chopped
30 g (1 oz) fresh turmeric,
peeled and finely chopped
1 head of garlic, cloves finely
chopped
10 fresh lime leaves, ribs
removed and finely shredded
2 tablespoons fish sauce

The num pang is the Cambodian version of bánh mì; or is it the
other way around? The answer is probably that they developed
around the same time, since both countries were part of French
Indochina, formed in Cambodia and Vietnam in 1887.

Kroeung, an important aromatic paste in Cambodian cuisine,
is used as the foundation of many dishes. There are actually five
versions; this yellow variant includes fresh turmeric, which
brings not only its colour to the pork, but the root's unique
earthiness too.

— Sprinkle the fennel with the salt and massage gently with
your hands for about 2 minutes, until it is soft and pliable.
— Combine the caster (superfine) sugar with the rice vinegar
and hot water in a bowl and stir until the sugar has dissolved.
Pour this liquid over the fennel and set aside for 1 hour
(the pickles will keep in a jar in the fridge for a few weeks).
— Make the kroeung paste by toasting the shrimp paste in
a dry pan over a medium heat until dark on all sides – about
15 minutes. It's ready when you can snap it in half easily,
like a biscuit. Crush it to a powder in a pestle and mortar.
Heat the oil in a frying pan over a medium heat, then add
everything except the shrimp paste and fish sauce. Cook for
about 5 minutes, stirring until just beginning to brown,
then add the shrimp powder and cook for a further minute or so.
Add everything to a blender with the fish sauce and blend to
a coarse paste.
— Lightly toast the peanuts for the baguettes in a dry pan
(taking care not to burn them). Allow to cool, then smash
to a coarse powder in a pestle and mortar. Set aside.
— Prepare the barbecue for direct cooking over medium heat.
— Combine the kroeung with the minced (ground) pork
in a bowl and mix really well.

Pickled fennel
250 g (9 oz) fennel bulbs,
trimmed and sliced thinly
lengthways (save any frilly
tops for garnishing the
sandwich)
1 teaspoon sea salt
50 g (1¾ oz/¼ cup) caster
(superfine) sugar
150 ml (5 fl oz/⅔ cup)
rice vinegar
150 ml (5 fl oz/⅔ cup)
hot tap water

To serve
2 tablespoons unsalted
peanuts
4 baguettes
4 tablespoons mayonnaise,
mixed with ½ teaspoon ground
white pepper
small handful Thai basil leaves
small handful Vietnamese
coriander or mint leaves
small handful coriander
(cilantro) leaves and
tender stems
1 green chilli, thinly sliced

— Divide the mixture evenly into 16 balls and flatten each one
slightly into a patty. Grill over direct heat on the barbecue for
about 10 minutes turning with tongs, until they've built up a
good caramelised crust on the outside and are cooked through.
— Spread each baguette with mayonnaise, then add some of the
meatballs, pickled fennel, herbs and chilli, and top with plenty
of peanut powder. Eat immediately.

To Cook Indoors: Fry the meatballs in neutral oil in a pan over
a medium heat for 5 minutes on each side, until cooked through.

Bún Chả:
Fish Sauce and
Street Fans

A fan is positioned behind the grill, its rotation a whirring thrum. The scent of caramelised pork is pushed through heavy air in tantalising gusts; the best form of advertising for a street-food vendor. It both attracts customers and fuels the fire, which should be fierce in order to quickly cook the pork patties and strips of marinated belly meat. They will join milky noodles and fragrant sprays of herbs alongside sweet and salty dipping sauce; I don't know it yet, but this is a meal that will carve itself a permanent and important nook in my memory.

There is a trope in food and travel writing along the lines of, 'I was hot and weary from my journey when I found this little street-food stall. I ordered a bowl of <insert dish name here> and felt revived,' which is annoying, because that's what happened when I ate my first bún chả. I am in Hanoi, North Vietnam, the city I think about returning to most often. I long for the controlled chaos and sticky, shimmering heat; the iced coffee viscous with the gloss of condensed milk and of course, the mind-blowing food.

One trip to Vietnam doesn't qualify me to start writing about Vietnamese food with any authority, but I really wanted to include this dish in this book because it's just one of the world's barbecue greats. I needed a guide to teach me the basics, so I contacted Liliane Nguyen, known as @family_feasting on Instagram. We follow each other but have never met, yet she agreed to come around to my house and teach me how to make bún chả. A few weeks later, we are standing at my kitchen counter prepping vegetables and picking herbs.

Liliane is an interior designer, a supper-club host and the founder of a food consultancy service called @thoughtfull_uk, which is 'driven by the need to ground food in its cultural and historical context'.

She explains why she started the business: 'The idea behind it all is to do more things like this, but also to connect with food publications. I see so many recipes in magazines and on websites – Thai curries, for example – that have been written by someone who is white and hasn't done their research or talked to anyone [about the cultural context of a dish]. They've got really random ingredients in there and I'm like, what?! I saw a sweet and sour recipe with balsamic vinegar in it. It's to avoid things like that really. The problem is that people think they want to learn but then they will back out at the last minute – they don't want to hear that what they're doing wrong.'

She describes bún chả as we stand at the counter, a mountain of perilla, mint and coriander leaves before us. 'It's barbecued pork with noodles and a dipping sauce. There's a northern and a southern variation of it, and this variation is the Northern one. In this version there are pork patties/meatballs and thinly sliced pork, which is usually shoulder or belly. Sometimes, some of the pork patties are also wrapped in betel leaves, and sometimes you can have some deep-fried crab spring rolls on the side. So, once you've barbecued the meat, you basically put it in a big bowl with dipping sauce and add the noodles and salad to your bowl rather than pouring the sauce over.

The dipping sauce is more of a savoury broth whereas with the southern version the meat, noodles and salad are already all in one bowl and then the whole thing is mixed up. The southern version includes rock sugar and is much sweeter (in the north we always complain that everything is too sweet!) and you don't have the pork patties, you use different vegetables and herbs …'

It's actually quite unusual to grill pork in Vietnam, says Liliane, with this being one of only a handful of dishes featuring it. 'We barbecue goat, and we barbecue seafood. We do a lot of barbecued shellfish mainly, so a lot of clams and cockles and mussels, and we call all shellfish 'snails'.

Top: Liliane loads pork into a cage for grilling.
Above: Pork patties are grilled hot and fast.

You have restaurants that specialise in barbecue seafood, so you can get clams grilled on the half shell with spring onion oil, for example, or we barbecue prawns and serve them with chilli salt. Like, really spicy chilli salt! We also barbecue things like chicken feet and cartilage a lot, that's a toothsome texture thing.'

The pork we are grilling for the bún chả has been marinated overnight in fish sauce, garlic, honey, MSG and nước màu, a sugar mixture used mainly for colour. 'Nước màu translates to coloured water,' explains Liliane, 'and to make it you basically burn sugar'.

It adds colour to this dish but it's also the basis of Vietnamese braises, for example braised pork belly or catfish. It brings the colour and that slightly burnt, bitter taste. You can buy it or make it – this one I bought and it's made of coconut sugar. If you don't have it you could use dark soy.'

We shape the pork mixture into balls then flatten them slightly into patties. 'Most recipes will say to buy a shoulder and grind your own meat at home so you can control the coarseness of it and the fattiness of the mixture, but most people don't have a meat grinder at home!' says Liliane. 'I guess it's the opposite of a dumpling where you want it to be homogenous – with this you want it to be a little bit chunkier. There's also a version on a skewer but that comes from a more midlands region. People forget how long Vietnam is - south to north is at least a 2-hour flight!'

We pack the strips of marinated shoulder meat into a fish cage, to stop them from falling through the barbecue grill. We also prepare all the accompaniments before grilling, as the process is very quick. 'It's the opposite of, like, American low and slow barbecue where the heat is very controlled,' Liliane tells me. 'You want the grill really fast and really hot, which is why there's always a fan to help with this.'

We prepare vermicelli noodles (which are served cold), and quick-pickle some slices of carrot and kohlrabi. Usually, green papaya would be used but it's so expensive here in the UK that it makes more sense to use something cheaper with a similar texture and flavour. What isn't negotiable however, is the type of vinegar used, 'it does have to be white vinegar - other vinegars have flavours that are too strong.'

We make the dipping sauce/broth by mixing fish sauce, sugar, lime, vinegar and water. 'Some people don't put this on the hob but it's nicer to have it served a little bit warm. There's also an old wives' tale/myth that if you warm it on the hob first, when you put your garlic and chilli in later on, it doesn't just float - it's more homogenous. I'm not sure that's true!

When I was researching recipes for this, a lot of recipes will just say "make it to taste", so if your personal taste is great, it's going to be a good dish! But they won't give you quantities, as it's not learned like that. It's a bit like, "do you have the skill or not?!"'

Once everything is ready, we sizzle the pork on the barbecue, the patties sitting directly on the grill until caramelised and charred in places. They are made with plenty of fat to stop them from drying out. The dish is assembled by adding some pork strips and patties to the broth, and arranging noodles and herbs alongside, for dipping, plunging, slurping. There is also a small bowl of very finely chopped garlic and bird's eye chilli: we both add too much and find ourselves sniffling through the dish, which is just as wonderfully aromatic, sweet, salty and full of fish sauce funk as I remember. We bathe jagged leaves of parilla in the liquid, which impart their electric citrus perfume to the dish. The dish is satisfying, yet light and invigorating.

It's not a quick dish to make, but it's also not something that would be made at home in Vietnam anyway, Liliane says: 'A lot of the time when people think of Vietnamese cooking, they think of noodle salads, baguettes and noodle soups. Dishes like these are things we would go outside and buy. We wouldn't really make them, ever, because you won't be able to make it as good as

the person who is doing it every day for like 30, 40, 50 years and it costs 30p on the street. An issue with Vietnamese food in the UK is - and this is the same with a lot of the cookbooks that are produced - that it's not the food you would eat at home. We would usually just cook the evening meal, and it would be like, soup, rice and vegetables. Maybe some fish or meat. A lot of dishes we eat are banged out in like, 10 minutes. Not with hundreds of different ingredients and aromatics in a broth.'

Of course, the dish is worth the effort if you don't have the option of buying it, and while South East London may not have the frantic atmosphere of Hanoi, the busy road outside my kitchen window with its stream of red buses, sirens and disgruntled cyclists is its own kind of chaos. While the original dish may have fortified and sustained me, this one has truly nourished.

Bún Chả

This is Liliane Nguyen's recipe for bún chả, which, as I said on page 123, I consider one of the greatest barbecue dishes of all time. The combination of salty caramelised pork, sweetened fish sauce and the various herbs is just incredible; this is the kind of dish you can't stop talking about as you're eating it, 'but it's SO good' 'it's just SO SO SO good' and so on, through inelegant (if you're me) mouthfuls of noodles and herb. You'll see. I hope you will join me in my campaign for Liliane to write a cookbook, because she really, really should.

Setup: Direct cooking
Equipment: Fish cage, tongs
Prep time: 45 minutes, plus overnight marinating time
Cook time: 30 minutes
Serves: 8

Pork patty
500 g (1 lb 2 oz) minced pork
minced shallots
1 tablespoon fish sauce
1 teaspoon nước màu (see below), or dark soy sauce

Nước màu
4 tablespoons caster (superfine) sugar
4 tablespoons water

Barbecue pork
750 g (1 lb 10 oz) pork belly, cut into thin strips
2 tablespoons fish sauce
2 teaspoons nước màu
1 tablespoon caster (superfine) sugar
2 teaspoons honey
5 smashed whole garlic cloves (not minced, just smashed with the side of your knife to release juices/aroma)
1 teaspoon Knorr chicken powder or MSG

Pickled vegetables
1 kohlrabi, peeled, cut in half, then each half cut into 8 wedges and thinly sliced
2 carrots, peeled and thinly sliced
3 tablespoons caster (superfine) sugar

To serve
vermicelli noodles
1 round (bibb) lettuce
large handful each Thai basil, mint, coriander, purple perilla (tía tô), Vietnamese balm/ Vietnamese Lemon Mint (kinh gi i)
5 cloves minced garlic
4 minced chillies (preferably bird's eye/Thai chillies, or rocket chillies for a less spicy kick)

Dipping sauce/broth
5 tablespoons fish sauce
2 tablespoons caster (superfine) sugar
2 limes
1 tablespoon distilled white vinegar (must be white distilled vinegar not white wine vinegar, if you cannot find white vinegar it is better to sub with only lime)
100 ml (3½ fl oz/ scant ½ cup) water

— The night before you want to cook the dish, combine all the pork patty ingredients into a bowl and mix it with your hands. Give it a good squish to make sure all the seasoning is absorbed but don't overwork the meat.
— Put all the pork ingredients into a bowl and repeat. Check the seasoning by either frying a small piece of the seasoned pork mixture (or microwaving for 30-60 seconds) until cooked, to check the seasoning. If you feel it needs more fish sauce or sugar then add some more. You're cooking it for you, and everyone's palate is different!
— Put your marinated meats into 2 containers, cover and place in the fridge.
— The next day, place the carrots and kohlrabi into a bowl and sprinkle with 1 teaspoon of salt, giving everything a stir. Leave for 30 minutes to 1 hour and then squeeze to remove the excess water.
— To lightly pickle the kohlrabi and carrots, combine the sugar and 3 tablespoons of water with the vegetables and mix well. Set aside.
— Cook the vermicelli noodles in boiling water for a few minutes, then drain and rinse under cold water. Set aside.
— Shape the pork patty mixture in small Babybel-sized rounds.
— Put all the dipping /broth ingredients except the water into a bowl and mix until all the sugar has dissolved. Taste and adjust accordingly by adding more sugar or vinegar.

The sauce should be a sweet and sour balance. Once adjusted to desired taste, put in a small pan over a low heat and add the 100 ml (31/2 fl oz/ ⅓ cup) of water. This will be warmed up prior to serving.

— Prepare a barbecue for direct cooking over high heat with the coals evenly spread over the base of the barbecue and just a small, cooler section to one side. Place the pork belly meat into the fish cage in one even single layer. You want every piece to have direct contact with the heat and to char a bit on the edges. Cook for 15-20 minutes, until everything is well caramelised and a little charred.

— At the same time, cook the pork patties over direct heat, turning them regularly with tongs, until cooked through and caramelised - around 15 minutes.

— To serve, arrange the noodles, herbs and salad on a serving platter.

— Each person should have a medium bowl. Each bowl should be filled with a few pork patties and barbecue belly, then topped with the drained kohlrabi and carrot and filled up with the dipping sauce.

— Minced chilli and garlic can be added to your bowl to taste.

— To eat, grab some noodles and vegetables and dip into your bowl and eat with the sauce and the meat out of the bowl. Often the noodle and vegetable plates are communal and placed in the middle of the table for people to continue helping themselves.

The various components of the dish are assembled.

Thai Barbecue: Smoke, Umami and the Long, Slow Sizzle

Ben Chapman, a restaurateur and expert in regional Thai food cooked over fire, is laughing: 'Yeah, so in Thailand, barbecuing is just called "cooking"' he says. What he means is that, historically, cooking outside was more common than cooking indoors in Thailand, and so barbecue is not a distinct culinary method as it is here in the UK and other parts of the world. I've called Ben because I am a fan of his work, particularly at his restaurant Kiln, which, despite being as firmly planted in London's primo Soho restaurant territory as it's possible to get, has no gas connected to its kitchen. Everything is cooked over live fire, from Northern Thai-style sausages to slow-grilled plaice and clay pot noodles.

While we chuckle about the emergence of barbecue as a movement here in the UK, compared with it being simply a method of putting a meal on the table in so many other countries, it emerges that the methods used in Thailand, both in terms of fuel preparation and cooking technique, are quite different from what we generally try to achieve in the West.

'A key component of Thai seasoning is smoke,' says Ben. 'A lot of Thai food relies on the different flavours you can extract from food by cooking over fire. There are typical dishes like moo yang, gai yang – pork and chicken marinated then grilled very slowly, a long distance away from the embers in order to get a little smokiness and a tickle of char. You're not going to get any of the blackening that you get in European cooking, that's just not a thing in Thai food.'

'When something is on the heat for a long time, you're really prioritising flavour over some of the texture. In Western cooking, people get excited about texture more than flavour, but to me that's less interesting. There are roadside places in Thailand where different parts of a pig are slowly grilled over gentle flaky white embers. You learn from that how you're going to preserve elements that aren't going to be there if you grill hard and fast.'

Slow-cooked ingredients might also be pounded into a paste to use in a marinade or sauce. 'Smoking ducks over coconut husk is quite typical, or smoking catfish in an enclosed chamber – quite similar to American-style barbecue – and they might be used in jungle curries. It all depends on the flavours you're looking to balance; you might be balancing saltiness with spiciness or bitterness with sweetness.' Smoke, says Ben, is a great way of harmonising those broad dimensions of flavour. 'There is a relationship between umami and smoke in Thai barbecue that is really important' He is referring to umami in the form of pla la [unfiltered freshwater fish sauce] and gapi [shrimp paste]. 'When you take those two things out, you can lose a dish.'

Cooking Thai cuisine in the UK is not straightforward due to the availability (or not) of ingredients. 'Our view is that by using ingredients we can get here, we accept that the dish is not verbatim but we should try to cook with an empathic spirit, so if the original dish is spicy, it should be as spicy, if the dish is bitter, it should be as bitter and so on – we are trying to honour the spirit of the original recipe, while accepting the new place it's going to go to.'

'At the restaurant, we cook using various forms of barbecue (as they do in Thailand), so we use charcoal grills to cook things a long way away from the fire. We do little red mullet and we take the offal and pound that into an aromatic paste, stuff the cavity and then grill them really gently over flaky white embers. We also do a lot of cooking on a tao, which is a traditional Thai barbecue.' The tao resembles a clay-lined bucket with an air vent at the bottom. The centre can be filled with fuel and a wok or grill placed on top. 'We use a highly engineered charcoal in the tao,' says Ben, 'which generates heat that is then held by the ceramic core.'

'We also use wood, which they wouldn't really use in Thailand, but we use it if we are looking for a more characterful smokiness; if you imagine the smokiness you would get grilling a piece of meat over vine wood for example: you get the character of the wood, whereas if you take the smokiness in, say,

smoked mackerel, it's not a characterful smokiness. We don't have words in English that are useful for describing these differences.'

I ask Ben where I should begin if I want to try grilling the Thai way. It has to be something slowly cooked, of course: 'I would start with the really classic Isaan (Northeast Thai) dishes, so gai yang, which is chicken marinated with coriander root, white pepper, turmeric ... That's going to teach you that slow grilling technique; you can't char it, it won't work – you have to have it a good distance from the fire and you have to be patient. All the bones are getting cooked all the way through – all the collagen is getting completely broken down into gelatine, all the skin has nice even colour. All the raw spice flavours in the marinade need to cook out. We always say that Thai food is really sophisticated and elegant, but it's done effortlessly, and this is a really good example of that.'

'Learning to grill fish in banana leaf with a simple curry paste is also a nice thing to do. It makes the fish easy to handle on the grill and the combination of fish, curry paste and banana leaf means it's going to retain a lot of moisture and the fish will be well cooked.

However, the idea is to get the raw curry paste cooked out, so you're thinking more about flavour and less about "cuisson" (a French term used to describe the degree to which fish or meat is cooked through), which is what people tend to think about with fish here; when you read a restaurant review they always say "the fish was cooked perfectly" not whether or not it tasted nice!'

I decided to develop the slow-grilled chicken with nam jim jaew: a salty, sweet, sour and slightly spicy dipping sauce, and fish steamed inside banana leaf (pages 130 and 133). The chicken is spectacular, slowly crisping until golden-tan, its flesh so tender there's the definite sense it was basted gently in its own fat. The fish, too, is glorious – herbs and paste softened yet still bold in flavour, pearly nuggets of cod, the grassiness of singed banana leaf permeating the fish. 'You're getting a sweet char as the banana leaf starts to catch,' says Ben 'and that gets into the food. The slow cooking is so important for the way the smokiness is used as a seasoning'. I pull another piece of meat from the chicken with my hands, wrapping it in a parcel of its own crisp skin, plunging it into the nam jim jaew. It's perfect, and I can see no reason at all to disagree with him.

Gai Yang with Nam Jim Jaew

Setup: Indirect cooking
Equipment: Tongs
Prep time: 15 minutes, plus overnight marinating time
Cook time: 1½ hours
Serves: 4

1 whole, large chicken approx 2–2.5 kg (4 lb 8 oz–5 lb 8 oz)

Marinade
3 tablespoons chopped coriander (cilantro) roots and stalks
1 head of garlic, cloves peeled
2 tablespoons light brown sugar
30 g (1 oz) fresh turmeric, grated and peeled
2 teaspoons white peppercorns
3 tablespoons fish sauce
1 teaspoon dark soy sauce

Nam jim jaew
1 tablespoon glutinous (sticky) rice
2 small Thai shallots, or 1 regular shallot, peeled and thinly sliced
1 spring onion, green part only, thinly sliced
2 tablespoons fish sauce
1–2 tablespoons light brown sugar
3–4 tablespoons lime juice
1 tablespoon dried chilli flakes

Gai yang is grilled chicken and nam jim jaew is a sauce from Isaan province in northeast Thailand. Best served with grilled meats, it is wildly popular. This dipping sauce is sweet, sour and a little spicy (although I do like to add a fair bit of chilli to mine, and you should adjust to your own taste). The roasted rice powder is easy to make and is essential to the sauce, adding a toasty flavour and a crunchy texture.

— To make the marinade for the chicken, pound the coriander roots and stalks, garlic, sugar, turmeric and peppercorns to a paste in a pestle and mortar, then mix in the fish sauce and soy sauce.
— Spatchcock the chicken by cutting either side of the backbone with sharp kitchen scissors. Remove the bone, turn the bird over and press down firmly with the heel of your hand. Rub the marinade all over the chicken and marinate in the fridge, covered, overnight.

— Toast the dry sticky rice in a pan or wok over a medium heat for about 10 minutes stirring continuously to stop it from burning. The toasted rice should have an even, golden colour. Allow the rice to cool completely, then grind to a coarse powder in a spice grinder or pestle and mortar. You want to retain some of the crunchy texture of the rice, so take care not to grind it to a fine powder.
— When you are ready to cook, prepare the barbecue for indirect cooking with the coals banked to one side. When the coals are ready, almost close the vents, leaving just a small gap at the top and the bottom. Wipe any large clumps of marinade off the chicken and cook the chicken offset, breast side up with the legs facing towards the hotter side, for 1½ hours.
— To make the nam jim jaew, combine all the ingredients with the toasted rice powder in a bowl. Allow the chicken to rest for 15 minutes before serving with the dipping sauce.

Grilled Fish
in Banana Leaf

Setup: Direct cooking
Equipment: Tongs, toothpicks
or small skewers
Prep time: 30 minutes
Cook time: 30 minutes
Makes: 4 small parcels

2 banana leaves, each cut into
several pieces and wiped
to remove dust and dirt
350 g (12 oz) meaty white fish
fillets (I used cod), cut into
large chunks
8 fresh lime leaves
a handful of Thai basil leaves
sea salt

Curry paste
2 lemongrass stalks, woody
outer parts removed and
tender part sliced
grated zest of 1 lime
(preferably makrut but
regular will do)
1 head of garlic, cloves
separated and peeled
5 small Thai shallots
(or 1 large shallot), sliced
8 small dry Thai red chillies
2 fresh bird's eye chillies
15 g ($\frac{1}{2}$ oz) fresh turmeric,
peeled and grated
2.5 cm (1 in) piece fresh
galangal, peeled and roughly
chopped

To serve
Thai basil leaves
limes, for juicing
sticky rice

This is such a simple method
for cooking fish. It allows the
fish to steam inside, taking
on the aroma of the singed
banana leaf. It should be
grilled gently to ensure that
the raw flavours of the curry
paste have time to soften –
this should the priority, rather
than the final texture of the
fish. Don't worry, it will taste
incredible. Trust the process.

— To make the curry paste,
pound everything in a pestle
and mortar with a generous
pinch of salt. Combine with
the fish pieces in a bowl
and set aside.
— Cut the banana leaves into
pieces large enough to wrap
around the fish. Lay a piece of
banana leaf, shiny green side
down, on a surface and lay
another piece on top of it to
make a cross shape. Place a
lime leaf on the banana leaves
and add a quarter of the fish
pieces on top. Add another
lime leaf, a small handful of
Thai basil leaves and a little
salt. Fold into a parcel and
secure with toothpicks or
small skewers. Repeat with
the remaining fish and leaves
to make 4 parcels.
— Prepare a barbecue
for direct cooking over
low-medium heat. Place the
parcels over direct heat and
cook for 30 minutes, turning
them halfway through. Don't
worry if the leaves go black –
the fish will steam inside.
— Serve the fish in the parcels
with extra Thai basil and lime
juice squeezed over the top,
and sticky rice on the side.

Pull-apart Garlic Bread

Setup: Indirect cooking
Equipment: A cast-iron frying pan – preferably with a flat lid, heatproof gloves
Prep time: 10 minutes, plus 30 minutes–1 hour rising time
Cook time: 30 minutes
Serves: 4–6

Dough
500 g (1 lb 2 oz/3 cups plus 2 tablespoons) '00' flour
7 g ($\frac{1}{4}$ oz) instant yeast
300 ml (10 fl oz/1$\frac{1}{4}$ cups) warm water
25 g (1 oz) sea salt

Garlic butter
250 g (9 oz) butter, softened
1 large head of garlic, cloves separated, peeled, and crushed or finely grated
large handful of parsley leaves, finely chopped

I first published this recipe in *Pit* magazine, but, since we printed hardly any copies barely anyone got to see it, and I really do want as many people to cook this as possible.
The best vessel for cooking it is a cast-iron frying pan with a lid, which will allow you to turn the bread over to brown the crust. If you don't have a lid though, it doesn't matter, it just won't be as brown on top. It will still taste incredible. I think I could actually eat a whole one of these to myself and not regret it – pillowy soft dough, freshly baked, soaked in garlic butter. Yup, definitely a whole one.

— Make the dough by combining all the ingredients in a bowl (or the bowl of a stand mixer with a dough hook). Bring together into a soft dough and knead for 5 minutes until you have a smooth elastic dough. Separate evenly into 8 balls and set aside in a warm place under a clean tea towel (dish towel) to rise until doubled in size – 30 minutes to 1 hour.
— To make the garlic butter, mash the butter in a bowl with the crushed garlic and parsley.
— Prepare the barbecue for indirect cooking with the coals banked to one side.
— Brush a cast-iron frying pan with neutral oil and place the dough balls into it, brushing them all over (gently) with lots of the garlic butter. Put the lid on the pan.
— Place the pan on the side of the barbecue without any coals, put the lid on and leave the vents half open. Cook for 25–30 minutes or until cooked through and very crisp on the bottom. After this time, carefully turn the pan over (it will be incredibly hot, so use heatproof gloves) and cook for a further 5 minutes.
— Brush with as much of the remaining butter as you like, and serve!

To Cook Indoors: Preheat the oven to 220°C (430°F/gas 9). Bake the bread in the oven with the lid on for 25–30 minutes, then remove the lid and cook for a further 5 minutes.

Setup: Direct cooking
Equipment: Tongs
Prep time: 5 minutes
Cook time: 10 minutes
Serves: 6-8

4 very ripe (black) plantains
60 g (2¼ oz/4 tablespoons)
salted butter
2 tablespoons honey
1 tablespoon dried chilli
flakes (or to taste)
lime wedges, to serve

Plantains
with Honey Butter, Chilli and Lime

The area of South East London where I live is home to one of the
largest diaspora populations of Nigerian people in the UK, which
means that the streets are lined with shops full of ingredients such as
technicolour scotch bonnet peppers (the reason I became fully
addicted to them), bulbous brown yams and plantains, which follow a
spectrum of light green through yellow to black, depending on their
level of ripeness.

The ripe (black) plantains caramelise beautifully on the barbecue,
especially in a honey-butter glaze. I love to serve them with Jamaican
Jerk Chicken (page 109), or with some vanilla or coconut ice cream.

— Trim the ends of the plantains but don't peel them. Slice each one
in half lengthways.
— Melt the butter with the honey and chilli flakes in a saucepan.
Set aside.
— Prepare a barbecue for direct cooking over medium heat.
— Use a piece of oiled kitchen paper or cloth and tongs to lightly oil
the grill. Brush the plantains with some of the glaze and grill flesh
side down over direct heat for a few minutes, until caramelised with
grill marks. Turn them over and brush again on the cut side with the
glaze. Continue grilling and glazing until soft – about 10 minutes.
— I like to take the soft plantain out of their skins, slice them into
pieces and serve them with any remaining glaze poured over, and
lime juice squeezed on top.

Setup: Direct cooking
Equipment: Tongs, a grill
basket or fish cage
Prep time: 15 minutes
Cook time: 10 minutes
Serves: 2

1 45 g (1½ oz) tin of anchovies
in olive oil
1 garlic clove, peeled
2 egg yolks
1 teaspoon Dijon mustard
3½ tablespoons light olive oil
400 g (14 oz) green beans,
topped and tailed
neutral oil, for cooking
the beans
1 tablespoon lemon juice
freshly ground black pepper
lemon wedges, to serve

Green Beans
with Anchovy Cream

Green beans may need some careful manoeuvring on the barbecue
(if you have a grill basket or fish cage, now is the time to use it!) but
they reward you by blistering into something much more interesting
than their boiled squeaky cousins. The anchovy cream is so silky;
this is a luxurious dish for a summer evening with focaccia or
sourdough to swish over the plate.

— Place the anchovies and their oil, the garlic, egg yolks
and mustard into a food processor and blitz to a rough paste.
With the motor running, add the olive oil very slowly, making sure
each drop is emulsified before adding the next. Once it thickens
a bit, add the oil in a steady stream. Add the lemon juice and a good
crack of black pepper.
— Prepare a barbecue for direct cooking over medium heat.
— Toss the beans in a little oil and grill over direct heat for about
10 minutes, or until soft, wrinkled and charred in places.
— Serve with the anchovy cream and a lemon wedge.

150 ml (5 fl oz/⅔ cup)
rice vinegar
350 ml (12 fl oz/1½ cups)
hot tap water
50 g (1¾ oz/¼ cup) caster
(superfine) sugar
1 tablespoon sea salt

My Standard Pickle Brine

Combine the rice vinegar, water, sugar and salt in a jug and stir until the sugar and salt have dissolved, then pour over your chosen fruit or vegetables.

Equipment: A sterilised jar
Prep time: 10 minutes
Makes: Fills a 1 litre
(34 fl oz) jar

4 ripe nectarines, stoned
and each cut into eighths
6 fresh lime leaves, bruised
2 thick slices of peeled ginger
1 quantity Standard Pickle
Brine (above)

Pickled Nectarines

Nectarines are my favourite fruit – like a slightly tart peach without the troubling fuzz. I'm always looking for new ways to eat them (see also the Upside-down Nectarine Cake with Thyme Cream on page 142 and the Halloumi with Nectarines, Tarragon and Basil on page 82).

— Sterilise your jar(s) first, as this is a quick process.
— Pack the nectarines into the jar, layering them up with the lime leaves and ginger.
— Pour over the brine, seal and refrigerate. The pickle will taste good after 2 days, and just gets better over a few weeks. They'll keep in the fridge like this for a couple of months.

Equipment: A sterilised jar
Prep time: 10 minutes
Makes: Fills a 1 litre
(34 fl oz) jar

450 g (1 lb) green beans,
washed, topped and tailed
4 garlic cloves, peeled and
smashed with the side of
a knife (or something heavy)
pared peel of 1 lemon,
in strips
3 sprigs of rosemary
½ teaspoon black peppercorns
large pinch of dried
chilli flakes
1 quantity Standard Pickle
Brine (above)

Pickled Green Beans

A barbecue classic! For me, at least. I also love how these look on the kitchen counter, all stood up in the jar.

— Sterilise your jar(s) first, as this is a quick process.
— Pack the beans into the jar (stand them up on their ends), along with the garlic, lemon peel, rosemary, peppercorns and chilli flakes.
— Pour over the brine, seal and refrigerate. They're good after 2 days, and just get better over a few weeks. They'll keep in the fridge like this for a couple of months.

Equipment: A sterilised jar
Prep time: 10 minutes
Makes: Fills a 1 litre
(34 fl oz) jar

2 fennel bulbs (about
500 g/1 lb 2 oz), tops and
bottom removed and bulbs cut
into thin slices lengthways
3 garlic cloves, peeled and
smashed with the side of
a knife (or something heavy)
3 dried chillies
1 tablespoon coriander seeds
1 teaspoon fennel seeds
1 quantity Standard Pickle
Brine (page 140)

Pickled Fennel

This goes very well with pork and fish. I also like to use it in
sandwiches, such as the Sticky Pork Bánh Mì on page 119.

— Sterilise your jar(s) first, as this is a quick process.
— Pack the fennel into the jar, layering it up with the garlic,
chillies, coriander and fennel seeds.
— Pour over the brine, seal and refrigerate. The pickle will taste
good after 2 days, and just gets better over a few weeks. It will
keep in the fridge like this for a couple of months.

Setup: Direct cooking
Equipment: Tongs
Prep time: 5 minutes
Cook time: 15 minutes,
plus an optional few hours
resting time
Serves: 4

600 g (1 lb 5 oz) ripe but
firm tomatoes
2 onions, peeled and halved
1 fat garlic clove, crushed
or finely grated
1 tablespoon lemon juice
large handful of coriander
(cilantro) leaves and stalks,
finely chopped
small handful of mint leaves,
chopped
1 tablespoon pomegranate
molasses
sea salt

Smoky Tomato Salsa

This salsa looks rather ordinary when you scan the ingredients,
but the charring of the tomatoes and onions and their
combination with pomegranate molasses makes it complex
in flavour.

— Prepare a barbecue for direct cooking over medium heat.
— Cook the tomatoes and onions (cut side down) in the centre
of the grill (so halfway between the hottest and coolest sides)
for about 15 minutes, until the tomatoes are starting to collapse,
and the onions are nicely charred. Turn with tongs to ensure
even cooking.
— Remove from the grill and, once cool enough to handle,
slip off the tomato skins and any stalks. Chop them roughly
and add them to a bowl along with any juice.
— Remove any tough outer skin from the onions, chop them
fairly finely and combine with the tomatoes. Add all the other
ingredients and season with salt. This salsa improves if left
for a couple of hours at room temperature before serving.

To Cook Indoors: Preheat a cast-iron griddle pan over a high
heat for at least 5 minutes. Char the tomatoes and onions for
about 15 minutes.

Upside-down Nectarine Cake
with Thyme Cream

Setup: Indirect cooking
Equipment: Skillet,
heatproof gloves
Prep time: 15 minutes,
plus 20 minutes infusing time
Cook time: 40–50 minutes
Serves: 8

125 g (4¼ oz/9 tablespoons)
butter, softened
125 g (4¼ oz/generous ½ cup)
golden caster (superfine) sugar
125 g (4¼ oz/1 cup)
self-raising flour
1 teaspoon baking powder
1 teaspoon vanilla extract
2 large eggs

Thyme cream
300 ml (10 fl oz/1¼ cups)
double (heavy) cream
2 sprigs of thyme
1 teaspoon caster
(superfine) sugar

Caramelised nectarine
50 g (1¾ oz) butter, softened
50 g (1¾ oz/generous ¼ cup)
light brown sugar
3 ripe but firm nectarines,
stoned and sliced into
6-8 wedges
leaves from 1 sprig of thyme

It is surprising how well this cake comes out, considering it's cooked on a barbecue. Upside-down cakes are particularly forgiving, and irresistible with their caramelised fruity base. Here I've combined my favourite fruit with a little thyme; herb flavours can be stunning when combined with sugar, as long as you don't overdo it. Of course, you could cook this in the oven, but where's your spirit of adventure?

— Gently heat the cream in a pan with the thyme sprigs, but don't let it boil. Set aside for 20 minutes to infuse, then strain and chill.
— Cut out a circle of parchment paper that is a bit larger than the skillet and use it to line the base. It will come up the sides a little bit and help to contain the caramel.
— Beat the 50 g (1¾ oz/3½ tablespoons) butter and 50 g (1¾ oz/ ¼ cup) sugar together with a wooden spoon (or use a mixer with a paddle attachment) until creamy, then spread it over the paper in the base of the skillet. Arrange the fruit slices in a nice pattern on top of the butter and sugar mixture. Add the leaves from 1 sprig of thyme. Place the skillet on top of a baking sheet (one that will fit inside the barbecue).
— Prepare a barbecue for indirect cooking with the coals banked to one side – you are looking for medium heat.
— Place all the cake ingredients in a bowl and use an electric whisk to beat to a soft consistency. Spoon on top of the fruit.
— Bake the cake on the opposite side to the coals for 40–50 minutes with the lid on and the vents open, or until a skewer inserted into the middle of the cake comes out clean. Remove from the barbecue and allow to stand for 5 minutes before turning out and removing the parchment paper.
— Serve the upside-down cake with the thyme cream.

To Cook Indoors: Preheat the oven to (320°F/gas 4). Bake the cake on a baking sheet in the oven for 35 minutes. Remove from the oven and allow to stand for 5 minutes before turning out.

Jammy Peaches and Cream
with Ginger Nut Biscuits

Setup: Indirect cooking
Wood: Choose from
Oak, Beech, sweet chestnut
or apple
Equipment: Roasting tray,
heatproof gloves
Prep time: 5 minutes
Cook time: 20 minutes
Serves: 3–4

6 ripe but firm peaches,
stoned and halved
250 ml (8 fl oz/1 cup) sweet
wine (I use a late-harvest
Chenin Blanc, or Muscat
Beaumes de Venise)
½ teaspoon vanilla extract
1 star anise
3 tablespoons light
brown sugar
a generous knob of
(1 oz/2 tablespoons) butter

To serve
a few scoops of vanilla ice
cream or clotted cream
a couple of ginger nut biscuits
(or similar) per serving

A still-warm squishy pile of lightly smoked fruit bathed in
spiced sweet wine – heaven on top of cold vanilla ice cream,
or even glossy wads of the clotted stuff. If I've some fuel left
after cooking the main event, I like to put these in the barbecue
and let them slowly give in until we are ready for them. They can
just as easily be cooked in the oven but, of course, you will miss
the smoke element.

— Prepare a barbecue for indirect cooking at low-medium heat,
with the coals banked to one side.
— Place the peach halves cut side up in a roasting tray and add
the sweet wine, vanilla extract and star anise. Scatter the sugar
over the peaches and dot the butter on top.
— Add a small piece of wood to the lit coals and let it smoulder.
Cook in the centre of the barbecue with the lid on and the vents
a quarter open for about 20 minutes, or until the peaches are
soft and a little collapsed and jammy. If they're not collapsing
fast enough, move them directly over the coals.
— Serve the jammy peaches with the cream or ice cream,
ginger nut biscuits and the poaching liquor.

To Cook Indoors: Preheat the oven to 160°C (320°F/gas 4).
Cook the peaches in the oven for 10–15 minutes, until the
peaches are soft and starting to collapse.

Smoked Cherry and
Whisky Butterscotch Sundae

Setup: Indirect cooking
Wood: Choose from oak,
beech, sweet chestnut or apple
Equipment: Roasting tray,
heatproof gloves
Prep time: 5 minutes
Cook time: 30 minutes
Serves: 3–4

Cherries
500 g (1 lb 2 oz) cherries,
pitted and halved
1 sprig of rosemary
juice of ½ lemon
2 tablespoons maple syrup
pinch of salt

Whisky butterscotch
50 g (1¾ oz/3½ tablespoons)
salted butter
50 g (1¾ oz/generous ¼ cup)
light brown sugar
200 ml (7 fl oz/scant 1 cup)
condensed milk
¼ teaspoon vanilla extract
2 tablespoons double
(heavy) cream
2 tablespoons whisky

To serve
vanilla ice cream

Serve this to the person who says that barbecue desserts are always rubbish (to be fair, they generally are). The combination of roasted cherries, rosemary, maple syrup and – most importantly – smoke, melds into something special. Layer the cherries and their juice up with ice cream and whisky caramel and you've got yourself a knockout.

— Prepare a barbecue for indirect cooking over medium heat, with the coals banked to one side.
— Place the halved cherries, rosemary sprig, lemon juice, maple syrup, salt and a splash of water into a roasting tray. Mix gently.
— Add a small piece of wood to the lit coals and let it smoulder. Place the roasting tray on the cooler side of the barbecue. Put the lid on and leave the vents a quarter open. Cook for 30 minutes, turning halfway through, until they have collapsed a little and given up some of their juice.
— Melt the butter and sugar for the butterscotch together in a saucepan, then turn up the heat and let it bubble for a minute or so, until you have a homogenous mixture. Add the condensed milk and vanilla extract, whisking continuously, and continue cooking and whisking for about 5 minutes, until the mixture thickens.
— Remove from the heat and whisk in the double (heavy) cream and whisky.
— Layer up the cherries and some of their cooking juices with vanilla ice cream and the whisky butterscotch in sundae glasses. Serve immediately.

To Cook Indoors: Preheat the oven to 180°C (350°F/gas 4). Cook the cherries in the oven for 30–35 minutes, until they have collapsed a little and given up some of their juice.

Smoked Tomato Soup
with Smoked Garlic Toast

Setup: Indirect cooking
Wood: Oak or beech
Equipment: Roasting tray,
heatproof gloves
Prep time: 10 minutes
Cook time: 1–1½ hours
Serves: 4

---

1 kg (2 lb 4 oz) tomatoes,
halved
2 onions, peeled and cut
into thick wedges
2 heads of garlic, cloves
separated but not peeled
olive oil
500 ml (17 fl oz/generous
2 cups) vegetable or
chicken stock
large handful of basil,
leaves only
1 teaspoon caster
(superfine) sugar
1 teaspoon sherry vinegar
100 ml (3½ fl oz/scant ½ cup)
double (heavy) cream
sea salt and freshly ground
black pepper

Smoked garlic toast
70 g (2½ oz/5 tablespoons)
salted butter, softened slightly
small handful of parsley
leaves, finely chopped
4 slices crusty bread or
sourdough

There's something about the aroma of a gently smouldering log in the barbecue on a crisp autumn morning that's irresistible; the mystery of it hangs in the air, a promise of good things to come later. This is like the tomato soup of my childhood wearing a lumberjack shirt. It's rich and creamy, with a gorgeous whiff of woodland, and – best of all – it comes with garlic bread.

— Place the tomatoes cut side up in a roasting tray, along with the onion wedges and garlic cloves. Coat with a slosh of olive oil.
— Prepare a barbecue for indirect cooking, with the coals banked to one side.
— Add a chunk of wood and, when it starts to smoulder, add the tray of tomatoes and onions on the cooler side of the barbecue, close the lid, leave the vents a quarter open, and cook for 1–1½ hours, rotating the tray halfway through or until the onions are golden and charred, and the tomatoes soft and broken down.
— Remove the tray from the barbecue using heatproof gloves or an oven mitt.
— Squeeze the garlic cloves from their skins. Keep half of the cloves for the soup and reserve the rest for the garlic toast. Remove the skins from the tomatoes and the first layer of the onions, plus any roots.
— Add the tomatoes, onions and garlic to a saucepan with the stock, basil and some salt and pepper. Make sure any juices from the roasting tray go into the saucepan, too. Use a stick blender to blend the soup until smooth, then gently reheat. Taste the soup and season with the sugar and the sherry vinegar, plus more salt and pepper if needed. Add the cream and mix well.
— Mash the butter with the remaining garlic cloves and parsley in a bowl. Toast the bread and spread it liberally with the butter. Serve the garlic toasts at once, with the soup.

To Cook Indoors: Obviously you're not going to get any of the smokiness cooking this indoors, but you will have a lovely tomato soup, so I guess it's okay. Preheat the oven to 140°C (280°F/gas 3) and cook the tomatoes, onions and garlic in a roasting tray for an hour or so.

Figs Two Ways

Setup: Direct cooking
Equipment: Tongs, foil (if not using fig leaves), cocktail sticks (if using fig leaves)
Prep time: 5 minutes
Cook time: 5 minutes
Serves: 2–3

6 figs
100 g (3½ oz) Stilton
½ teaspoon runny honey per fig
6 fig leaves

Stilton-stuffed Figs Cooked in Their Own Leaves

Is it mean to cook figs in their own leaves? The large, waxy leaves are just right for wrapping the soft, stuffed fruits and it's an attractive way to serve them. If you don't have a fig tree near you, then, obviously, just use foil instead.

— This is a bit like a hot cheeseboard, I guess: sweet fruit and sharp, funky cheese.
— Prepare a barbecue for direct cooking over a low-ish heat.
— Cut a cross in the top of the figs and fill with the Stilton. Top each fig with ½ teaspoon of honey.
— Wrap each fig in a leaf and secure with a cocktail stick (or wrap in foil, loosely closed at the top). Cook over direct heat for about 5 minutes, or until soft and the cheese is melted.

Setup: Direct cooking
Equipment: Tongs
Prep time: 10 minutes
Cook time: 5 minutes
Serves: 4

8 figs
neutral oil, for brushing the figs
4 tablespoons caster (superfine) sugar
grated zest of 1 orange
2 teaspoons thyme leaves
2 tablespoons pomegranate molasses, plus a little extra to serve
vanilla ice cream, to serve

Sticky Grilled Figs with Vanilla Ice Cream

These taste alarmingly boozy when they come off the grill and I can't help thinking it wouldn't be a bad idea to have them with a glass of something like a dessert Riesling - all electric acidity and honeyed, herbal notes.

— Prepare a barbecue for direct cooking over medium heat.
— Trim the stems off the figs and cut them in half lengthways. Brush the skin side of each with a little neutral oil.
— Combine the sugar, orange zest and thyme leaves in a bowl and rub together with your fingers until you have a lovely orange sugar. Brush the cut sides of the figs with the pomegranate molasses and sprinkle with the orange and thyme sugar.
— Place the figs over direct medium heat, cut side up. Put the lid on, vents half closed and cook for about 5 minutes, until the topping starts to bubble and the figs are soft.
— Serve with vanilla ice cream, and a little more pomegranate molasses swirled on top, if you like.

To Cook Indoors: Cook the figs under a medium-hot grill for about 5 minutes until hot and bubbling, taking care not to burn them.

Mackerel

Near to where I live in South East London there is a series of railway arches occupied by various businesses, old and new. Some could be considered signs of gentrification – the multiple (and excellent) craft beer breweries, for example – while others are established, their worn footpaths and accumulated grime forming part of the structural fabric. One such business is a mechanics yard, full of twisted metal and terrifying tools. One day a mate of mine (hi, Iso!) was cycling past when she caught a whiff of smoke and stopped to investigate; she found a group of men huddled around an old oil drum and asked what they were up to – it turns out they'd converted the drum into a mackerel smoker. I absolutely love this story. The idea of these men with their calloused, oily hands that spend all day grappling with the underside of cars delicately lowering fresh fish into the smoking barrel, then sitting down to eat it together. Why should they be eating a soggy sandwich? Where there's a will, there's a way.

It pleased me that this fragment of our fish smoking tradition happened in my little corner of London. Its history dates back hundreds of years, with herrings smoked at Great Yarmouth, Norfolk, as far back as the 13th century where they were soaked in brine then hung in chimneys until golden.

The Yarmouth bloater was particularly popular during Victorian times, so called because it was smoked with the guts still inside, giving it a portly appearance. I can relate. Grimsby, on England's north east coast, has a tradition of cod and haddock smoking that stretches back 150 years, and a few smokehouses survive, such as Alfred Enderby with its traditional rotating iron chimney cowls. In Scotland, haddock is used to make the famous Arbroath smokie, using techniques similar to ancient Scandinavian methods, and salmon is smoked up and down the country thanks to the Jewish people from Russia and Poland who brought their method to London's East End in the late 19th century (read more about salmon smoking traditions on page 26).

It's reasonable to conclude that we've been smoking mackerel for as long as we've been catching them, and while there are still plenty in the sea they're a strong choice for the barbecue. These fierce, pearlescent-skinned predators can be found whooshing around our coastline once the weather starts to warm up, and they're very easy to catch, which is why mackerel fishing trips are so popular with tourists.

They travel about in massive shoals, constantly looking for food and are ridiculously fast – a mackerel can cover 50 metres (55 yards) in just ten seconds, which feels a little bit like showing off. They spoil quickly once caught, however – much more so than other fish – so look for bright eyes and nice firm flesh. If buying fillets (in the supermarket for example, where you should look for the Marine Stewardship Council's 'blue tick'), they're likely to be pretty fresh already due to the aforementioned spoilage rate. Basically, fresher is better when it comes to eating mackerel.

Mackerel is one of few fish that may be prepared using both hot or cold smoking methods. Hot smoking involves cooking the fish over fire, then putting out that fire in a way that produces lots of smoke. Cold smoking on the other hand doesn't cook the fish with heat but exposes it to a small amount of smoke over a long period (24 hours or more). Either way, the results are astonishing. Smoked mackerel doesn't have PGI (Protected Geographical Indication) status like the Arbroath smokie but it's certainly one of the finest smoked fish you can eat and very easy to make at home. Once you've tasted home-smoked mackerel you'll be looking into protecting that product with a special status of its own, trust me. Find a method on page 155.

But wait! There's more than one way to cook a mackerel. That oily flesh and robust flavour means they hold up very well on the grill, and their skin can really take a bit of char. They make a lovely meal served with something crunchy and sour to cut the richness – quick pickled vegetables, for example – and I also love to serve them with a salad dressed with pickling spices, which brings pops of flavour from coriander and fennel seeds (page 155).

When barbecuing such a full-flavoured fish, you'll need to be really confident with the salt and pepper as they take a lot of seasoning; you could also try adding woody herbs like rosemary or branches of bay to the coals for scented smoke, or caramelising lemons to sweeten them a little before squeezing over the cooked fish.

Home-smoked Mackerel *and a Salad Dressed with Pickling Spices*

Setup: Indirect cooking
Wood: Oak or beech
Equipment: Tongs
Prep time: 10 minutes
Cook time: 10 minutes
Serves: 2

½ small red onion, peeled and thinly sliced
4 mackerel fillets
neutral oil, for the mackerel
2 handfuls of watercress
1 soft butter lettuce, leaves separated
sea salt and freshly ground black pepper

Dressing
1 teaspoon brown mustard seeds
1 teaspoon fennel seeds
1 teaspoon coriander seeds
1 teaspoon Dijon mustard
1 teaspoon honey
2 tablespoons lemon juice
4 tablespoons extra virgin olive oil

Of course, I now want to build a smoker in an old oil drum like the fellas in the story on page 152, but I also know I'm never going to get around to it. This is a recipe for a lightly smoked mackerel instead – one that's cooked briefly with wood in the barbecue, rather than the very strongly smoked stuff you get in shops. I love that style, but I also appreciate something more delicate, and it works well in a salad dressed with whole spices that burst in the mouth and are surprising, even when you know they're there.

You could use any mixed salad leaves for this, but I like the combination of the soft, floppy butterhead lettuce and fiercely curled and peppery watercress.

— Put the sliced red onion into a bowl of iced water – this will take the sting out of it.
— Prepare a barbecue for indirect cooking, with just a few lit coals.
— Rub the mackerel skin with a little neutral oil, then season both sides with salt. Place skin side down on the opposite side of the grill to the coals and place a small piece of wood or some chips on the lit coals. Close the lid, leaving a very small gap in the top and bottom vents, and smoke the mackerel for 5–10 minutes – basically, it's done when it's cooked.

— Make the dressing. Toast the mustard seeds, fennel seeds and coriander seeds in a dry frying pan (skillet) over a medium heat, moving them around so they don't burn. When the mustard seeds start to pop, transfer the toasted spices to a clean lidded jar or a bowl. Add the remaining dressing ingredients, along with some salt and pepper, and shake or whisk to combine.
— Combine the watercress and lettuce leaves in a bowl. Drain the red onion slices and add them too, then add some of the dressing and mix well.
— Arrange the salad leaves on two plates then gently flake the smoked mackerel, including the skin, if you like, and add that too. Add a little more of the dressing on top, if you like, and serve.

Whole Barbecued Pumpkin
Stuffed with Beer and Sage Fondue

Setup: Indirect cooking
Wood: Oak, beech or apple
Equipment: Disposable foil
tray (or another heatproof tray
that will fit inside the
barbecue), heatproof gloves
are also handy here but, as
ever, not essential
Prep time: 20 minutes
Cook time: 1 hour 15 minutes
–1 hour 45 minutes
Serves: 4–6

1 whole pumpkin
(about 1.5 kg/3 lb 5 oz)
200 g (7 oz) Gruyère, grated
100 g (3½ oz) mature
Cheddar, grated
1 tablespoon cornflour
(cornstarch)
200 ml (7 fl oz/scant 1 cup)
beer
2 garlic cloves, peeled
and crushed or grated
a few sage leaves
2 thick slices of sourdough,
torn in chunks, plus extra
to serve
small pickled onions (the
small, white cocktail ones are
perfect for this), to serve
sea salt and freshly ground
black pepper

This one's a bit of a party piece, and just the thing for
a Halloween or Bonfire Night gathering if that's something
you do. Pumpkins vary from the completely tasteless
to the sweet but more expensive – if you want to eat the
bowl then I'd suggest seeking out the latter variety, e.g. Delica.
You will need extra bread for dipping, and I like to serve some
of those little white cocktail onions, for punctuating the
richness and aiding stamina.

— Prepare a barbecue for indirect cooking over medium heat,
with the coals banked on both sides.
— Remove the top of the pumpkin (keep the top), scoop out the
insides and discard them. Place the pumpkin in the disposable
tray in the centre of the grill and cook, with the lid on leaving
the vents half open and cook for 45 minutes.
— Combine the grated cheeses with the cornflour in a bowl
and toss well.
— Mix the beer, garlic, sage leaves and some salt and pepper
in a jug.
— Carefully layer up the chunks of sourdough, cheese and beer
mixture inside the pumpkin. Put the pumpkin in a foil (or other
heatproof) tray and put its hat on. Place a small chunk of wood
on the lit coals (if using) until it starts to smoulder. Place the
pumpkin back on the grill and cook for a further 30 minutes–
1 hour (turning the tray around halfway through) or until the
pumpkin is completely soft.
— Serve the pumpkin as a centrepiece with the extra bread
and pickled onions.

To Cook Indoors: Preheat the oven to 160°C (320°F/gas 4).
Bake the hollowed-out pumpkin for 45 minutes, then increase
the heat to 180°C (350°F/gas 4). Fill the pumpkin as described
above and cook for a further 30 minutes–1 hour, or until
completely soft.

Prawns
with Sweetcorn and Special Seafood Seasoning Dust

Setup: Direct cooking
Equipment: Tongs
Prep time: 10 minutes
Cook time: 10 minutes
Serves: 4–6

Prawns and corns
4 corn cobs (or 1 per person),
preferably in their husks
about 20 shell-on king prawns
neutral oil, for cooking
150 g (5½ oz/10½ tablespoons)
butter
1 green chilli, finely chopped
lemon wedges, to serve

*Special seafood
seasoning dust*
2 teaspoons fennel seeds
1 tablespoon paprika
2 teaspoons onion powder
2 teaspoons garlic powder
1 teaspoon cayenne
1 tablespoon sea salt
1½ teaspoons ground
white pepper
1 teaspoon dried thyme
1 teaspoon dried oregano

This is reminiscent of a Louisiana shrimp boil, only grilled. Why not? I actually use this seasoning dust on lots of different seafood, not least my beloved crabs – it's incredibly satisfying to suck the dust from pieces of shell and swipe quivering claw meat through the pools of spiced butter that collect on the table. Adding grilled small potatoes like the ones on page 71 would be a very good idea, to bulk this out.

— Prepare a barbecue for direct cooking over medium heat.
— Lightly toast the fennel seeds in a dry frying pan over a medium heat for a couple of minutes, until fragrant, moving them around so they don't burn. Transfer to a spice grinder or pestle and mortar and grind or crush to a powder. Combine in a bowl with the paprika, onion and garlic powders, cayenne, salt, white pepper, thyme and oregano.
— If using in-husk corn, snip off any long silky parts using kitchen scissors then place the cobs over direct medium heat for 15 minutes, or until the husks are black and the corn inside is soft and yellow (you can peel a little husk back to check). If you want to char the corn, now is the time to peel off the husks and do that, taking care not to leave it on the grill more than a few minutes longer.
— If using pre-prepared corn cobs, rub them with a little neutral oil. Grill over direct heat medium heat, turning occasionally with tongs, for about 10 minutes until soft, golden and charred.
— Rub the prawns with a little neutral oil and grill them over direct heat for 1–2 minutes on each side, until completely pink.
— Combine the butter and 2 tablespoons of the seasoning dust in a saucepan and melt to combine. Arrange the grilled corn and prawns on a plate and pour over the spiced butter, then scatter over the green chilli and add lemon wedges, to serve.

To Cook Indoors: Preheat a cast-iron griddle pan over a high heat for at least 5 minutes. Cook the corn cobs on the griddle for 10 minutes or until soft and charred, turning them so they char evenly. Cook the prawns, lightly oiled, in the same pan for a couple of minutes on each side or until totally pink and cooked through.

Chicken Shawarma

Setup: Indirect cooking
Equipment: 4 long metal skewers (if your skewers are quite thick, just use 2), drip tray
Prep time: 30 minutes, plus overnight marinating time
Cook time: 45 minutes–1 hour
Serves: 6

1 kg (2 lb 4 oz) skinless, boneless chicken thighs

Baharat spice mix
1 tablespoon black peppercorns
1 tablespoon coriander seeds
2 teaspoons cumin seeds
2 cloves
½ teaspoon green cardamom seeds (from roughly 6 pods)
2 teaspoons paprika
¼ teaspoon grated nutmeg

Chicken marinade
3 tablespoons lemon juice
2 tablespoons Baharat spice mix (above)
2 teaspoons chilli flakes
1 tablespoon sea salt
1 tablespoon neutral oil

This is an attempt at recreating a chicken shawarma I ate in Beirut, in particular one from a strip-lit, late-night, in-and-out kinda place; the sort of place where your food is unceremoniously slapped together and handed to you with no pleasure whatsoever. I remember the garlic sauce most of all: toum. I was remembering it well into the next day, because it's made with lots and lots (and lots) of blended raw garlic, lemon juice and oil. Its fierce pungency can be unexpected, since it looks like an unassuming bowl of white fluff, but this is serious. If you are 'a bit funny' about raw garlic, then you want to stay well away from this sauce. I (along with millions of other people) think it's heavenly and it is part of this kebab's identity. However, I suppose you could soak a little bit of crushed garlic in lemon juice and then add it to yoghurt if the idea of eating a truly amazing kebab is too intimidating (or you have to talk to literally anyone else in person within the next 24 hours).

Ideally, you'd want a rotisserie for this, and if any of you fancy-pants barbecue crew have one, then this is the time to use it. However, it is by no means essential. If the centre of your grill is a removable circle, then remove it, place the coals underneath and rest the skewers on either side – this means it's not in direct contact with the grill. If neither of these options apply, don't worry about it! This will still be incredible cooked right on the bars. I've not provided an oven method for this, because I think you'll lose the personality of the dish.

Baharat is a Middle Eastern spice blend (the word baharat means 'spices' in Arabic), which comes in various iterations. It is available to buy ready-made, but freshly ground spices always taste better and it's simple to put together.

— First, make the baharat spice mix. Toast the black peppercorns, coriander seeds, cumin seeds and cloves in a dry frying pan for a minute or two, until fragrant (moving them around so they don't burn), then add to a spice grinder or pestle and mortar with the cardamom seeds and grind or crush to a fine powder. Combine with the paprika and nutmeg.
— Combine the chicken marinade ingredients in a bowl and spread all over the chicken thighs, mixing well. Cover and put in the fridge to marinate overnight.
— Prepare a barbecue for indirect cooking using a whole chimney starter of coals, with the coals banked on either side.

Toum
1½ heads of garlic, cloves
separated and peeled
large pinch of sea salt
2 tablespoons lemon juice
300 ml (10 fl oz/1¼ cups)
neutral oil (such as vegetable
or groundnut)
2 tablespoons iced water

Cabbage salad
½ red cabbage, cored and
finely shredded
1 red onion, peeled and
thinly sliced
really generous pinch
of sea salt
handful of parsley leaves,
roughly chopped
2 tablespoons sumac

To serve
lavash, pitta or flatbreads
(my Easy Flatbreads on
page 60 would be perfect)
pickled chillies

— When you're ready to cook, get your 4 long metal skewers ready. Take a marinated chicken thigh and position it so that you are ready to thread the skewers through the shortest sides of each thigh. You are going to thread each thigh on top of the other to make one large kebab. Take two skewers and thread them through one end of the chicken thigh, then do the same on the other side with the other skewers. Thread the chicken thigh all the way down the skewers, then repeat, layering up the thighs.

— Position a drip tray in the centre of the coals on the bottom of the barbecue, and pour in around 1 litre (34 fl oz/4 ¼ cups) of water. Place the chicken shawarma on the grill over the drip tray and close the lid, leaving the vents one-third open at the top and bottom of the barbecue. Cook for 45 minutes to 1 hour, turning the shawarma halfway through.

— Make the toum by pureeing the garlic, salt and 1 tablespoon of the lemon juice in a blender. With the motor running, add the other tablespoon of lemon juice, then very slowly pour in 100 ml (3½ fl oz/scant ½ cup) of the oil. Add a tablespoon of iced water, then follow with another 100 ml (3½ fl oz/scant ½ cup) of oil. Finally, add a second tablespoon of iced water and the final 100 ml (3½ fl oz/scant ½ cup) of oil. The toum should be light, fluffy and white.

— To make the salad, combine the cabbage and onion in a bowl, add the salt, and use your hands to scrunch the cabbage and onion together until the vegetables soften and begin to release their juice. Mix in the parsley and sumac.

— Remove the chicken from the skewers and slice, serving it with the toum, cabbage salad, bread and pickled chillies.

Chicken Wings
with Miso Fish Sauce Caramel

Setup: Indirect cooking
Equipment: Tongs
Prep time: 15 minutes, plus
minimum 3 hours marinating
time (overnight if possible)
Cook time: 30 minutes
Serves: 2–4

12 chicken wings, separated
into flats and drums if you like
(discard the tips or put them
in the freezer as I do, to use
for making chicken stock)
bunch of spring onions
(scallions), halved widthways
then sliced lengthways
into strips

Rub
1 teaspoon ground ginger
2 teaspoons garlic powder
1 teaspoon turmeric
1 teaspoon bicarbonate
of soda
large pinch of salt

Miso fish sauce caramel
1 tablespoon white miso
1 tablespoon fish sauce
1 teaspoon dried chilli flakes
1 tablespoon lime juice,
plus 1 lime cut into wedges,
to serve
100 g (3½ oz/scant ½ cup)
granulated sugar
50 ml (1¾ fl oz/3½ tablespoons)
water

Sweet, salty, funky and spicy: these wings have it all.

It's not essential to leave the rubbed wings overnight, but if you're oven-cooking them I would encourage you to do so, as the bicarbonate of soda helps them crisp up. It's a really good technique for getting crisp chicken wings without grilling or frying. If you just want some barbecued wings in a hurry, put the rub on before cooking and leave out the bicarbonate of soda.

I love to serve these with a giant tangle of spring onions (scallions) on top, in homage to a Korean restaurant close to my home in London. I'm not sure the food is that good, to be honest, but I do love the way they serve their fried chicken with a tumbleweed nest of curly spring onions. The drama!

— Combine the ground ginger, garlic powder, turmeric, bicarb and salt in a bowl and mix well. Combine this mixture with the wings and mix well. Arrange the wings on a rack over a baking tray in the fridge, uncovered, for at least 3 hours or overnight.
— To make the miso fish sauce caramel, first combine the miso, fish sauce, chilli flakes and lime juice in a small bowl until smooth. Make the caramel by combining the sugar and water in a pan. Dissolve over a low heat until it's no longer grainy, then turn up the heat and boil until it's a lovely golden amber colour. Avoid stirring the mixture during this time. Remove from the heat and stir in the miso mixture (it will splutter wildly).
— Put the spring onion (scallion) strips in a bowl of iced water.
— Prepare a barbecue for indirect cooking over medium heat, with the coals arranged in the centre, leaving a circle with no coals around the edge of the barbecue.
— Arrange the wings on the grill around the edge of the coals, so that they're not quite over the heat but are close to it. Cook for about 30 minutes, moving the wings around so that they crisp evenly (you may need to move them closer to the coals as they start to burn down).
— Once the wings are cooked, gently reheat the caramel until it's just thin enough to pour and pour it over the grilled wings. Mix well and top with a giant tangle of the spring onions.

To Cook Indoors: Preheat the oven to 220°C (430°F/gas 9) and cook the wings, spread out on a roasting tray for 40 minutes, turning them once. Pour the caramel over and top with the spring onions.

Iran in South East London

I struggle now to remember when I first met Sally Butcher, but it was probably around 15 years ago when I moved to Peckham, an area of South East London. Once a district that was mocked and feared, Peckham is rapidly changing, and yet it has managed to dodge the predictable path of gentrification. For now, at least, it has retained its character, developing a unique patchwork: of barbers and nail salons; Pakistani butchers; Nigerian grocers; wine and Campari bars; fried chicken shops; Aladura churches; bougie, expensive delis; and some of London's best suya spots.

Sally and her husband Jamshid opened their bright-yellow corner shop Persepolis on the High Street in 2001, importing Iranian foods and other products and selling them alongside, well, pretty much anything else actually (in recent years they have also set up a vegetarian cafe, and Sally has published an incredible seven cookbooks). I'd been meaning to investigate the place for weeks before I first walked through the door, peering through shisha-stacked windows at a tumble of jars and boxes. Shopping with Sally became a weekly routine. I'd waft past the sugared-and-syruped pastries and into dried fruits (sour cherries! Dried limes!) always on my way, ultimately, to the shelves containing 10-year-old pickled garlic, burnished with age, it's flavour caramel and salt, sharpness and creamy pungency. Sally's shop was a big part of my life when I moved to the area, and it seemed right to revisit when I started writing this book, particularly since fire is such an important theme in Iranian culture.

At the start of the Persian new year (Nowruz), Iranian people jump over fire as a symbolic gesture, which is thought to bring good health and luck for the year ahead. Fire worshipping and related rituals have firm roots in ancient Iranian culture, when Zoroastrianism was the dominant religion. Fire plays a central role in worship for Zoroastrians, symbolising the spirit of God, and fires are kept perpetually burning in temples known as the Atashkadeh, or 'house of fire'.

It won't surprise you then to learn that Iranian people are very keen on barbecuing. 'A lot of Iranians – even those who live in cities – will have a little barbecue on their balcony,' says Sally. 'On public holidays, the parks are designed to have little regular private areas where families can relax, women can maybe take their scarves off and be protected from public view and have a barbecue. London park-keepers are horrified by this and regularly shut parks when they know Iranians will be out feasting for the Iranian New Year. In North London they actually shut whole parks, which is very antisocial.'

When Sally first moved to Peckham, barbecuing was done out of necessity as well as for fun. 'When I got shacked up with my man 26 years ago his family regularly cooked over an open fire here in Peckham,' she says, 'Indoors or outdoors if the weather was good enough. Entertaining was cooking over a wood fire, and some things were buried in the embers – baked potatoes and so on – and some stuff was cooked on top. We've had a long hard journey to get to where we are. We weren't very well off at all, so when we first started out, I was "minister of wood" and I used to go out and forage for pallets and things all around Peckham. Mainly we would cook kebab. Kebab is the essence of what Persians think they want to eat all the time. What Persians eat at home most of the time is actually completely different, but this is what they aspire to eat. If you ask my dear sweet husband what he would like, he will always say "kebab with the occasional steak thrown in" – the great irony is that I run a vegetarian restaurant here with a great carnivore as a husband.'

'The greatest Persian kebab – kabab koobideh – is a very simple minced (ground) lamb kebab with three ingredients: salt, meat and a pinch of bicarb. Some people add sumac or herbs and it's served on these long skewers.

It's the ratio of fat to lamb that makes them so good – it has to be fatty, partly so it sticks to the skewer and partly to give it the flavour – lean lamb just doesn't do it for anyone. So really, it's all about the fat, and sometimes it's about the spice, but that's the basic recipe [find Sally's recipe on page 167]. The other really famous one is chicken with lemon and saffron, that's lovely: really salty, really lemony. If you go to a Persian restaurant, the choice of kebabs can be really overwhelming, especially as there doesn't seem to be a lot of difference between them. It's amazing how much detail and how many combinations they go into (some have bones and some don't). Before you know it you've got 60 different kebabs.'

While kebabs are aspirational, then, everyday Iranian food is different. 'They have a very rich vegetable culture', Sally tells me. 'Cooking vegetables over fire, it's fairly basic – tomatoes, onions, peppers on skewers. Vegetables that can be cooked in the embers are root vegetables, so turnips, beetroots, corn if you like. Baked potatoes. I'm happy to say though that I'm generally not that impressed by barbecued vegetables – I think it's probably not my thing.' (Obviously, I disagree with Sally on this point but that won't bother her at all.) She's not predictable when it comes to her views on meat, either: 'If I eat a steak I have it blue. I'm not some lily-livered

vegetarian; I just don't really like meat very much.' Marrying into an Iranian family and not loving kebabs! Imagine.

Sally has created a space that serves the Iranian community as much as it does the local art students, who come for their platters of meze, topped with a proud cheesy Wotsit – Sally's humour on the plate. They come for Turkish delight ice-cream sundaes, pomegranate juice and Afghan green tea ('separates the men from the boys'). Sally's shop was one of my first windows into a cuisine I knew absolutely nothing about, and I felt enveloped in the traditions of Iranian culture. 'A famous fact about me is that I've never actually been to Iran,' Sally says over a quick cup of tea one morning, 'although I'm not a fraud, as I have recreated Iran here. I'm what they call kâseh dâghtar az âsh – the bowl hotter than the soup'. She explains that this is a slightly derogatory term implying that she knows more about Iranian food than most Iranian people do. This – like many things – will be likely be a source of amusement for Sally, a woman who knows not only how to enjoy good food but how to look sideways at life, and be all the wiser for it.

Sally Butcher's Kebab Koobideh

Setup: Direct cooking
Equipment: 6 flat skewers
Prep time: 20 minutes
Cook time: 10 minutes
Serves: 6

2 medium onions, peeled
1 kg (2 lb 4 oz) really good
quality minced lamb
(shoulder works best:
the kebab needs some fat in
it to make it cohere)
2 level teaspoons salt
(Iranians would use
a lot more)
1 teaspoon ground
black pepper
⅔ teaspoon bicarbonate of soda
(baking soda)
2 teaspoons ground cumin
(optional)
6 tomatoes, halved

To serve
6 flatbread (preferably lavash)
ground sumac

Sally describes this as 'the most basic-and-yet-popular of the Iranian kebab family.' It's incredibly simple… at first sight. The skill lies in forming the kebabs around the wide, flat skewers, which can apparently be a source of amusement for Iranians as they try to school the uninitiated. I suggest that you do as Sally advises, and either use two long skewers side by side, or do away with them entirely.

Taken from Sally Butcher's *Snackistan: Street Food, Comfort Meze: Informal eating in the Middle East & Beyond* (Pavilion Books).

— Light the barbecue or preheat the grill or oven to 220°C (425°F/gas 7). Put the bowl end of 2 teaspoons in your mouth so that they cross over, then grate the onions. This is as close to non-crying as you can hope to get in the weepy world of onions: really, it works.
— Mix the onion into the lamb and add the seasoning, bicarbonate of soda, and cumin, if using. Pound the mixture well with your hands: generally the less you play with food the better, but in this case the mixture benefits from the warmth of your hands, as this causes the fat to soften and the whole thing to come together.
— Using wet hands, mould the meat onto skewers (these kebabs are usually around 18 cm/7 in long), allowing the impression left by our fingers to show - the kebab should still display these wavy crenellations once it's cooked. Pop your skewers onto a hot barbecue, under a hot grill or even into the oven on a baking tray. They will need about 5 minutes on each side to cook (longer in the oven).
— If you don't have any skewers, just arm the meat into sausage shapes and use a spatula to lift them on to your grill.
— Thread the tomato halves on to (any old) skewers and grill them alongside the meat. Pop a sheet of folded lavash (or other bread) on to a plate. As each of the skewers of lamb is cooked, lift the folded over part of the bread over the skewer, pressing it down on top of the kebab. If you exert enough gentle pressure, you should now be able to withdraw the skewer, leaving the kebab nestled inside the bread. Add a couple of tomato halves, sprinkle with sumac, then tuck the ends of the bread in to make the kebab more wieldy.
— These kebabs are just a s often enjoyed with buttered saffron rice, when they become known as chelow kebab. Noshe jan! (Which kind of means 'enjoy!' and 'bon appetit!' and 'you're welcome!' all in one expression.)

Tandoor,
Mixed Grill,
Lamb Chops

I'm not sure when I first became alerted to the tandoor's magic but it was almost certainly via the 'curry house' takeaway that to teenage me – woefully ignorant of the regional variety of food in the world's second most-populous country – meant 'Indian food' (the broadest of terms, it is practically meaningless). Oh, how I loved that food – and I wasn't alone. London's Brick Lane, Manchester's 'Curry Mile' and Birmingham's 'Balti Triangle' were all thriving in the mid 90s. The thrill of ripping into a steaming garlic naan, fingers shimmering with ghee; the smoke whispering through a seekh kebab; a crisp, straggly onion bhaji, a little too gooey in the middle; chicken tikka with its wedge of lemon and shredded iceberg in a tiny plastic bag. This was all I wanted or needed. Ignorance was truly blissful.

Later, I discovered the joys of eating the mixed grill actually inside a restaurant, delighting in the sizzling, black cast-iron platter that could be heard approaching from the kitchen, its contrail of spiced steam fizzling behind a mound of tandoor-cooked delights. I became a one-woman mixed grill appreciation society.

Anyone on 'London food Twitter' around 2010 will remember there was only one mixed grill that people were talking about, and it came from the kitchens of Tayyabs, a Pakistani restaurant in Whitechapel, in the East End. Tayyabs had been going since 1972, but one day a restaurant critic called Charles Campion (sadly no longer with us) gave it a rave in his newspaper column and this 'off the beaten track' restaurant's popularity blew up. People queued to get in before queuing for restaurants was even 'a thing'. Tayyabs became famous overnight.

Over the years I became friends with Wasim, whose father Tayyab started the business, 'Dad came here in the late '50s; it was always a passion for him, to come here. When he arrived he moved in with five or six other men from Pakistan; a two-bedroom house with a kitchen and a toilet, no bath – they used to go to the public baths every two or three days.'

When Tayyab's family later came from Pakistan, he quickly became known for his culinary skills, 'Whenever it was Dad's turn to cook at home people would get excited, rubbing their hands together. He would make some chicken, some lamb, some biryani,' says Wasim. When the owner of the greasy spoon opposite his house was selling up, he saw his chance – 'He used to say there's no food that is authentic in this area, nothing for the people that live here. He borrowed money,

Below: Chef Fazal Wahab shapes seekh kebabs onto their skewers.
Right: Tayyabs' famous lamb chops on the grill.

took it over and did it up – very basic with wooden chairs and tables from the market near Brick Lane. He had just two things on the menu: meat and dal, and my auntie she used to cook the chapattis.'

'When my mother came, she added a few more dishes: mixed vegetables, some chickpeas, some saag gosht. They used to make small batches and I can still see it now. One corner used to be dry meat, another was meat curry, then potato meat, vegetable, dal and the chickpeas out on a tray. Then we would have specialities like lamb trotters on Mondays, and Fridays used to be very popular after prayers – the meat biryani was outstanding. My father was a military man; he wanted everything to have its proper place. This glass, that spoon, that stock pot. That plate. We used to come and help Dad with sweeping, peeling the onions, melting the butter to make ghee – that's how we learnt, me and my brother – we did that and then bed after the 9 o'clock news.'

Tayyabs gradually expanded and installed a tandoor: 'I remember going somewhere in South London in a transit van to buy a tandoor with clay inside' says Wasim, 'It was a turning point – people wanted tandoor-cooked food all of a sudden. We bricked around it, put sand in, and sealed it from the top. It was run by charcoal in those days. We were constantly refilling it!

Most tandoor ovens are now run on gas, for reasons of convenience. The first tandoors were found in excavations of Harappan sites – the earliest known urban culture of the Indian subcontinent, with the very earliest example found in 'the Ganganagar district of Rajastan, about 400 km from Delhi' writes Ranjit Rai in his book *Tandoor*. Designs were apparently not so different from the ovens in use today. A cylindrical clay (or metal) oven, the tandoor retains heat incredibly well, with temperatures reaching ~480°C.

Sanjay Battycharya, a cookery teacher and chef living in Perth, Scotland, has memories of cooking in a tandoor at home with his father, from West Bengal (Calcutta), 'When I was 10 my father purchased a tandoor, and we set out on a journey to master it. There are not a lot of books or content online – it's an ancient skill and unless you're in the trade, there aren't many ways to learn. We spent a long time getting proficient at building a fire and working with it.'

'Bread is the most traditional item to cook in the tandoor. The dark art comes in the way in which you place the bread on the wall of the tandoor – it must be well seasoned. You must use a salt water solution to coat the inside of the tandoor so that it forms a good surface for the naan to stick to; if you don't do that first, the naan will fall off. Then you take bread dough, roll it out and transfer

it to what's called a gaddi, which is a cushion filled with straw and covered with muslin.' The naan dough is stretched over the tandoor and quickly – woompf – slapped inside the raging funnel. At Tayyabs, where the naan mother dough is 45 years old, I am transfixed by baking; dough is stretched over the gaddi, baked in seconds and retrieved from the screaming tandoor by two implements on long poles – one a hook, the other a scraper. The hot naan are immediately brushed with ghee. I notice the cook has no hair on his forearms.

While tandoors were originally used for bread, their role has expanded, 'Meat cooking in a tandoor is a relatively new thing,' says Sanjay, 'but we can imagine that eventually seekh kebabs were cooked in a tandoor to make use of the residual heat.' Ah yes, my beloved seekh kebab. Named for the thick, square skewer the meat is shaped around, this spiced log of lamb is an essential mixed grill component. Sanjay has spent time developing his own recipe, 'Their success lies in ensuring that the mixture has the right ratio of meat to fat, the right amount of water, and defining the perfect bind,' he says, 'We use minced lamb shoulder, as we found it has enough fat and flavour.'

Below top: Chef Kadir
Tanha prepares naan for
the tandoor. He has no hair
on his forearms.
Below: naan in the tandoor.

We also blend or grate the onions – not to a puree but to a coarse paste, then salt them and drain the moisture until it's really quite dry. Wet onions will cause your kebabs to disintegrate. The last part is the binder, and we use roasted channa dal (split chickpeas), ground to a fine powder using a spice grinder. It adds a roasted background flavour, a chewiness, and it's just a really good way to help the kebabs stick.'

'Kneading the meat is also important as that helps to stop it falling off the skewer, but you must be careful not to over work it, or it will be tough. I think the most important part is the cooking in the tandoor; the skewers are so thick they conduct a large amount of heat into the kebab and once it's immersed in the hot coals it will transfer that heat very quickly. You don't want the kebabs to be too thin, but conversely you don't want them too thick because they will slide down the seekh before they finish cooking.'

For reasons of practicality then, Tayyabs' cook their seekh kebabs on a grill mounted on top of the tandoor, along with their famous lamb chops, 'We currently sell 150 kg [330 lb] of lamb chops daily' says Wasim, 'although before the pandemic it was double that amount.'

The lamb chops are something of a phenomenon: a thick spice paste surrounds tenderised meat, fat charred and crackled around the edges. A three-bite job at most, plus finger licking. 'They are marinated the night before' says Wasim, 'We use vinegar to tenderise them and we also bash them out a bit.'

The spice mix is a secret, 'I know the spice blends, and my brothers and my mum know, but nobody else. They are actually basic, there is nothing that secret, but if you ask 10 chefs to make garam masala, none of them will do it the same, so we try to keep it consistent.'

Sanjay spent years experimenting with different spice combinations for his seekh kebabs, 'We tried lots of different blends for garam masala and have come up with one we think works best with lamb,' he tells me, before generously offering the recipe. It is warm, with a buzzing current of black and china/cubeb peppercorns (a tailed peppercorn with hints of allspice). You can find seekh kebab and lamb chop recipes on pages 172 and 173 – the seekh kebab heavily based on Sanjay's recipe, and the lamb chops more my attempt at coming close to the Tayyabs version. Both can be cooked on a standard kettle barbecue and both include nostalgic nods to the style of 'Indian food' I grew up with and which still comforts me today. You can take the girl out of the curry house …

Seekh Kebabs

Setup: Direct cooking
Equipment: Tongs, 6 long skewers
Prep time: 2 hours if using channa dal, 30 minutes if not
Cook time: 10 minutes
Serves: 6

---

45 g (1½ oz) dried channa dal
200 ml (7 fl oz/1 scant cup) water
1 large onion
500 g (1 lb 2 oz) minced (ground) lamb shoulder
4 tablespoons finely chopped coriander (cilantro)
3 garlic cloves, crushed
1.5 cm (½ in) piece of ginger, peeled and very finely chopped
1 tablespoon Sanjay's Garam Masala #5 for Lamb
2 teaspoons Kashmiri chilli powder
1 green chilli, very finely chopped
sea salt

Sanjay's Garam Masala #5 for Lamb
15 black peppercorns
15 kebab chini (cubeb peppercorns)
4 green cardamom pods
3 mace blades
1 teaspoon hot chilli flakes

To serve
6 naan
1 cucumber, sliced thinly lengthways
150 g (5 oz) natural yoghurt
1 red onion, thinly sliced and soaked in iced water for 10 minutes

This recipe has two major influences: chef Sanjay Battychara (page 170), who was so kind to share his tips for making seekh kebabs and his garam masala recipe with me, and a hole-in-the-wall tandoor place near my house, which is simply called 'Asian Takeaway'. It's a basic, one-man-and-a-tandoor situation, with a few daily specials. For a while, I was very into their seekh kebab wrap, which was as simple as yoghurt, cucumber, onion and kebab inside a freshly baked naan. It stuck with me, so here's a recipe for a similar seekh kebab wrap. The barbecue naan on page 216 would be marvellous here, but chapatti would be perfect too. Suggested stockists for cubeb pepper, and Kashmiri chilli powder are provided on page 17.

— If you are using channa dal, soak it in water for 1 hour, then drain and place in a saucepan with the water and some salt. Bring to the boil, reduce the heat and cook for about 30 minutes until all the water has been absorbed.
— Preheat the oven to 200°C (400°F/gas 6).
— Spread the channa dal on a lightly oiled baking tray and cook in the oven for about 20 minutes, shaking halfway through. The channa dal will crisp up. Once cool, grind to a fine powder in a spice grinder or pestle and mortar.
— Sprinkle the cucumber slices with a generous pinch of salt, toss to combine and leave to drain in a colander over the sink.
— To make the garam masala, toast the whole spices in a dry pan over a medium heat for a minute or two until aromatic (move them around so they don't burn), then grind in a spice grinder or pestle and mortar until very fine. Pass through a sieve to remove any strands of cardamom hull.
— Put the onion in a food processor and whizz to a slushy paste. Place the onion in a clean tea towel, piece of muslin or new cloth and squeeze out as much moisture as you can.
— In a bowl, combine the minced (ground) lamb, onion, coriander stalks and leaves, garlic, ginger, garam masala, chilli powder, green chilli, ground channa dal (if using) and a few generous pinches of salt. Mix well with your hands, kneading the meat against the bottom of the bowl for a couple of minutes as if you are making bread.
— Divide the mixture into 6 balls, then shape each ball onto a skewer using a 'grabbing' motion (this is easiest with wet hands). If this doesn't work out, shape into logs.
— Prepare a barbecue for direct cooking over low-medium heat, with the coals banked to one side. Once the coals are ready, cook the kebabs directly over the coals for about 5 minutes each side, or until just cooked through. If the fat starts to flare up too much, just move them to the cooler side of the grill until the flames die down.
— Serve the kebabs with the naan, cucumber, yoghurt and onion.

Tandoori
Lamb Chops

Setup: Direct cooking
Equipment: Tongs
Prep time: 30 minutes, plus
overnight marinating time
Cook time: 5 minutes
Serves: 4

---

1 kg (2 lb 4 oz) lamb chops
sea salt
naan or chapatti, to serve

Tandoori marinade
250 g (9 oz/1 cup) natural
yoghurt, plus extra to serve
1 tablespoon Sanjay's Garam
Masala #5 for Lamb (see
opposite)
2 tablespoons lime juice
1 tablespoon tomato puree
(paste)
5 garlic cloves, crushed
5 cm (2 in) piece of ginger,
peeled and very finely chopped
or grated
1 teaspoon ground turmeric
2 teaspoons Kashmiri
chilli powder
½ teaspoon ground cinnamon

Salad
1 red or white onion,
peeled and thinly sliced
1 iceberg lettuce, very finely
shredded
1 tomato, finely diced
½ cucumber, finely diced
small handful of mint leaves,
finely chopped
1 tablespoon lemon juice
2 tablespoons olive oil

These are a riff on Tayyabs'
lamb chops (page 168) and
while not exactly the same,
I think they're a pretty good
approximation. The iceberg
lettuce salad is a nostalgic nod
to those little plastic bags of
salad that used to come
alongside a curry-house
takeaway mixed grill
(sometimes, they still do!).
I've seen numerous people
tweeting things along the lines
of 'Who actually eats those
little bags of salad anyway?!'
– I do guys, I do!

— Using a meat tenderiser or
something heavy (e.g., a rolling
pin), bash the meaty part of
the lamb chops until the meat
is around 1 cm (½ in) thick.
— Combine the yoghurt,
garam masala, lime juice,
tomato puree (paste), garlic,
ginger, turmeric, Kashmiri
chilli powder and cinnamon
in a bowl with a couple of
generous pinches of salt
and mix very well.
— Combine the chops and
marinade in a large container,
rubbing the marinade onto
the chops, to coat. Cover
and marinate in the
fridge overnight.
— When you are ready
to cook the chops, prepare the
onion for the salad by soaking
the slices in very cold or iced
water for 10 minutes, then
drain. Combine the sliced
onion with all the other
vegetables in a bowl. Combine
the lemon juice and olive oil
with some salt and pepper
in a clean lidded jar or bowl
and shake or whisk to
combine. Pour over the
salad and mix well.

— Prepare a barbecue for
direct cooking over medium
heat. Once the coals are ready,
brush off most of the marinade
and cook the chops over direct
heat for a minute or so on each
side to get some colour on
them. Once the fat starts to
melt they will cause flare ups,
so move them just next to the
coals when this happens, to
finish cooking through – a few
minutes more.
— Divide the naan between
serving plates and divide the
lamb chops between them,
placing them on top of the
bread. Serve immediately with
the salad and yoghurt.

Sheftalia and Psychotherapy

My first contact with psychotherapist and writer Andrea Oskis was when I commissioned her to write about the food of her Greek Cypriot heritage for *Pit*, weaving in her work in the field of human attachment. Andrea's work focuses on the emotional bond we feel between ourselves and other humans, places and foods: we are always searching for nourishment, whether it be from the obvious nutrients present in food or the emotional nourishment that we get from other people.

I thought of Andrea again when I began researching this book, as she had told me a little of her childhood growing up in North London's Cypriot community. Her stories of barbecued lamb intrigued me, but there was something else besides. A retired academic with a PhD in psychology myself, I was interested to know more about her work. During our conversation it became apparent that the research study I cut my teeth on as a budding young psychologist 20 years ago formed the foundation of Andrea's work now. A long-term investigation of the link between life events and depression in women, it's now a famous piece of work, but I hadn't expected to discuss it with anyone for this book, especially not when I'd phoned them up to talk about kebabs.

'You are kidding!' Angela is animated. 'That is some of the most powerful work on the origins of depression that we will ever know, I'm so proud to have a link to it!'

Now, Andrea's work steers towards the emotional bonds we form with particular foods. 'Attachment and food is my USP, so I've started asking more questions about early food memories of my clients. You can get lots of information about peoples' wants and needs and deep unconscious desires if you integrate that. I was only brave enough to start my blog (cupboard-love.co.uk) a year ago, but all of it is client-inspired. Food and people – you can't separate them.'

As a young person – a psychologist forming – Angela noticed differences between the way her family dined at home around a table, and the way they dined in Cyprus, around the barbecue. 'In the UK we would have a formal dinner and we were at the table at 6 or 7. Then we went to Cyprus on holiday and all that went out the window. You would decide you're doing a barbecue an hour before you're doing it. A quick dash to the shops… it has a casualness about it but it's not stressful. I always remember being really struck by that.'

'Mum would always get really stressed about getting dinner on the table, but barbecues were off the cuff and fun. You wouldn't have a big elaborate spread, you would do a few things well – a bit of meat, a bit of salad, a bit of bread. I was struck by how

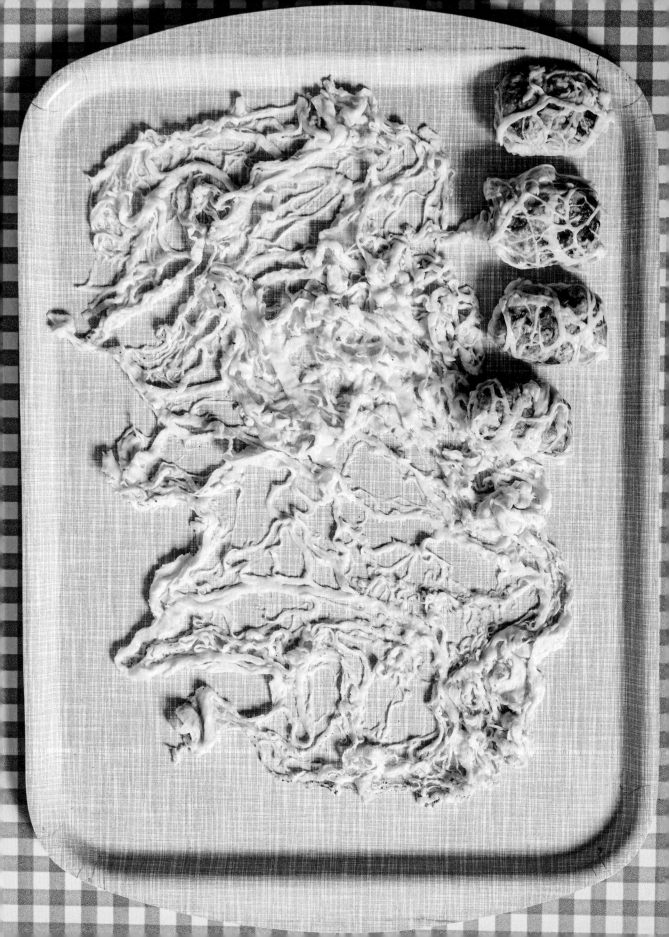

little we sat around a table; the food came off the barbecue and you ate it standing around. Some people would sit down – my elderly grandparents or whatever – but there was less, *right let's get a knife and fork and get ready to eat*, and I loved it. My memories of barbecue always link to play and fun. We never had a barbecue where we didn't jump in the pool at the end of it. So there was a focus on food, but there was also a focus on what we were doing afterwards.'

I ask Andrea who the protagonists of the story were; was there a designated cook? ' It would be uncles of mine cooking outside and women in the kitchen. Cypriot culture is pretty patriarchal, but I was always struck by the synergy of it; it was a collaboration.'

Among the dishes most commonly cooked, says Andrea, was sheftalia. Pronounced sheftayia (the 'l' sound is a guttural 'y' in Greek), they are small lamb 'kebabs' flavoured with onion and parsley. 'My auntie Androula is the person I always go to for cooking advice,' Andrea tells me, 'she's the one I trust to make sheftalia. I've got my mum too, of course – she hates cooking, but she knows a few things. Mostly though, I will go to Auntie Androula.'

'She's given me a couple of tips to pass on to you. Firstly, she said she goes to the butcher and chooses her lamb, then asks them to grind it for her. And it should always be ground twice. She said if it's too coarse it just won't cook evenly, so you need it to be fine. Apparently some commercial sheftalia have breadcrumbs in the mixture to pad them out, but that is also a big no-no.'

'She also said to grate the onion, as it disperses better than very finely diced onion. The herb must be parsley only – there is no other herb choice. The Cypriots don't do competing herbs. You have one shining star. Parsley is a big go-to. A lot of other recipes would use mint.'

Once the mixture is ready, the sheftalia are wrapped in caul fat, which is fat from the abdominal cavity of a sheep. A thin membrane laced with webbed deposits of milky fat, it is ideal for encasing ground (minced) meat, while simultaneously basting the mixture. 'Auntie Androula said that you must wash the caul fat three times – I don't know if this is a father, son and holy ghost thing – but you wash it with vinegar. She said some people use lemon but basically you want a bit of acid in there. Then you roll it up like you would a dolma. And that's it!'

Well, apart from the cooking, of course, which absolutely must be done on the barbecue. 'The closest thing to sheftalia [in British cuisine] is faggots,' says Andrea, 'which are cooked in the oven, but I've tried doing that with sheftalia and it just doesn't work.

The charcoal is an ingredient and you need that burnt flavour to balance the dish. You won't get that if you shove them in the oven: they will just taste quite fatty and greasy – and not in the right way. They must also always be started over a low barbecue; that charring, the Dalmatian spottiness will happen but you have to start it low… you have to get them cooked first and then you can add the final charring to get the burnt bits, which are so essential to the flavour.'

Sheftalia is such an everyday dish, says Andrea ('it's ordinary; it's "let's have a barbecue" at 7pm on Wednesday night'), and yet cooks are particular about their methods. When I cook the sheftalia to Auntie Androula's recipe, I think about how many times it has been made to these exact instructions, and enjoyed around the swimming pool in Cyprus. 'Now that Auntie Androula is nearly 80,' Andrea says, 'these conversations that I have with her are really precious, and it's mad because I think I just want to get all this information out of you because one day, you won't be here.'

'It feels really important to keep the recipe alive?', I ask. 'Yeah, Greek Cypriot cookbooks are quite hard to come by,' says Andrea, 'and I don't mean glammed-up glossy photo ones, I mean proper cookbooks from the village. My mum's got one and it's great – it has the most awful photos, the grammar is all over the shop and it hasn't been translated properly but the recipes work and you can feel the love on the page, you know.'

Auntie Androula's Sheftalia

Setup: Indirect cooking
Equipment: Tongs,
metal skewers
Prep time: 30 minutes
Cook time: 15-20 minutes
Serves: 8

---

300 g (10 ½ oz) caul
(approximately – it's better
to have more than less, see
rolling note in step 4 of
the method)
white vinegar or white wine
vinegar, for washing the caul
750 g (1 lb 10 oz) minced pork
(shoulder is the best cut for
sheftalia, never use loin
because the lack of fat will
make them dry. Ask your
butcher to grind it twice – the
finer the better as the sheftalia
will cook more evenly)
2 large onions, grated
60 g (2 ¼ oz) flat-leaf parsley,
finely chopped
1 ½ teaspoons salt
½ teaspoon ground
black pepper
½ teaspoon ground cinnamon

To serve
8–10 pitta breads
6 tomatoes, diced
1 cucumber, diced
1 large onion, diced
large handful of finely
chopped parsley
2 lemons, cut into wedges

— Start by washing the caul
in water mixed with vinegar
– white or wine vinegar is best
and you want a ratio of 4 parts
water to 1 part vinegar.
Wash the caul and leave to
drain in a sieve.
— Mix the rest of the
ingredients together until
well-combined – using your
hands is best for this.
— Prepare the barbecue
for indirect cooking.
— Cut squares of caul,
approximately 12 × 12 cm
(5 × 5 in). Take about
2 tablespoons of the mince
mixture and spoon it about 2.5
cm (1 in) from the side that is
closest to you. Roll it over
once, then fold over both sides
and continue rolling into
a squat sausage shape.
When wrapping sheftalia you
need to make sure that they
are tight, yet not overstuffed;
if they are too thin they will
burn easily. Also, the caul
is fragile and can rip when
rolling so it is better to have
more rather than less,
as you might have to do
some patchwork.
— Thread the sheftalia onto
skewers; it is best to use
2 skewers to create a 'ladder'
of sheftalia, as this makes
them easier to turn on
the barbecue.

— Cook over low heat on the
barbecue – there should be
no flame at all, and this will
ensure they cook through.
Turn the skewers every
2-3 minutes and cook for 15-20
minutes, or until the caul
is light brown all over and
charred in spots. Move them
to the cooler side of the grill if
they flare up too much, and
wait for the flames to die down
before proceeding.
— Serve in pittas with diced
tomatoes, cucumber and
onions, finely chopped parsley
and a spritz of lemon.

Butterflied Leg of Lamb
with Mustard and Mint

Setup: Indirect cooking
Equipment: Tongs
Prep time: 10 minutes, plus
minimum 2 hours marinating
time (overnight if possible)
Cook time: 20 minutes,
plus resting time
Serves: 6

1 lamb leg, butterflied
(a butcher will do this for you)

Rub
1 tablespoon English mustard
1 tablespoon dried mint
grated zest of 1 lemon
1 teaspoon ground cumin
6 tablespoons neutral oil
1 tablespoon sea salt

Mint and mustard
basting sauce
handful of mint leaves, finely
chopped
1 tablespoon English mustard
grated zest and juice
of 2 lemons
4 garlic cloves, crushed
or finely grated
6 tablespoons olive oil
a generous pinch of sea salt

I'm always astonished by how quickly a butterflied leg of lamb cooks on the barbecue, despite it making perfect sense – it has been opened out and laid flat for entirely that reason. Some very British flavours here: the rip-searing fire of hot mustard and fresh, country-garden sweetness of mint. I've taken a two-pronged approach by marinating the meat first, then basting it on the grill to really hammer the message home – it's like a Sunday roast, only fresher and with scraggly fatty caramelised edge bits and a tender pinkness within.

I like to serve this with the Autumn Coleslaw on page 195 or the Green Beans with Anchovy Cream on page 137 and some buttered potatoes.

— Unfold the butterflied lamb and trim off any large pieces of fat or sinew.
— Combine the ingredients for the rub and mix well, then rub it all over the lamb, making sure you get into every part of the meat. Set aside in the fridge for a couple of hours, or overnight, if you can.
— Combine the ingredients for the basting sauce and divide between two bowls (you will use one bowl to baste the lamb towards the end of cooking).
— Remove the meat from the fridge 1 hour before you want to cook it.
— Prepare a barbecue for indirect cooking using a whole chimney of coals, and bank them to one side.
— Grill the lamb over high direct heat on both sides to get some colour – around 5 minutes, then move it to indirect heat to finish cooking – it will take about 20 minutes to cook to medium. Turn and baste the lamb regularly with the mint and mustard sauce.
— Rest the lamb for 15 minutes before slicing and serving with the remaining sauce.

To Cook Indoors: Preheat the oven to 200°C (400°F/gas 6). Roast the lamb in a roasting tray for 15 minutes, basting twice with the sauce, then reduce the temperature to 180°C (350°F/gas 4) and cook for a further 15 minutes, basting twice again. Rest for 15 minutes before serving.

Barbacoa-style Lamb Tacos

Setup: Indirect cooking
Equipment: Roasting tray,
heatproof gloves
Prep time: 1 hour, plus
minimum 4 hours marinating
time (overnight if possible)
Cook time: 3–4 hours
Serves: 4–6

1 bone-in lamb shoulder,
around 2 kg (4 lb 8 oz)
400 g (14 oz) banana leaves,
for wrapping the lamb
sea salt

Adobo
2 dried chipotle chillies
10 dried guajillo chillies
3 dried pasilla chillies
3 dried ancho chillies
500 ml (17 fl oz/generous
2 cups) water
1 tablespoon cumin seeds
1 teaspoon allspice berries
1 cinnamon stick
2 cloves
2 heads of garlic
2 tablespoons sea salt
3 tablespoons cider vinegar
1 tablespoon dried thyme

Barbacoa is a cooking method that originated with the
Caribbean Taino people, the first to use green wood in 'earth
ovens' – basically dug-for-purpose pits that were used to cook
meat slowly, over long periods. They called this original cooking
style 'babarbicu', meaning 'sacred fire pit', and … well, I think
you can see where this is going. That word evolved over time
to what we know today as 'barbecue'.

   This style of pit cooking eventually made it to Mexico, where
it is still used to cook lamb or goat under maguey (agave) leaves,
which bring their scent to the dish. In the absence of both
a garden to dig a hole in and maguey leaves, I use a kettle
barbecue and banana leaves – they add a grassy flavour, and you
can find them in the freezer cabinet of Asian supermarkets and
online. They are important for containing all the cooking juices
here too, which are heady with smoky chillies, allspice and
garlic, and are mixed back through the meat before frying
at the end.

— Put the dried chillies in a saucepan, cover with the water and
bring to the boil. Cook for a few minutes, then drain, reserving
the water. Pull the stalks off the chillies and discard.
— Toast the whole spices in a dry frying pan (skillet) over
a medium heat until fragrant (moving them around so they don't
burn), then grind to a coarse powder using a spice grinder or
pestle and mortar. Process to a smooth-ish paste in a blender
with the drained chillies, garlic, salt, vinegar, thyme and 100 ml
(3½ fl oz/scant ½ cup) of the chilli cooking liquid.
— Make deep slashes all over the lamb and add the adobo
paste, rubbing it all over the lamb and getting into all the
slashes. Leave in the fridge, covered, overnight, or for
a minimum of 4 hours.
— Allow the marinated lamb to come to room temperature
(for about 1 hour) before cooking.

Salsa verde cruda
large handful of coriander
(cilantro) leaves and stalks,
finely chopped
small handful of mint leaves,
finely chopped
2 green chillies, finely chopped
2 garlic cloves, finely chopped
2 medium white onions,
finely chopped
3–4 tablespoons lime juice
a couple of generous pinches
sea salt

To serve
at least 20 corn tortillas
|(store bought, or see my
recipe on page 244)
200ml sour cream
large bunch coriander
(cilantro), leaves picked

— Prepare a barbecue for indirect cooking using half a chimney starter of coals.
— Place some banana leaves overlapping and criss-crossing on a roasting tray and put the lamb inside, then wrap the banana leaves around it – you want it completely enclosed. Tuck the banana leaves down at the sides so that they are secure.
— Place the roasting tray on the grill on the cooler side of the barbecue and put the lid on with the vents about ¼ open. Cook for 3–4 hours, or until the meat can be pulled apart with a fork.
— To make the salsa verde cruda, combine all the ingredients in a bowl with a pinch of salt – the salsa should be good and sour.
— When the meat is ready, unwrap it carefully, preserving the juices. Pull it apart, removing the bones, and toss the meat in its cooking juices, adding some salt to season it right through.
— Fry the meat briefly in a heavy-based frying pan (skillet) over high heat, to crisp it up.
— Serve the crisped-up meat with the corn tortillas, salsa verde cruda, sour cream and coriander (cilantro).

To Cook Indoors: Preheat the oven to 140°C (280°F/gas 3). Cook the lamb shoulder in a roasting tray, covered tightly with foil (no banana leaves), for about 4 hours or until falling apart. Once cooked, pull the meat apart and combine with the juices, then fry in a frying pan (skillet) over high heat, to crisp it up.

Squid
with Chilli, Fennel, Garlic and Mint

Setup: Direct cooking
Equipment: Tongs
Prep time: 10 minutes, plus
a few hours marinating time
Cook time: 5 minutes
Serves: 2–4

400 g (14 oz) medium squid
tubes, cleaned and tentacles
removed (keep these if you
have them)
2 teaspoons fennel seeds
1–2 red chillies, finely chopped
2 tablespoons lemon juice
2 garlic cloves, crushed or
finely grated
5 tablespoons extra virgin
olive oil
handful of mint leaves,
finely chopped
sea salt and freshly ground
black pepper

This is a real crowd-pleaser for a scorching day: just make sure to cook the squid hot and fast so that it stays tender (bonus: you won't need to stand in front of a grill for long). I like to serve the squid sliced on a big platter with the sauce poured over so people can help themselves. It won't last long. The recipe is easy to scale up, too.

— Open out the squid tubes using a sharp knife and score the inside surface in a cross-hatch pattern, taking care not to cut all the way through the squid.
— Lightly toast the fennel seeds in a dry frying pan (skillet), moving them around so they don't burn. Crush roughly in a pestle and mortar. Combine the fennel seeds with all the other ingredients, except the fresh mint, season with salt and pepper, and whisk to a sauce.
— Toss the scored squid in half the sauce and leave to marinate for a couple of hours in the fridge.
— Prepare a barbecue for direct cooking over high heat, and grill the marinated squid over direct heat for a couple of minutes on each side, turning it with tongs.
— Cut the squid into chunky slices, transfer to a platter, drizzle with the remaining sauce and garnish with the chopped mint.

To Cook Indoors: Preheat a cast-iron griddle pan over a high heat for at least 5 minutes, then add the squid and cook for a couple of minutes on each side.

Lamb Breast
with a Malt Vinegar Dipping Sauce

Setup: Indirect cooking
Equipment: Tongs
Prep time: 10 minutes,
plus 3 hours marinating time
(overnight if possible)
Cook time: 3 hours
Serves: 4

2 lamb breasts

Marinade
10 dried bay leaves
1 tablespoon dried mint
1 tablespoon English
mustard powder
1 tablespoon flaky sea salt
1 tablespoon light
brown sugar
1 tablespoon garlic powder
1 tablespoon onion powder
1 teaspoon ground
white pepper
neutral oil, to make a paste

Malt vinegar dipping sauce
60 ml (2 fl oz/4 tablespoons)
malt vinegar
1 tablespoon caster
(superfine) sugar
4 tablespoons mayonnaise
½ teaspoon English mustard
small dash of Worcestershire
sauce
pinch of salt
pinch of freshly ground
white pepper
handful of mint leaves,
finely chopped

I have written various iterations of this recipe over the years but I think this is my favourite: honed and toned. The original inspiration was to make something with very British flavours like mustard, mint and bay, then serve it with a riff on a white barbecue sauce. My version uses malt vinegar and I love it because it's so sharp against the rich lamb with its irresistible scrackly fat. It really is a dipping sauce, though – a quick dunk is enough!

— To make the marinade, combine all the ingredients except the oil in a spice grinder or small blender and blitz to a fine powder. Combine with enough oil to make a spreadable paste. Rub the paste all over the lamb breasts. Cover and put in the fridge for at least a few hours, or overnight if you can.
— Prepare a barbecue for indirect cooking with half a chimney starter of coals, with the coals banked to one side.
— Place the lamb breasts skin side down on the opposite side of the grill to the coals and close the lid. Set the vents to a quarter open at the base and leave a small crack (2 mm) in the vent holes on the lid. Cook the lamb for 3 hours, turning it every 45 minutes. Rest for 10 minutes before cutting into slices, following the rib bones.
— To make the sauce, combine all the ingredients except for the mint leaves and mix well. Stir in the mint and serve with the ribs.

To Cook Indoors: Preheat the oven to 130°C (260°F/gas 2). Roast the lamb breasts (on two trays if necessary) for 2–2½ hours, or until very tender.

Flank Steak
with Seaweed Butter

Setup: Indirect cooking
Equipment: Tongs
Prep time: 10 minutes
Cook time: 5 minutes
Serves: 4

20 × 10 cm (8 × 4 in) piece nori (I've used nori here as it's widely available in shops, but you should definitely experiment with different types of dried seaweed)
100 g (3½ oz/7 tablespoons) butter, softened
1 flank steak, around 800 g (1 lb 12 oz)
sea salt

You could serve this seaweed butter with any cut of steak; I like to use flank (bavette) as it has so much texture, and there's something very fun about that combination of rich, slightly offaly meat and the murky iodine twang of seaweed. Gnarly.

Seaweed works so well as a seasoning because it has a ton of umami and it's a particularly rich source of naturally occurring monosodium glutamate (MSG). This nori seaweed butter recipe is just a starting point; there are so many different types of seaweed available now, all of which have their own characteristics. Dulse, for example, is peppery and smoky (some compare it to bacon once cooked), while brown seaweeds such as kelp are milder but still full of savoury depth.

— Crumble the nori into the smallest pieces you can and mash it into the softened butter.
— Prepare a barbecue for indirect cooking over high heat, with the coals banked to one side.
— Rub the steaks with a little neutral oil and season with salt. Sear on the grill for a couple of minutes, flipping once or twice, then move it to a cooler spot and grill for a few minutes more, flipping once or twice more. You don't want to overcook it. Wrap the steak in foil and rest for 10 minutes.
— Flank steak must be sliced against the grain, otherwise it will be inedibly tough. Cut lovely thin slices and top with plenty of the seaweed butter.

To Cook Indoors: Preheat a cast-iron griddle pan over a high heat for at least 5 minutes. Rub the steak with a little neutral oil, season with salt and cook as directed above.

Eritrean-London Barbecue: Smoking Shanks and Sweating Onions

I have been in Makda Ghermai-Harlow and her husband Jack's house for approximately five minutes before Makda is thrusting a glass of Araki – an Eritrean spirit similar to ouzo – into my hand. 'In Eritrea when you have a barbecue, you also have araki,' she says, as we clink our tiny glasses and down them in one swift and surprisingly smooth shot. I have come here for a lesson in Eritrean cooking from Makda, who left Eritrea at the age of 16, first for New York and then the UK, in 2004.

Did I mention it was 9am when I arrived at their North London home? Makda, worried that I might start feeling the effects of liquor on an empty stomach, spontaneously decides to make fit-fit, a traditional Eritrean breakfast dish that uses up leftover injera – the pancake-like flatbread made from fermented teff flour that forms a staple food in both Eritrea and Ethiopia. Sour in flavour from the fermentation process, it is thin and bubbly. Soon, I am handed a steaming bowl, the shredded injera flavoured with tomatoes, chillies, and the essential ingredient: berbere, a spice blend that defines the flavour of Eritrean and Ethiopian cuisine. But more on that later.

It is fitting that we are drinking together now, as the first time I met Makda and Jack at their stall Lemlem Kitchen in an East London market I had been er... doing a little day drinking. On the hunt for something to soak it up, the incredible scents emanating from their stall drew me in. Lemlem means 'bloom and flourish' in Amharic and that is exactly what happened to their business, as, over the years, they developed a loyal fan base and went on to host pop-ups and supper clubs.

I became one of their regulars thanks to their incredible Awaze Wings – double fried chicken wings in a richly spiced sauce – and their innovative injera 'tacos'. 'Eritrean food was a big part of our lives, but the idea of just giving people a plate of injera wasn't going to work,' says Jack. 'In Eritrea all dishes are served on top of a very large plate of injera, which everyone then shares. That just wasn't practical for street food.' Instead they cut small circles of injera and topped them, like tortillas. 'We started doing the little injera tacos almost as a joke and then they ended up becoming the main thing we did. It was also about balancing the amount of injera with the amount of sauce and spice, so that people weren't having too much of one thing, otherwise you don't get the right balance of flavours.'

None of the cooking at Lemlem was grilled, but plenty is cooked over fire in Eritrea, and I had the idea

Right: Smoked lamb shanks are added to the rich, slow cooked zigni sauce to become tender.

that I could collaborate with Makda and Jack, two of my favourite cooks in London. We decide to make the awaze sauce to dress grilled (instead of fried) chicken wings and we also come up with an entirely new idea, which is to smoke lamb shanks and simmer them in zigni sauce, a famous sauce for stews, made with lots and lots of slowly cooked onions.

When I arrive, Makda has already been stewing down the onions in the back garden, on a small induction hob (stovetop). 'It makes the house smell very strongly of onions otherwise, and in Eritrea most of the cooking would be done outside over charcoal anyway,' she explains. The onions are cooked in their own juice for hours. 'If you see a recipe for zigni that cooks the onions for a short amount of time then that is not the right method. The only thing to do is add a little bit of water if it looks like it's drying out,' says Jack.

Once the onions have cooked down sufficiently, Makda adds berbere. 'Berbere is a mixture of spices, and it is the flavour of Eritrea. It has chilli powder from the chillies that grow in the region and then garlic, ginger, cinnamon, black cardamom, cloves and also some people add more or less of the allspice.' Peppercorns such as long pepper feature too; a knobbly peppercorn native to India, it resembles a dried catkin. 'We can make berbere here,' says Makda, 'but it won't be the same as the blends we have in Eritrea, because of the sun, the heat, the soil, and the

ingredients. It's not going to taste the same – like if you made a sun-dried tomato in London it won't taste the same as a sun-dried tomato in Italy.'

'In Eritrea, they have huge mills where they are grinding all the spices with these huge machines,' says Jack, 'and everything from the ceiling to the floor is the colour of berbere. The air is full of berbere. People also take their own spices there to be ground for them.'

Next, Makda adds the berbere to the onions and allows it to cook more. 'After 3 hours this is still young,' she explains, even though to my taste buds it already has an incredible depth of flavour. 'We will then add the garlic, ginger and clarified butter later on.' I have brought two smoked lamb shanks with me, which we drop into the sauce after berbere has been added and leave it for another 2 hours, until the shanks have become very tender.

We take another shot of Araki and put some chicken wings on the barbecue to let them slowly grill and take on some smoke. A small, well-used drum sits at the end of the garden. 'Yes, that has seen some use,' laughs Jack, 'and has followed us through several house moves.' The wings will be tossed in the awaze sauce once cooked and crisp.

'So awaze traditionally is just a mix of berbere and water, or some people mix it with araki so it's almost like a paste,' explains Jack. 'In Ethiopia they do it differently; they ferment it or do different variations. 'Awaze' is almost a generic term for a paste that's based on berbere. When we made our wing sauce we actually took influence from other wing sauces, like Korean sauces with garlic and ginger, which you would never put in awaze, then we added loads of berbere, white wine vinegar, olive oil and honey – lots of things you wouldn't normally add. We also add tamari soy sauce, which gives it that fermented depth and umami. So, although you'd never find these ingredients in awaze normally, the essence of it is there, like an Asian-influenced wing sauce.'

So Makda and Jack fused Asian and Eritrean influences for their wings and fused their own version of Eritrean-meets-Mexican-meets-British cuisine for their tacos. Eritrean food, of course, was already heavily influenced by the Italians who colonised the country from 1882 to 1941. 'Eritrean cuisine is very similar to Ethiopian cuisine,' says Makda, 'but we use a lot more tomatoes and it's lighter, with less fat. It's more Mediterranean. We also eat a lot of pasta because we inherited it from the Italians. When I left Eritrea, it was still occupied by Ethiopia, and there was not one cafe or restaurant you could go to that didn't serve Italian food,

Top: Makda and Helen taste the zigni sauce.
Bottom: Helen grills the wings ready for tossing with the awaze sauce.

or something that had a mash-up of Italian and Eritrean cuisines, e.g. Bolognese with berbere. Now, since independence, there is injera everywhere.'

'The cafe and restaurant culture was also inherited from the Italians, for example cappuccinos and fast food, which for me as a kid was a mortadella sandwich with jalapeños. I bet that outside of Bologna the second biggest city that consumed mortadella was Asmara!' says Makda. 'We did that sandwich as a course at a supper club actually, and served it wrapped in an Eritrean newspaper. All food is evolving as people are adapting. When we did our stall, Eritrean dishes evolved into London food, and now you are here and we are changing these recipes and they are evolving again.'

Jack tosses the wings in the awaze sauce as we start laying the table. Makda pours spiced tea. 'It's a very simple mix of spices – cardamom, cinnamon and cloves – and you bring it up to the boil slowly, slowly.' The finished tea is sweet, fragrant and very comforting. The injera, bought from nearby Finsbury Park, is spread out ready to receive the zigni lamb shanks. 'Injera is the most complicated thing to make in this country because of the climate,' says Makda. For this reason, many restaurateurs and cooks in the UK use a combination of wheat and teff flour, 'But now we can buy 100 per cent legit injera made by the experts,

locally,' says Jack. 'This is what I love about London, the food cultures. You find there are so many shared methods, styles and motivations behind cooking and I love that.'

We all dig into the injera, tearing pieces off with our right hands and using them to scoop up food. This is the only way people eat in Eritrea, explains Makda. 'There is no street food culture in Eritrea. People eat at home. People eat together. Traditionally everyone would eat from the same spread. It's the lifestyle. You don't eat alone, it's very strange to do that. It's just not done.' The tender shanks and sweet, spiced zigni sauce are incredibly addictive. The depth and richness of the sauces Makda has cooked is incredible: the secret ingredient, other than berbere, is time. This level of umami can only come from long, slow cooking, and combined with smoke it is out of this world. The combination of Makda and Jack's expertise and hospitality, and my curiosity and eagerness to just invite myself the heck over to their house, has borne some very fun results: two entirely new (to us, at least) barbecue dishes that we are proud to share here in these pages.

Awaze Wings

Setup: Indirect cooking
Equipment: Tongs
Prep time: 5 minutes
Cook time: 30 minutes
Serves: 6–8

20 chicken wings, jointed

Awaze sauce
5 garlic cloves, crushed
or finely grated
thumb-sized piece of ginger,
grated (about the same volume
as the garlic)
3 tablespoons tamari
soy sauce
3 tablespoons berbere
(page 190)
2 tablespoons white
wine vinegar
1 tablespoon extra virgin
olive oil
1 tablespoon honey

As described on page 184–187, this is a combination of Makda Ghermai-Harlow and her husband Jack's awaze sauce, with grilled (rather than fried) wings. I will let them introduce it: 'Traditional awaze is quite different from our wing sauce. At its simplest it's a paste made from berbere (a spice mix used in Eritrean and Ethiopian cuisine) and a liquid (often alcohol), and the consistency can range from a runny dip to a thicker paste - then it can be fresh or aged, and there are no strict proportions either. Our awaze wing sauce was inspired by Korean-style wing sauces, and uses berbere and Mediterranean ingredients.'

— Combine all the sauce ingredients in a food processor and blend to a smooth sauce.
— Prepare a barbecue for indirect cooking over medium heat, with the coals arranged in the centre of the barbecue and space around the edge.
— Once the barbecue is ready, arrange the wings in a circle around the coals, but not directly over them. Cook the wings for about 30 minutes, turning them every so often, until cooked through and caramelised. You can move the wings further into the centre of the barbecue as the coals burn down.
— Warm through the awaze sauce then toss the wings in the sauce.

Berbere

30–50 g (1–1 ¾ oz) dried red chilli pepper (dried bird's eye chillies or a chilli powder – weight needed depends on the strength of the chilli. This is the key element of the mix – so avoid supermarket chilli powders)
1 teaspoon black cardamom seeds (korerima) – if you can't find these, substitute with green cardamom seeds
2 teaspoons coriander seeds
2 teaspoons cumin seeds
½ teaspoon cloves
2 teaspoons fenugreek seeds
1 teaspoon ground ginger
1 teaspoon garlic powder
1 teaspoon red onion powder
1 teaspoon freshly grated nutmeg
1 teaspoon ground cinnamon
1 teaspoon salt
1 teaspoon dried Thai basil
1 teaspoon dried thyme
1 teaspoon freshly ground black pepper

According to Makda and Jack, 'The best place to source berbere is from an Ethiopian or Eritrean shop – or look online. We saw an article recently that used the analogy of terroir when describing berbere: many of the ingredients are sundried and the proportions vary from family to family, each of which has their own recipe and uses different chillies with different strengths. So, if you approach buying berbere like buying wine, it helps. Consider where it came from, how recently it was ground, and get to know the colour and smell. If you trawl the internet for berbere recipes, one thing that is consistent is that they are all different!'

—— If using whole seeds and/or dried chillies, toast them in a dry pan until fragrant, then grind before mixing with the powdered ingredients.

Zigni Lamb Shanks

Setup: Indirect cooking
Equipment: Roasting tray
Wood: Oak
Prep time: 1 hour
Cook time: 4–5 hours
Serves: 4–6

---

4 lamb shanks

Zigni sauce
3 kg (6 lb 8 oz) brown or red onions, finely chopped
3 tablespoons salt
100 ml (3½ fl oz/scant ½ cup) sunflower oil
120 g (4¼ oz) berbere (see opposite)
3 tablespoons minced garlic
3 tablespoons minced ginger
½ tablespoon mekelesha (a finishing spice mix – see Stockists page 17)
½ tablespoon black cardamom seeds (korerima), or green cardamom seeds
400ml (14 floz / 1¾ cups) passata or 3 tablespoons double concentrate tomato paste (puree) (optional)

Tesmi
500 g (1 lb 2 oz) butter
½ teaspoon cardamom seeds
½ teaspoon fenugreek seeds
½ teaspoon cumin seeds
½ teaspoon nigella seeds

Zigni sauce is made with lots of very gently cooked onions that are stewed for hours, releasing their sweetness and depth of flavour. Once berbere and clarified butter are added, the sauce becomes exceptionally rich and intense. In this recipe, the lamb shanks are smoked, then simmered in the sauce, adding another dimension of flavour. Serve with injera, or another carb such as rice or potatoes if you can't get hold of injera.

— To make the tesmi, coarsely grind the spices in a spice grinder or pestle and mortar and add to a heavy saucepan with the butter. Clarify the butter by melting it gently over a low heat. Skim off the froth from the surface leaving behind a clear yellow layer on top of the spices and white milky deposits. Carefully pour the yellow layer off into a container, leaving behind the spices and milky deposits.
— Cook the onion in a large saucepan over a very low heat without oil for 1 hour, stirring occasionally.
— Prepare a barbecue for indirect cooking, with just a few lit coals. Place a small piece of wood on top of the coals and let it smoulder.
— Place the lamb shanks in a roasting tray on the opposite side of the grill to the coals, put the lid on and leave the vents a quarter open. Cook offset with a piece of wood for 2 hours, topping up the coals and wood if necessary.

— After the onions have been cooking for an hour, add the salt then continue to cook over very low heat for another hour. The onion should not burn or caramelise – it should look like a very pale mush with the consistency of jam.
— After the second hour, add the sunflower oil and berbere and mix well – you should now have a bright red sauce developing. If it looks pale you may need to add more berbere. Cook slowly for another hour, stirring occasionally. If it seems to be drying out, add a little water.
— Add the smoked lamb shanks to the sauce, along with the garlic and ginger. You can adjust the sauce with a little water if it seems too thick and add the tomato passata or tomato paste (puree), if using. Finally, add the mekelesha, korerima and around 100ml tesmi for a lovely shiny finish and cook for another 1–2 hours over a very low heat until the lamb shanks are tender. Season to taste.

Venison Kebabs
with Watercress Zhoug and Hazelnut Dukkah

Setup: Direct cooking
Equipment: Tongs, skewers
Prep time: 30 minutes
Cook time: 10 minutes
Serves: 6

This is one of my favourite autumnal kebabs. Venison is fun to cook with, so long as you're aware that it's lean and therefore needs a bit of help in the form of additional fat.

A great kebab is like a great sandwich: it's all about the contrasts. Which is why I serve this one with a zippy zhoug (a spiced Yemenite hot sauce of admirable herbal intensity) and a woodsy hazelnut dukkah, which brings crunch and crackles of spice to the plate. All this sounds quite romantic, but ultimately, it's about wanting to roll it up and point it into your face as fast as possible, and I think these elements work together to achieve that goal nicely.

— Toast the cumin and coriander seeds for the kebabs in a dry frying pan over a medium heat until fragrant (moving them around so they don't burn), then add to a spice grinder or pestle and mortar with the cloves and grind or crush to a fine powder. Combine the spices with the minced (ground) venison, pork, parsley stalks, Urfa chilli, sumac, black pepper and salt in a bowl and mix everything really well using your hands. If you like, fry a small piece of the mixture to check the seasoning.
— Divide the mixture equally into 12 balls, then flatten and lengthen the balls into small kebabs, or - alternatively - shape around metal skewers.
— To make the zhoug, combine all the ingredients in a blender with a big pinch of salt and blend to a smooth sauce. Set aside.

Venison kebabs

1 tablespoon cumin seeds
1 tablespoon coriander seeds
2 cloves
500 g (1 lb 2 oz) minced (ground) venison
500 g (1 lb 2 oz) minced (ground) pork
4 tablespoons finely chopped parsley stalks
1 tablespoon Urfa chilli
1 tablespoon sumac
½ teaspoon freshly ground black pepper
1 tablespoon sea salt

Watercress zhoug

80 g (2¾ oz) watercress
small bunch of coriander (cilantro) leaves
2 green chillies
4 garlic cloves
3 tablespoons lemon juice
3 tablespoons olive oil
1 teaspoon ground cumin
seeds of 5 cardamom pods, crushed
2 tablespoons pul biber

Hazelnut dukkah

50 g (1¾ oz) blanched hazelnuts
2 tablespoons coriander seeds
1 tablespoon cumin seeds
1 tablespoon sesame seeds
1 teaspoon salt

To serve

6 flatbreads (page 60)
200g natural yoghurt
½ small white or red cabbage, very thinly sliced

— To make the dukkah, lightly toast the nuts in a dry frying pan over a medium heat until just starting to colour, then set aside and roughly chop. Toast the coriander and cumin seeds in the same pan over a medium heat (moving them around so they don't burn) and crush those in a spice grinder or pestle and mortar before combining them with the nuts. Stir through the sesame seeds and salt and set aside.
— Prepare a barbecue for direct cooking over medium heat.
— Grill the kebabs directly over the coals for about 8 minutes, turning them regularly, or until cooked through. Take care not to overcook these, as they will dry out a bit.
— Serve with the zhoug, dukkah, flatbread, yoghurt and cabbage.

To Cook Indoors: Cook the kebabs under a medium-hot grill for about 4 minutes on each side.

Cider-brined Pork Chops

Setup: Indirect cooking
Equipment: Tongs, plastic tub
for brining
Prep time: 10 minutes,
plus overnight brining
Cook time: 10–15 minutes
Serves: 2

2 thick-cut pork chops
(Gloucester Old Spot would
be wonderful!)
500 ml (17 fl oz/generous
2 cups) sweet cider
1 tablespoon sea salt
2 bay leaves
1 teaspoon brown mustard
seeds
2 garlic cloves
2 sprigs of rosemary
pared zest of 1 lemon
neutral oil, for cooking

N.B. My friend and cookery
writer, Ed Smith, likes to
score the removed piece of fat,
salt it, let it sit for 30 minutes,
and then roast it in the oven
for 15–20 minutes at 230°C
(440°F/gas 9) to make a giant
crackling to eat alongside
the chop. I can't really argue
with that.

I don't do masses of brining, only when I think it's really worth it.
I find there's a very fine line between meat being juicy and having
an off-putting 'fake' texture. I think pork chops really benefit
from brining though, as they can dry out easily on the barbecue.
The cider also adds a lot of flavour. I was raised in
Gloucestershire and I like to think this is a little nod to that.
You can take the girl out of The Shire...
These are very good with either of the potato salads on
pages 68 and 195.

— Trim the outer layer of fat from the pork chops if it's thick,
using the natural line visible between the skin and meat of the
pork chop as a guide (you'll be trimming around half of the
fat off).
— Combine the cider with the salt in a bowl or jug and stir until
the salt has dissolved. Place the pork chops in a shallow dish
and pour over the brine, making sure the chops are completely
covered. Add the bay leaves, mustard seeds, garlic, rosemary
and lemon zest. Cover and refrigerate overnight.
— Remove the pork chops from the brine and pat dry.
Make a series of lateral cuts into the fat of the chops (knife
starting from the outside and pointing in towards the meat),
taking care not to cut into the meat. This will stop the chops
from warping on the grill.
— Prepare a barbecue for indirect cooking with the coals
banked to one side.
— Lightly oil the chops on both sides.
— Grill the pork chops over direct heat for 5 minutes on each
side, depending on the thickness of the chops. The fat will drip
and flare up, so stay with the pork chops, moving them around as
necessary with the tongs. Move to the cooler side of the barbecue
to finish cooking through, around 5 minutes more per side.
— Allow to rest for a few minutes before serving.

To Cook Indoors: You want to get crisp fat here, so begin by
using a cold heavy-based frying pan to gently render the fat down
before you start cooking the chops – use tongs to hold the chops
upright so that only the fat is touching the surface of the pan.
Once the fat is crisp (after about 15 minutes), turn up the heat
and cook the chop for a few minutes on each side, or until just
cooked through. Rest for a few minutes before serving.

Setup: Indoors
Prep Time: 10 minutes
Cook Time: 15 minutes, plus
minimum 30 minutes resting
(overnight if possible)
Serves: 4–6

1 kg (2 lb 4 oz) waxy potatoes,
sliced fairly thickly
70 ml (2¼ fl oz/5 tablespoons)
white wine vinegar
50 ml (1¾ fl oz/3½ tablespoons)
olive oil
1 tablespoon Dijon mustard
1 teaspoon wholegrain mustard
2 teaspoons caster (superfine)
sugar
100 ml (3½ fl oz/scant ½ cup)
hot chicken stock
1 small red onion, very finely
chopped
2 tablespoons finely chopped
chives
1 tablespoon very finely
chopped parsley (optional)
sea salt and freshly ground
black pepper

Pickled Potato Salad

This is a version of a recipe kindly sent to me by Marion
Woracziczky, the patron of a restaurant in Vienna called
Woracziczky Gasthaus. It's the kind of pickly, saucy potato
salad that's very good with sausages and other rich, grilled
meats. I find it irresistible and can't be trusted not to swipe a
mouthful every time it passes within my field of vision.

— Cook the potatoes in boiling salted water for about 15
minutes until tender.
— Mix the vinegar, olive oil, mustards, sugar, stock and some
salt and pepper in a large bowl. Add the hot potatoes and allow
to cool.
— Once cool, add the onion and herbs and mix the salad quite
roughly – this will agitate the potatoes, releasing their starch,
and help thicken the potato salad.
— Rest for at least 30 minutes, but ideally overnight.
Allow to come back to room temperature before serving.

Setup: Indoors
Prep time: 15 minutes
Cook time: 1 minute
Serves: 6

350 g (12 oz) celeriac (celery
root), grated or cut into very
fine strips
1 medium onion, thinly sliced
1 large carrot, grated or cut
into very fine strips
100 g (3½ oz/generous ⅓ cup)
natural full-fat yoghurt
100 g (3½ oz) mayonnaise
1 tablespoon Dijon mustard
3 tablespoons lemon juice
small handful of chives,
finely chopped
1 tablespoon coriander seeds
2 tablespoons mixed seeds
sea salt and freshly ground white
or black pepper

Autumn Coleslaw

This is like the lovechild of a coleslaw and a remoulade,
with rootsy earthiness from celeriac (celery root) and a dressing
that's like a pumped-up yoghurt or a freshened mayonnaise,
depending on your point of view. Coriander seeds are one of my
favourite spices to use in dressings and salads because of their
warmth and citrus notes: they lift this coleslaw and bring life
to it alongside the toasted seeds.

— Combine the celeriac (celery root), onion and carrot in a bowl.
— Combine the yoghurt, mayonnaise, mustard, lemon juice,
chives and some salt and pepper, and mix well, then combine
with the vegetables.
— Lightly toast the coriander seeds and mixed seeds (pumpkin
and sunflower is a nice combination) in a dry frying pan over a
medium heat (moving them around so they don't burn), then
add to the coleslaw. Check the seasoning and serve immediately.

Smoking Pigs: Burnt Bangers and Whole Hog Roasts

It's sad, but sausages are still a symbol for poorly cooked barbecue food in the UK. I know many people who could tell you a tale of biting into a blackened crust only to find cold, raw meat in the middle. I actually feel like that happened at every barbecue I went to during my childhood and teenage years. The incinerated banger became a metaphor for how little effort some of us have put into fire-cooked food over the past few decades, which is a great shame in light of our rich fresh-sausage making history and vast range of regional products, many of which are PGI protected.

Consider the coarse, peppery Cumberland, coiled and cooked whole, snail-fashion. There's the loaf-shaped Scottish Lorne, sliced into squares of spiced beef and/or pork, casing absent. We have sage-laced Lincolnshire and richly spiced Yorkshire sausages; squat, ceremonial haggis (haggi?); and hog's pudding, white pudding and black pudding. There are sausages named after Gloucester, Manchester, Newmarket, Oxford and Marylebone. There is even a vegetarian sausage in the Welsh Glamorgan, made with leeks, cheese and breadcrumbs.

People have been making sausages since they've been eating pigs - a very long time. Once the pig was domesticated (some time before 2,000BC), we became adept at using up offal, trotters, fat and so on. Pigs would be slaughtered in late autumn (fall) after fattening on plentiful roots and before the cold weather, when food for them would become scarce. British sausages tend to be fresh, not cured, with the latter historically produced in countries where 'a dry wind could be counted on to help with the cure,' says Alan Davidson in his *Oxford Companion to Food* (1999): 'Here damp countries like England were at a disadvantage. This may account for the failure of England to produce a range of cured sausages to rival those of the Continent, and for the preference they have shown for fresh sausages.'

Some sausages were home-smoked, however, (though rarely named), particularly during the Middle Ages when pigs were 'salted and smoked, much [of it] made into sausages kept hanging near the hearth,' writes Colin Spencer in his book *British Food: An Extraordinary Thousand Years of History* (2002). There is a notable exception to our tradition of nameless smoked sausages: the saveloy. This centuries-old, highly seasoned sausage, often red due to saltpetre or, later, red food colouring, was originally made from pigs' brains but is now made from the more usual pork fat, meat and fillers. In the UK, it's most often found in fish and chip shops, and can be battered and deep fried. It is considered a 'guilty pleasure' (a particularly pointless and judgemental phrase) or a late-night snack for drunk people, probably because it is mass produced and highly emulsified. Even in Dickensian times the saveloy was dinner for undesirables. In *Oliver Twist*, criminal mastermind Fagin sits over a fire 'with a saveloy and a small loaf in his hand'.

In the north of England, the saveloy is honoured better by the Saveloy Dip ('Sav Dip'): a sandwich consisting of a soft white bun spread with butter and pease pudding (slow-cooked yellow split peas), a skinned sav', sage and onion stuffing and fierce English mustard. The whole thing is then dipped in the layer of fat on the water the saveloy was boiled in or, more recently, gravy. A triumph. The origins of the sandwich lie with the German people who settled in the North East of England in the late 19th century, bringing their pork butchery traditions with them. Their shops became anglicised as a means of defence against the abuse they received, particularly after the second world war, and while their German heritage visibly faded, their products remained popular and became an indelible part of the fast-food landscape of the North.

In Devon, towards England's westernmost coastal tip, Graham and Ruth Waddington of Rare and Pasture are attempting to steer Southerners towards a new saveloy made from free-range pork and smoked over oak. Rare and Pasture's revamped sav' reflects the move in recent decades to revive the art of sausage-making in the UK, which took a hammering after the war. In *British Food:*

An Extraordinary Thousand Years of History, Colin Spencer laments, 'it was impossible to defend the quality of the wartime sausage,' as 'sausages were unrationed and became the butt for jokes' due to their very low meat content, which was 'not less than thirty percent. Before 1939 it has been eighty.'

There is another live-fire pork tradition that deserves special mention: the hog roast. A fixture at weddings, community events and markets, it involves cooking a whole pig on a spit, originally using live fire but now using gas for consistent heat and results. The pig is cooked until the meat is very tender and the crackling golden, then carved and served, typically, inside soft white baps with apple sauce. Every roll should contain plenty of soft, pulled meat and a generous piece of crackling. Any hog roast diner will tell you that an absence of crackling is unacceptable.

There is a unifying power to the hog roast, and this may have been its original purpose. A study of the Neolithic henge complexes of southern Britain published in the journal *Science Advances* (2019) found that massive pork feasts were held during winter. While researchers previously thought the pigs had been raised locally, they now think they were raised elsewhere and herded vast distances (as far as Scotland), foraging in prehistoric forests on the way. The end goal, researchers speculate, may have been to forge

alliances between neighbouring groups. If crackling can't do it, nothing can.

By the 15th century, roasted boar was also a fixture at Yuletide feasts. The Boar's Head Carol describes the presentation of the head at such a banquet, apple still in mouth. Transported into the dining hall on a gold or silver platter, it would be accompanied by trumpeting and singing.

The boar's head, as I understand,
Is the rarest dish in all this land,
Which thus bedeck'd with a gay garland
Let us *servire cantico* (let us serve with a song)

What would those diners think of a modern-day hog roast? Its ceremony stripped and methods adapted for efficiency and in line with technological developments. Sorry, 15th century revellers, but I'm going to push that concept further. I haven't yet gotten around to spit-roasting a whole pig (although friends have), and it's not practical for the home cook. At the end of the day, what we want is tender meat, crisp fat and a zippy apple sauce to accompany, which you will absolutely achieve if you follow my recipe on page 199. I think the results are as good as any you'll get from a whole hog roast. To utilise a charming British phrase dating back to the late 1800s, you'll be 'as happy as a pig in shit'.

Crispy Pork Belly *and Apple Sauce Sandwich*

Setup: Indirect cooking
Wood: Choose from oak, beech, silver birch or a pple
Equipment: Drip tray, gloves, tongs, probe thermometer
Prep time: 15 minutes, plus overnight drying
Cook time: about 1 hour 20 minutes, plus resting time
Makes: 4 generous sandwiches, with leftovers

Pork belly
about 1 kg (2 lb 4 oz) pork belly, skin scored (ask a butcher to do this for you or use a very sharp knife or Stanley knife)
1 fennel bulb, thinly sliced widthways
4 sturdy white buns, such as crusty baps or focaccia (you want something with a bit of chew that won't fall apart before you've finished the sandwich)
English mustard
sea salt

Apple sauce
neutral oil, for cooking
1 large onion, finely chopped
5 apples, peeled, cored and diced (such as Cox's)
4 tablespoons cider vinegar
4 tablespoons caster (superfine) sugar
1 teaspoon rosemary leaves, finely chopped
1 teaspoon chilli flakes

How could I write about hog roasts and then not offer a recipe for a pork sandwich? I'm not a monster.

The hot water and air-drying method will guarantee crispy crackling, so don't skip it. No-one wants pork belly without crispy crackling. I have tried various methods of getting it super bubbly on the barbecue but none of them work as well as shoving it under the indoor grill briefly at the end, so that's what I suggest you do for the optimum crunch-to-soft-meat ratio. All it needs then is some thinly sliced fennel, a big dollop of apple sauce and a swipe of English mustard on the bun and it's a trip down memory lane, only much better than you remember.

— Place the pork belly on a wire rack over the sink, skin side up, and pour a kettle of boiling water over the skin.
— Place the pork belly in the fridge overnight, uncovered, on a rack over a baking tray, to allow it to dry out.
— The next day, remove the belly from the fridge and allow to come to room temperature.
— Prepare a barbecue for indirect cooking over medium heat. I like to set up the coals on either side for this recipe, with a drip tray in the middle on the base of the barbecue, but banking the coals to one side will work just fine too.
— Put the lid on and let the temperature come up to 250°C/480°F. Add a large chunk of wood to the coals and let it smoulder. Salt the skin of your pork belly heavily with

sea salt, rubbing it in and place it skin side up on the grill, over the drip tray. Put the lid on with the vents open and cook for 20 minutes.
— Remove the lid and add 600 ml (20 fl oz/2 ½ cups) to the drip tray - this will cool any fat that drips down. Close the vents, leaving a small gap at both the top and bottom, and put the lid back on and the vents ¼ open. The temperature will slowly drop and the pork will take about 1 hour to cook. It's ready when a thermometer reads 71°C (160°F).
— To make the apple sauce, heat a splash of neutral oil in a saucepan over a medium heat, add the onion and cook for about 10 minutes until soft but not coloured. Stir in the diced apple, vinegar, sugar, rosemary, chilli flakes and about 5 tablespoons water. Cook over a low heat for 20 minutes, until the apple is very soft. Remove from the heat.
— Either transfer some of the sauce to a blender or use a stick blender in the pan to blend around half of the sauce. I like it chunky, but you could blend the lot if you want.
— It's likely that you'll want to crisp up the crackling on the pork once it's done, and I always do this under the grill. Preheat a grill to high, pop the pork under and watch it carefully until it's bubbled and crisp. Rest the pork for 10–15 minutes.
— Assemble the sandwiches, starting with a layer of mustard, some fennel, sliced pork and crackling and apple sauce. Eat hot!

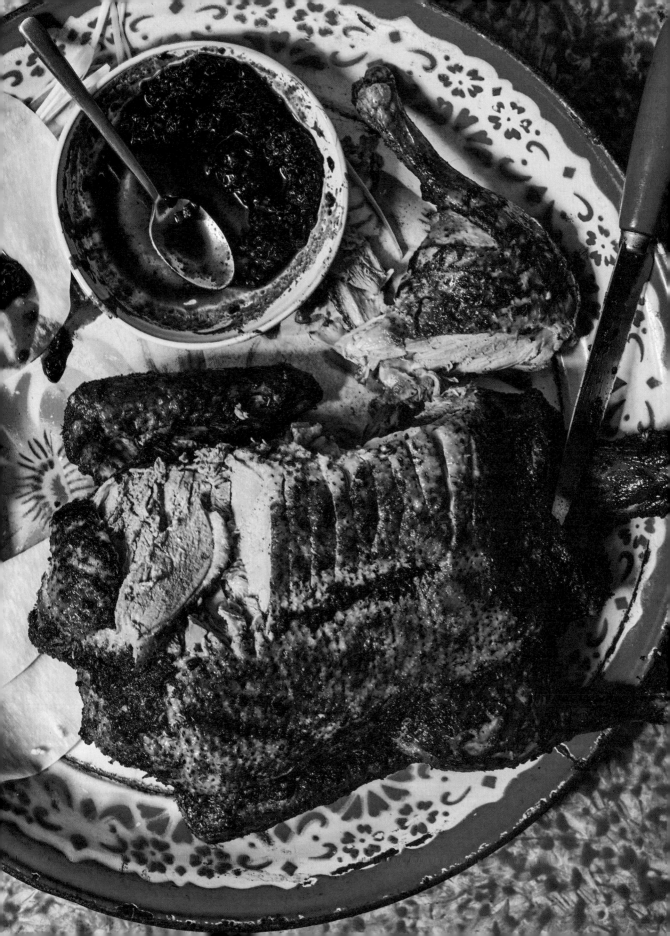

Smoked Duck
with Pancakes and Blackberry Hoi Sin

Setup: Indirect cooking
Wood: Choose from oak,
beech, sweet chestnut
or silver birch
Equipment: Drip tray,
heatproof gloves
Prep time: 10 minutes, plus a
few hours drying (or overnight,
if you have time)
Cook time: 1 hour, plus 30
minutes resting time
Serves: 4–6

1 whole duck (about 2.5 kg
/5 lb 8 oz)
1 tablespoon neutral oil
2 tablespoons Chinese
five spice
salt

Blackberry hoi sin
450 g (1 lb) blackberries
100 g (3½ oz/½ cup) light
brown sugar
3 tablespoons black
bean sauce
2 tablespoons light soy sauce
1 tablespoon Chinese
rice vinegar
1 teaspoon Chinese five spice
½ teaspoon toasted sesame oil

To serve
8 spring onions (scallions) cut
into thin, short strips
Chinese pancakes or bao buns

This is based on the Cantonese dish of deep-fried duck with
hoi sin, cucumber and spring onions (scallions). I'd originally
thought this would just be a fun experiment and nothing else,
but it turned out to be one of my favourite recipes in this book.
The smoked duck stays incredibly tender, and the blackberries
add a touch of sourness to the hoi sin that is a perfect contrast
to the fatty meat. The pancakes can be bought in Asian grocery
shops or larger supermarkets.

— The day before you want to serve the duck (or a few hours
before if you don't have time), position the duck on a rack either
over the sink (with the rack balancing on either side) or over
a roasting tray, and pour a kettle of boiling water over it.
Place in the fridge uncovered for a few hours if possible,
or overnight, to dry out.
— Remove the duck from the fridge 30 minutes before cooking
and prick the skin all over the breasts with a toothpick or metal
skewer, then combine the oil, five spice and a couple of pinches
of salt and rub it all over the duck.
— Prepare a barbecue for indirect cooking with a whole
chimney starter of coals banked to one side and a drip tray
positioned in the base of the barbecue on the opposite side.
— Add a piece of wood onto the lit coals and wait until it starts
to smoulder. Place the duck breast side up on the grill directly
over the drip tray. Cook the duck for about 1 hour, with the lid
on and the vents half open, rotating once to ensure even
cooking, until the duck is cooked through. The leg joints should
feel loose when they're wiggled – if they're not, cook the duck
a little longer.
— While the duck is cooking, make the blackberry hoi sin.
Combine all the ingredients except the sesame oil in a saucepan
with a splash of water and simmer for about 10 minutes,
or until the fruit is broken down but there are still some
chunks. Remove from the heat and add the sesame oil.
— Once the duck is cooked, let it rest for 30 minutes before
pulling it apart and serving with the blackberry hoi sin, spring
onion strips and pancakes.

To Cook Indoors: Preheat the oven to 200°C (400°F/gas 6).
Place the duck on a rack over a roasting tray and roast for
1½–2 hours, or until cooked through and golden.

Adana Kebabs

Setup: Direct cooking
Equipment: Tongs
Prep time: 20 minutes
Cook time: 10 minutes
Serves: 6

Adana kebab
500 g (1 lb 2 oz) minced
(ground) lamb (try to get a
nice fatty mix from a butcher
– if you're buying it from the
supermarket, get the highest
fat content – ideally 20% fat)
2 tablespoons pul biber
1 tablespoon Urfa chilli flakes
1 tablespoon sumac
2 teaspoons ground cumin
2 tablespoons parsley stalks,
finely chopped
3 garlic cloves, crushed

Sumac onions
1 onion, sliced
chopped parsley leaves
1 tablespoon sumac
salt

To serve
6 flatbreads (store bought
or see my Easy Flatbreads
recipe on page 60)
natural yoghurt
large handful parsley leaves
sliced tomato
pickled chillies

These kebabs – named after the Turkish city of Adana –
are predominantly flavoured with chilli and sumac. They're
traditionally cooked on wide, flat skewers but a) I don't have any
so don't use them and, b) they can be a bit tricky to work with.
People – like Mustafa (page 210) – spend a lifetime mastering
how to shape Adana onto flat skewers. Rather than skewering
them at all, then, I tend to place them directly onto the grill.

The meat would usually be chopped using a huge, curved
knife called a zirh. I might not have flat skewers but my
boyfriend and I (my partner and I? Why is there no good word
for the other person in your life?) did once buy a zihr in Istanbul
and bring it back to London. We no longer have it (long story),
so I just use a good, fatty mince.

An Adana kebab wouldn't usually be that highly seasoned,
but I like a lot of pul biber in mine because I enjoy the flavour
of it. I think that's a good enough reason?

— Place the onion for the onion salad in a bowl of iced water for
about 20 minutes. Drain and combine in a bowl with the parsley
leaves, a generous pinch of salt and the sumac.
Prepare a barbecue for direct cooking over medium heat.
— To make the kebab mixture, combine the lamb in a bowl with
all the other ingredients and a couple of generous pinches of
salt. Mix very well with your hands, almost as if you are
kneading bread. Do this for 5 minutes, then form the mixture
into 6 kebabs. You can thread these onto skewers, but they cook
well when placed directly onto the grill, too.
— Grill over direct heat and, once they start to caramelise and
release juice (a couple of minutes) pick them up with tongs and
wipe them on the bread, then return to the grill. They will take
around 5 minutes each side to cook through. When the kebabs
are nearly cooked, place the breads on top of them to warm up
and pick up some of the fatty juices.
— Serve the kebabs with the bread and accompaniments.

To Cook Indoors: Cook the kebabs under a medium-hot grill for
8 minutes, or until just cooked, turning them once.

Mushroom Shawarma

Setup: Direct cooking
Equipment: Long metal skewers
Prep time: 15 minutes, plus minimum 1 hour marinating time (overnight if possible)
Cook time: 20 minutes
Serves: 4

1 tablespoon sea salt
200 ml (7 fl oz/scant 1 cup) olive oil
1 kg (2 lb 4 oz) portobello mushrooms (about 15), stalks trimmed

Shawarma spice mix
2 tablespoons cumin seeds
2 teaspoons black peppercorns
2 teaspoons coriander seeds
1 teaspoon fennel seeds
½ teaspoon fenugreek seeds
5 cloves
½ cinnamon stick
seeds from 3 cardamom pods
1 tablespoon paprika

To say this shawarma is a 'great meat alternative' is to do it a disservice; it's excellent in its own right. The mushrooms are threaded onto large skewers then shaved off in slices, which gives the sense of serving a 'proper' kebab. Their gills – like damp woodland tutus – do a very good job of holding onto the spice mixture, and no matter how shrivelled the 'shrooms look on the outside, they're always juicy within. Dare I say this is one of my favourite kebabs?

The yoghurt sauce here is a bona fide riff on the garlic sauce you get at your local kebab shop – it goes without saying that it can be used with any kebabs. The dried mint is an integral part of the 'bab shop flavour, so while you can use fresh mint instead, just be aware that you'll end up with something quite different – more of a tzatziki vibe.

Yoghurt sauce
200 g (7 oz/generous ¾ cup)
natural yoghurt
2 garlic cloves, crushed
1 teaspoon dried mint
4 teaspoons lemon juice

Cabbage salad
½ red cabbage, cored and
finely shredded
1 red onion, peeled and
thinly sliced
really generous pinch of
sea salt
handful of parsley leaves,
roughly chopped
2 tablespoons sumac

To serve
flatbreads (use store-bought
flatbreads or try my Easy
Everyday Flatbreads recipe
on page 60)
pickled chillies

— First, make the shawarma spice mix. Toast the whole spices in a dry frying pan (skillet) over medium-low heat until fragrant. Add to a spice grinder or pestle and mortar and grind or crush to a powder. Mix with the paprika, sea salt and olive oil. Brush the mushrooms all over with the spice paste, making sure to get into the gills too. Leave to marinate for 1 hour at room temperature, or overnight in the fridge if you can.
— Prepare a barbecue for direct cooking over medium heat.
— To make the yoghurt sauce, combine the yoghurt, garlic, dried mint and lemon juice in a bowl with a generous pinch of salt. Set aside.
— To make the salad, combine the cabbage and onion in a bowl, add the salt, and use your hands to scrunch the cabbage and onion until the vegetables soften and begin to release juice.
— When the barbecue is ready, thread the mushrooms onto two skewers with the skewers piercing both sides, to keep them steady. The mushrooms should be quite tightly packed. Grill over direct heat with the lid on and vents ½ open for about 20 minutes, or until cooked through, turning them often.
— To serve, pull the mushrooms off the skewers and slice or roughly chop, arranging on a platter. Serve the mushrooms with the yoghurt, salad, flatbreads and pickled chillies.

To Cook Indoors: Cook the mushroom shawarma under a hot grill, turning occasionally, until lightly charred and cooked through, around 20 minutes.

The Ocakbasi and Me

Ocakbasi translates from Turkish as 'fireside' or 'stand by the grill', which is something I am partial to doing, you may have noticed. The food in ocakbasi is cooked on a rectangular grill called a mangal, the width of which matches that of a long kebab skewer, which negates the need for a grill on top and allows fat to drip, creating smoke and therefore flavour. Charcoal is lit at one end of the grill and kept alight in a continuously burning pile, allowing the chef to move coals along as he needs them; he (I have never seen a woman cook at a mangal, but here's hopin') will have full control of the heat level this way, which will vary along the length of the mangal according to the amount of coals in each section.

Watching a mangal chef at work is mesmerising. In Istanbul, in particular, I have enjoyed eating right in front of the grill, which is sometimes built in the centre of the restaurant; these seats are coveted and often require advance booking. I was as happy as a clam watching the chef pat puffy flatbreads between his hands and flip skewers of onion or chicken wings, sizzling minced (ground) lamb or mini racks of ribs. The mangal master becomes a sort of kebab-spinning octopus, arms crossing and bending. He dances for your dinner.

Almost everyone who visits ocakbasi will know that a common dining mistake is to fill up on bread and dips before the kebabs arrive. And yet it's virtually impossible, in my extensive experience, to resist spice-smeared flatbread that has been warming on top of an Adana kebab as it cooks, sucking up its rich fat and flavour. It's also very hard to stop dipping that bread into a pot of purple pomegranate dip, and to resist scooping out the charred onion petals and squidgy garlic cloves that bob within. I am talking specifically now about the bread and dip at my local ocakbasi in Camberwell, South East London, which is called FM Mangal, and has been part of my life for around 10 years (almost as long as it's been open, it turns out), even before I moved to a flat that is, handily, located approximately 2 minutes from the restaurant door.

The bread and dip in question are quite famous in this tiny corner of the world: the bread a slightly puffy flatbread, larger than pitta but smaller than lavash, which is covered in a slightly oily, rust-coloured spice mix. The dip is thin and tastes faintly of pomegranate juice, yet has a mysterious depth of flavour that's hard to identify. Within it are blistered wedges of onion, their layers scorched black, and whole creamy cloves of garlic; both may be plucked from the liquid using a flatbread pincer.

When I ask Mustafa Akpinar – owner of FM Mangal and its head chef – how the famous dip became so popular, he grins: 'Our speciality! Everybody thinks that the dip has meat juices mixed into it, but it doesn't. We don't rest the bread on the meat kebabs as they cook either. It is spices and olive oil on top, things like that – but it is a secret I'm afraid.'

Mustafa has been cooking 'for more than 30 years', originally up in North London, before opening FM Mangal. His son, Şiyar, who runs the family grocery store elaborates: 'Yeah, but he's actually been in this job since he was 11, which is normal in Turkey, especially back in those days. They lived in the country and when they moved to the city everyone had to work to survive.'

'People come to Europe for a new life, for freedom, that's why we came here,' says Mustafa. While FM Mangal is widely thought to be a Turkish kitchen, Mustafa is actually Kurdish. 'In the south of Turkey there are many Kurdish people – in Urfa, Gaziantep,' he explains. 'There are millions of us but back home we are scared to say we are Kurdish, because of the politics. My food here is Kurdish and Middle Eastern. Turkish food has influences from Greece and Armenia – everybody leaves something.

The Greek influences come from dishes like tzatziki with yogurt, the use of vine leaves for dolma and they do lahmacun (page 214), which is more similar to Armenian food.'

Mustafa's best dish, according to my extensive research (*pats stomach*), is the Adana kebab. Named after the fifth largest city in Turkey, it is made from spiced minced (ground) lamb, which is shaped onto a long skewer before grilling. I have always wondered what Mustafa's secret is, so relished the chance to ask him, 'We use shoulder of lamb blended with rib meat to make our Adana, as this gives the right flavour and amount of fat. We also use British meat, which some restaurants don't. It's also in the teaching, as we shape it by hand onto the skewer. This can be tricky but it depends on how clever the chef is! Some people they go years and years and they learn nothing but some people they just sit down and they do it. The charcoal must also be burning correctly because if it hasn't burnt down, then it will not taste nice. It needs to be no flames. If I go to another restaurant I can taste if the charcoal has been burned correctly or not.'

Mustafa also emphasises that Adana must be cooked slowly, 'Fast is not good. The oil from the fat must come slowly from the lamb and make the flavour; it drips onto the coals and that smoke goes back onto the meat. Where we come from, for this type of barbecue, you come with your

Above: a variety of skewers sizzle gently on the mangal. Below: Chillies are charred over a higher flame. Page 211: Mustafa's famous Adana.

family and you sit down and you say can I have one Adana skewer, and it is cooked slowly, slowly, and before it is finished you say, can I have one more? And maybe two tomatoes and two peppers and they cook very slowly, and then if you're not full you say, can I have some lamb ribs?' He smiles. This is the way this food is eaten. You must take some time.'

This sums up my favourite part of the ocaskbasi experience, and also why the bread and dips are so often my downfall. The moment that basket of fresh bread is set down on the table, the meal opens up before me, a path paved with glittering possibilities. Lingering for hours over the dips is both the best and worst part; variety is key and yet they can never be finished by fewer than five people. I know that the Adana is yet to come. My advice is to order everything to arrive at the same time, thus preserving capacity. Better still would be to follow Mustafa's advice and do it properly, enjoying a kebab that has been cooked slowly in front of you, before deciding if you'd like another. Fortunately, cooking at home makes this scenario achievable. I don't pretend to have Mustafa's expertise, but these recipes have served me and my friends very well over the years.

HG Mangal
Bread and Dip

Setup: Indirect cooking for
the dip, direct cooking
for the bread
Equipment: Tongs,
metal skewers
Prep time: 15 minutes
Cook time: 40 minutes
Serves: 8

HG Mangal dip
1 onion, peeled and quartered
1 head of garlic, cloves
separated and peeled
1 tablespoon pomegranate
molasses
1 teaspoon sumac
1½ teaspoons MSG
1 teaspoon olive oil
1 teaspoon turnip juice
(optional, but a must for the
niche fans as it really
completes the dip)
100 ml (3½ fl oz/scant ½ cup)
warm water

HG Mangal bread
2 teaspoons MSG
2 teaspoons paprika
2 teaspoons smoked
sweet paprika
2 teaspoons sea salt
4 tablespoons neutral oil
8 shop-bought flatbreads or
lavash, or a batch of flatbreads
such as the ones on page 60
(needless to say, this is 1,000x
better with freshly-made
flatbreads)

Fans of South East London
restaurant FM Mangal (the
'HG' above = my own initials)
talk about this bread and
dip in hushed tones. What
is the recipe? Can it ever be
replicated? What are the
secrets? Well, I'm not sure,
but I'll tell you the secret
to my 'kebab shop bread':
MSG. Monosodium glutamate:
the flavour enhancer that
brings intensity to the flavour
of crisps, stock cubes,
KFC and instant gravies.
I found out about this 'kebab
shop secret' thanks to Hasan
'Big Has' Semay, a chef who is
also a columnist for *Pit* and
who wrote about it for our
MSG issue. The whole issue
– guest edited by Burmese
food writer MiMi Aye – was
themed entirely around MSG
and delved deep into the
reason it's so wonderful,
and all the misinformation
surrounding it, which is rooted
in racism. Writer Cheryl
Chow's powerful piece for
the issue explained all of
this, and it's one of the best
pieces of food writing
I've read in a long time.
We were honoured to publish
it. MSG is not harmful.
The human brain makes no
distinction between the stuff
produced in a factory and the
MSG that occurs naturally
in tomatoes, Parmesan and
mushrooms. There is simply
no scientific evidence to
support claims that it
produces so called 'Chinese
Restaurant Syndrome'.
So, with that in mind, here
are two recipes absolutely
laden with it. That's why they
taste so good.

— Prepare a barbecue for
indirect cooking over low heat.
— Separate the onion quarters
into petals with 2–3 layers
each. Thread onto a skewer.
— On a separate skewer,
do the same with the
garlic cloves.
— Cook the onions and garlic
over a low direct heat for
25–30 minutes, until well
charred and fully softened.
The heat needs to be low,
otherwise they won't soften
inside, so move them to
a cooler part of the grill
if you need to, turning
them frequently so that they
cook evenly.
— Combine the pomegranate
molasses, sumac, MSG, olive
oil, turnip juice (if using)
and water in a bowl.
— Once the onions and garlic
are ready, add them to the
liquid and set aside while
you make the bread.

— To make the bread, combine
all the ingredients in a bowl
to make a paste then brush
the paste onto the flatbreads
while fresh and warm.
If serving kebabs alongside,
brush the spice mix on the
breads, then re-warm the
flatbreads on top of the
kebabs. Serve with the dip.

Barbecue Lahmacun

Setup: Indirect cooking
Equipment: Tongs, pizza peel
or baking tray
Prep time: 15 minutes,
plus 45 minutes rising time
Cook time: 5 minutes
per lahmacun
Makes: 12 lahmacun

Dough
600 g (1 lb 5 oz/generous
5 cups) plain (all-purpose)
flour
2 teaspoons caster
(superfine) sugar
2 teaspoons fine sea salt
3 teaspoons instant yeast
5 tablespoons olive oil
300 ml (10 fl oz/1¼ cups)
warm water
extra flour or fine cornmeal,
for dusting

Sumac onions
1 red onion, thinly sliced
handful of parsley leaves,
roughly chopped
sea salt
1 tablespoon sumac

Lahmacun is not a 'Turkish pizza', it is lahmacun: a thin bread topped sparingly with spiced lamb, typically rolled up with salad before eating. Its golden bottom cracks into soft shards as it rolls around crisp salad and its shower of lemon juice. I also add finely chopped lamb's liver to my version, which pumps up the lambiness a notch, but you could sub it for the same quantity of minced (ground) lamb if it's not your thing.

— Combine the flour and sugar in a bowl, adding the yeast on one side and salt on the other. Add the olive oil and water and knead for about 5 minutes until smooth and elastic (you can do this either by hand or in a stand mixer fitted with the dough hook attachment). Place in a lightly oiled bowl, cover and set aside in a warm place to let it rise for about 45 minutes, or until doubled in size.
— Place the onion for the sumac onions in a bowl of iced water for about 20 minutes. Drain and combine in a bowl with the parsley leaves, a generous pinch of salt and the sumac.
— Skin the tomato by cutting a cross shape in the skin on the bottom, placing it in a heatproof bowl and pouring over boiling water. Leave for no more than a minute, then remove, refresh under cold water and peel off the skin.
— Put the peppers, onion and tomatoes in a blender and blend until they form a smooth paste. Put the paste into a colander or sieve and stir it to allow excess liquid to drain away.
Mix the paste in a bowl with the rest of the topping ingredients, the chillies and a generous pinch salt.

Lamb topping
1 large tomato
1 red (bell) pepper,
roughly chopped
1 green (bell) pepper,
roughly chopped
1 onion, roughly chopped
200 g (7 oz) minced (ground)
lamb (at least 20% fat if
possible)
200 g (7 oz) lamb's liver,
finely chopped
1 tablespoon Urfa chilli
1 tablespoon pul biber
handful of parsley leaves,
finely chopped
3 garlic cloves, crushed
or finely grated

To serve
mint leaves
pickled chillies
sliced tomatoes
lemon wedges

— Prepare a barbecue for indirect cooking over medium heat, with the coals banked to one side.
— Divide the dough into 12 balls. On a lightly floured surface, roll out the balls one at a time to the size of a large side plate then place a couple of tablespoons of topping in the centre. Use your fingertips to spread the topping out towards the edges – the topping should be spread thinly and have gaps.
— Dust a pizza peel or the underside of a baking tray with flour or fine cornmeal and drag the lahmacun onto it.
— Using one swift movement, quickly slide the lahmacun off the peel or tray onto the grill directly over the coals. Once it's crisp on the bottom, slide it across to the other side and put the lid on with the vents open, to finish cooking the top.
— Once cooked, serve the lahmacun topped with some of the sumac onions, mint, pickled chilli, tomato slices and a squeeze of lemon juice. Roll it up and eat immediately.

Quick and Easy Barbecued Naan

Setup: Direct cooking
Equipment: Tongs
Prep time: 25 minutes
Cook time: 10 minutes
Makes: 8 naan

500 g (1 lb 2 oz/3 cups plus
2 tablespoons) strong white
bread flour, plus extra for
dusting
4 teaspoons baking powder
2 teaspoons fine sea salt
1 tablespoon caster
(superfine) sugar
1 tablespoon nigella seeds
200 ml (7 fl oz/3/4 cup)
whole milk
200 g (7 oz/generous ¾ cup)
natural full-fat yoghurt
100 g (3½ oz/7 tablespoons)
butter or ghee
handful of coriander (cilantro)
leaves, chopped

This isn't a traditional naan, which would be leavened with yeast and cooked in a tandoor as discussed on page 170, but it's a quick and easy version that works on the grill. The milk and yoghurt make the dough very soft, and the nigella seeds add their unmistakable allium perfume.

— Combine the flour, baking powder, salt, sugar and nigella seeds in the bowl of a stand mixer fitted with the dough hook, or in a large mixing bowl.
— Warm the milk and yoghurt in a small saucepan – you should still be able to dip your finger in it comfortably – then combine it with the dry ingredients. Knead using with the dough hook, or by hand on a work surface, for 5 minutes until smooth.
— Cover lightly with a tea towel and allow to sit at room temperature for 15 minutes while you prepare a barbecue for direct cooking over medium heat.
— Melt the butter or ghee and add the coriander (cilantro).
— On a lightly floured surface, divide the dough into 8 pieces and roll them out into a naan shape roughly 15 × 20 cm (6 × 8 in). You want to take the naan dough outside, but whatever you do don't rest it next to the hot barbecue – the dough will become unmanageably sloppy in moments and you won't be able to get it on the grill.
— Grill over direct heat very briefly (they will take as little as 20 seconds to cook on each side, depending on how hot your grill is), and brush with the melted butter mixture while still warm.

To Cook Indoors: Preheat a cast-iron griddle pan over a high heat for at least 5 minutes, then cook each naan for 30 seconds or so on each side, or until puffed and beginning to colour.

Quince and Scotch Bonnet
Hot Sauce

Setup: Indoors
Prep Time: 10 minutes
Cook Time: 20 minutes
Makes: about 1.2 litres
(40 fl oz/5 cups)

3 large quinces, peeled, cut
into eighths and any core
and gnarly bits removed
500 ml (17 fl oz/generous
2 cups) cold water
70 g (2¾ oz/⅓ cup) caster
(superfine) sugar
1 tablespoon sea salt
10 large scotch bonnet chillies,
stalks and seeds removed
(wear gloves or wash your
hands very thoroughly
afterwards)
125 ml (4¼ fl oz/generous ½ cup)
cider vinegar

I've realised over the years that the key to making a good hot sauce is to keep it simple. It's very tempting to add lots of spices, garlic and so on, but what you really want – or at least what I really want – is to taste the flavour of the chilli and whatever it is paired with (if anything). Extra ingredients just muddy the waters.

I'm not interested in sauces that are hot for the sake of it either – you can keep your 'Triple X Double Hard B*stard Sauce', thank you. I want heat, yes, but also purity of flavour, be it the fruity tropical tones of scotch bonnet or the searing green fire of jalapeño.

The intense perfume of both chilli and quince make for a particularly aromatic sauce, which goes particularly well with grilled pork.

— Put the quince pieces in a saucepan and cover with the water plus the sugar and salt. Add a little more water if the pieces aren't quite covered. Bring to the boil, then reduce to a simmer and cook for 20 minutes, or until the quince pieces are soft.
— Remove from the heat and leave the quince to cool in the liquid, then transfer the fruit to a blender with the chillies and vinegar. Blend, adding a little of the cooking liquid if you want a runnier sauce.
— Store in sterilised, sealed jars in the fridge. The sauce will mellow and develop over time, becoming a little less spicy with a more rounded profile. It will keep for a few weeks.

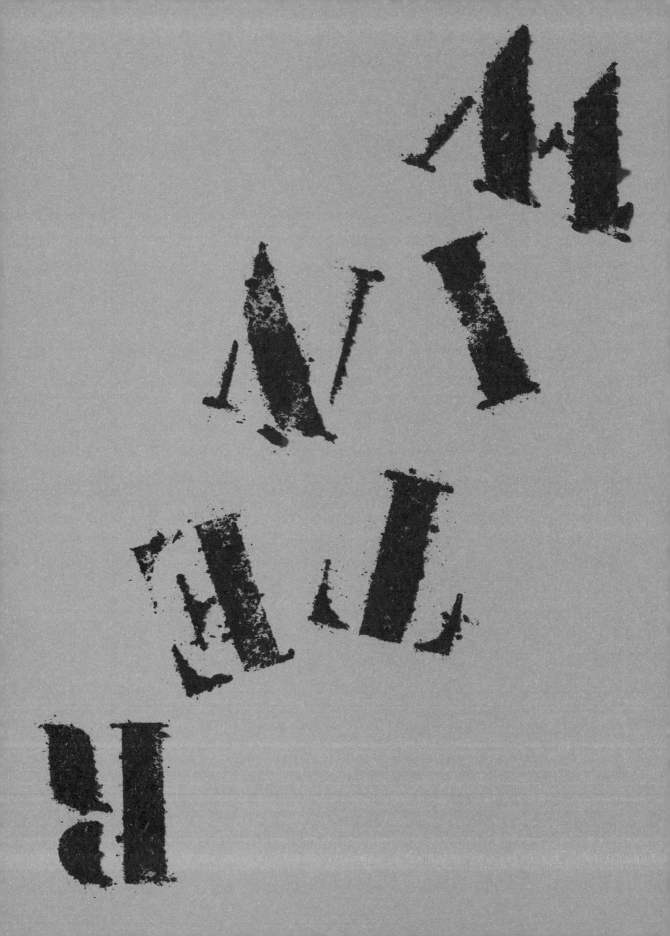

Charred Purple Sprouting Broccoli
with Spicy Fish Sauce and Clementine Caramel

Setup: Direct cooking
Equipment: Tongs
Prep time: 15 minutes
Cook time: 30–40 minutes
Serves: 4 as a side dish,
2 generously

400 g (14 oz) purple
sprouting broccoli
neutral oil, for cooking
50 g (1¾ oz) blanched hazelnuts
80 g (2¾ oz/generous ⅓ cup)
granulated sugar
175 ml (6 fl oz/¾ cup) water
1 teaspoon clementine juice
3 tablespoons sherry vinegar
2 tablespoons fish sauce
1–2 red chillies, thinly sliced
2 clementines, peeled and
segments separated
sea salt

This dish is inspired by Vietnamese flavours. The 'dressing'
is salty and hot, with umami funk from the fish sauce;
I particularly love the combination of charred, bitter broccoli
with its glossy, sweet sharpness. The vegetables quite literally
shine, given such glamorous treatment.

— Prepare a barbecue for direct cooking over medium heat.
— Blanch the broccoli in boiling salted water for 1 minute,
then drain.
— Toss the broccoli with a little oil and season with salt.
Grill it over direct heat for 5–10 minutes on each side until
slightly blackened. Transfer to a bowl and cover and keep warm.
— Lightly toast the hazelnuts in a dry frying pan (skillet) over
a medium heat until beginning to colour, moving them around
so they don't burn. Roughly chop and set aside.
— Combine the sugar and water in a saucepan and heat gently
until the sugar has dissolved (do not allow it to boil). Once the
sugar has dissolved, add the teaspoon of clementine juice and
continue heating to boiling point. Boil for about 20 minutes
until the liquid has reduced and is the colour of amber caramel.
Remove from the heat and carefully (it will spit) whisk in the
sherry vinegar, fish sauce and 1 tablespoon of water. If the
caramel forms any hard lumps, keep heating gently until they
dissolve. Stir well, remove from the heat and add the chilli and
clementine segments. Mix gently.
— Place the broccoli on a plate and pour the dressing over.
Top with the chopped hazelnuts and serve.

To Cook Indoors: Preheat a cast-iron griddle pan over a high
heat for at least 5 minutes then add the oiled and seasoned
broccoli and cook for 5–10 minutes, or until slightly blackened.
Remove to a bowl and cover while you continue with the rest
of the dish.

Marinated Grilled Carrots
with Yoghurt and Spiced Butter

Setup: Direct cooking
Equipment: Tongs
Prep time: 10 minutes,
plus a few hours marinating
time (overnight if possible)
Cook time: 20 minutes
Serves: 4

2 teaspoons cumin seeds
2 teaspoons coriander seeds
1 teaspoon fennel seeds
2 green cardamom pods,
crushed and seeds removed
3 tablespoons lime juice
4 garlic cloves, peeled and
crushed or grated
4 tablespoons neutral oil
500 g (1 lb 2 oz) carrots, peeled
and quartered lengthways
25 g (1 oz/2 tablespoons)
butter
2 teaspoons pul biber
150 g (5½ oz/scant ⅔ cup) thick
yoghurt (either strained
natural yoghurt or thick
Greek yoghurt)
sea salt

We marinate meat and fish, so why not vegetables? Carrots aren't exactly the first ingredient that comes to mind when thinking about barbecue food, I grant you, but please trust me when I say that this is a really good way to eat them. I hope you will be surprised by how exciting they are on the plate. The contrast between hot carrots, cold yoghurt and warm butter is pretty special.

There are so many ways to vary this: try adding different spices to the butter, for example, or stir in a paste such as harissa.

— Toast the cumin, coriander and fennel seeds in a dry frying pan (skillet) over a medium heat until fragrant, moving them around so they don't burn). Add to a spice grinder or pestle and mortar with the cardamom seeds and grind or crush to a fine powder. Combine the spices with the lime juice, garlic and oil in a bowl.
— Cook the carrots in boiling salted water for 3 minutes, then drain. Add them to the marinade, cover and leave overnight in the fridge or for at least a few hours.
— Prepare a barbecue for direct cooking over medium heat.
— Grill the marinated carrots for 15–20 minutes over direct heat (facing in the opposite direction to the bars), turning with tongs, until soft and lightly charred.
— Melt the butter and add the pul biber.
— Spread the yoghurt on a plate, add a sprinkle of salt and pile on the grilled carrots. Pour the spiced butter on top and serve.

To Cook Indoors: Preheat a cast-iron griddle pan over a high heat for at least 5 minutes, then cook the marinated carrots over medium heat for 15–20 minutes, turning them with tongs, until cooked through and charred.

Smoked Onion and Garlic Soup
with White Miso Butter

Setup: Indirect cooking
Wood: Oak or hickory
Equipment: Heatproof gloves,
a roasting tray large enough to
hold the onions and garlic
Prep time: 5 minutes
Cook time: 1 hour 10 minutes
Serves: 4 as a light meal or
starter, 2 for a generous bowl

4 onions, unpeeled, halved
lengthways
neutral oil, for rubbing
the vegetables
2 heads of garlic, unpeeled
500 ml (17 fl oz/generous
2 cups) chicken or vegetable
stock (I prefer chicken)
2 tablespoons full-fat
crème fraîche
¾ teaspoon ground
white pepper
sea salt
small handful of chives, finely
chopped, to serve

White miso butter
30 g (1 oz/2 tablespoons)
unsalted butter
1 tablespoon white miso

This soup is one of my favourites, and I say that as someone who has never been totally convinced by a bowl of liquid as a meal. The onions and garlic are smoked to provide a creamy base, which is finished with miso and melted butter. It's full of salty-savouriness and can be dressed up or down: it feels elegant in a bowl but absolutely at home in a Thermos or mug around a campfire. The smoke is critical to this recipe, hence the absence of instructions for cooking indoors.

— Prepare a barbecue for indirect cooking over medium heat, with the coals banked to one side.
— Place the onions in the roasting tray and rub the cut sides with a little oil. Slice the tops off the garlic bulbs to reveal the cloves and rub those lightly with oil too. Add to the roasting tray.
— Place a large chunk of wood or handful of chips onto the hot coals, put the roasting tray onto the opposite side of the grill - as far away as possible from the coals - and close the lid. Position the air vents to about halfway open. Cook the onion and garlic for 1 hour, rotating the tray halfway through and adding more wood chunks or chips as necessary to keep the smoke fairly constant throughout the cooking time.
— Remove the roasting tray from the barbecue then remove the skins, roots and any papery outer layers from the onions and garlic and put them into a blender with half of the stock (be careful not to fill the blender more than halfway if the stock is hot). Blend until very smooth.
— Pour into a saucepan with the remaining stock and bring to the boil. Reduce to a simmer, add the white pepper and remove from the heat. Stir in the crème fraîche.
— To make the miso butter, melt the butter in a pan and add the miso, stirring until incorporated. Stir the butter into the soup. Check the seasoning - miso is salty but you will likely need some extra salt. This soup should be highly seasoned.
— Serve scattered with the chives.

Blackened Leeks
with Garlic Mayonnaise, Romesco and Charred Sourdough

Setup: Direct cooking
Equipment: Tongs, old newspaper
Prep time: 30 minutes
Cook time: 15 minutes
Serves: 4–6

16 small leeks
sliced sourdough (a few slices per person)

Garlic mayonnaise
2 egg yolks
160 ml (5½ fl oz/ ⅔ cup) sunflower oil
40 ml (1¼ fl oz/2½ tablespoons) olive oil
2 tablespoons lemon juice
2 garlic cloves, crushed or finely grated
sea salt

Romesco
3 red (bell) peppers
100 g (3½ oz) blanched almonds
3 large tomatoes
100 g (3½ oz) stale white bread (no crusts)
3 garlic cloves
1 teaspoon smoked hot paprika
2 tablespoons sherry vinegar
3 tablespoons lemon juice
6 tablespoons olive oil, plus a little extra for drizzling

This method of cooking leeks is inspired by the Catalan calçotada – a festival where vegetables called calçots (very much like large spring onions/scallions, or small leeks) are cooked over fire until blackened, then wrapped in newspaper and served on terracotta tiles. They are eaten with a sauce called salvitxada, which is similar to romesco, with the addition of blended, garlic-scrubbed toast. It's fantastically messy, particularly in light of the fact that it's served with red wine, poured directly into the mouth from a vessel called a porron.

— First, make the mayonnaise. Whisk the egg yolks in the bowl of a stand mixer fitted with the whisk attachment, or in a bowl if you are using a hand whisk. With the motor running (or the hand whisking), very slowly begin adding the sunflower oil, a drop at a time, making sure each drop is incorporated before adding the next. Once the mayonnaise starts to thicken, you can start adding the oil in a thin, steady stream, whisking constantly. Once it's used up, add the olive oil in the same way. Whisk in the lemon and garlic and season with salt. Set aside.
— Prepare a barbecue for direct cooking over medium heat.
— Grill the red (bell) peppers over direct heat and cook until black all over, turning with tongs – about 10 minutes. Transfer to a bowl and cover with a plate or put in a sealed bag and set aside for 2 minutes. Remove the skin, stalks and seeds.
— Toast the almonds in a dry frying pan over a medium heat then remove and set aside. Skin the tomatoes by cutting a cross shape in the skin on the bottom, placing them in a heatproof bowl and pouring over boiling water. Leave for a minute, then remove, refresh under cold water and peel off the skin.
— Place the almonds and tomatoes in a blender with the remaining romesco ingredients and a couple of big pinches of salt and pulse to a coarsely textured sauce.
— Trim some of the long green ends off the leeks to make them tidier (you won't eat the green parts anyway). Grill the leeks for about 10 minutes over direct heat, turning them regularly until totally blackened. Wrap them in newspaper, in bundles of 3–4, and leave to steam for 5 minutes.
— Grill the sourdough on the barbecue over direct heat, until lightly charred on both sides.
— Serve the leek bundles with the sourdough, romesco and garlic mayonnaise.

Wood: Oak, beech or apple
Equipment: Tongs, roasting
tray, heatproof gloves
Prep time: 5 minutes
Cook time: 45 minutes–1 hour
Serves: 4

600 g (1 lb 5 oz) parsnips,
peeled and quartered
lengthways and tough
core removed
1 tablespoon neutral oil
a few sprigs of thyme
sea salt and freshly ground
black pepper

Dressing
1 red chilli, finely chopped
1 tablespoon cider vinegar
2 tablespoons honey

Smoked Parsnips with Quick Pickled Chilli Dressing

Parsnips were a once-a-year thing for me (yup, Christmas
dinner) until I tried smoking them. They go very soft and gooey
in places, and take on the smoke so well. I bathe them in a sweet
and slightly sharp dressing which both contrasts with and
enhances their natural sweetness. Sugary weirdos.

— Prepare a barbecue for indirect cooking over medium heat,
with the coals banked to one side.
— Add a chunk of wood directly to the coals and wait until
it starts to smoulder.
— Place the parsnips in a roasting tray, toss with the oil, thyme
sprigs, season with some salt and pepper and place on the grill
on the opposite side to the coals. Put the lid on and set the vents
a quarter open, then cook for 45 minutes–1 hour, rotating the
tray and turning the parsnips every so often with tongs to
ensure even cooking.
— Meanwhile, make the dressing. Place the chopped chilli in
a bowl and add the cider vinegar, honey and a good pinch of salt.
Mix well and set aside.
— Once the parsnips are cooked, combine them with the
dressing while they're still warm. Mix well and serve.

To Cook Indoors: Preheat the oven to 170°C (340°F/gas 3).
Parboil the parsnips for 5 minutes then drain, toss with the oil,
and season with salt and pepper. Roast in the oven for 45
minutes to 1 hour, turning once.

Setup: Direct cooking
Equipment: Tongs
Prep time: 10 minutes
Cook time: 5 minutes
Serves: 4

2 tablespoons pomegranate
molasses
2 tablespoons lemon juice
2 tablespoons extra
virgin olive oil
2 tablespoons sumac
1 radicchio, quartered
lengthways
2 red chicory, halved
lengthways
neutral oil, for cooking
a few pomegranate seeds,
to garnish (optional)
sea salt

Charred Bitter Leaves with Pomegranate Molasses and Sumac

As a general rule I can't stand bitterness, which just goes to
show how important balance is in cookery: the bitterness of
these leaves is actually enhanced by charring, but offered
a counterpoint from sweet-sour pomegranate molasses and
the citric snap of sumac I really dig it. Go figure.

— Prepare a barbecue for direct cooking over medium heat.
— Combine the molasses, lemon juice, oil, sumac and a big pinch
of salt in a clean lidded jar and shake to combine. Set aside.
— Brush the cut sides of the radicchio and chicory with neutral
oil and grill cut side down on the barbecue for a few minutes,
turning them with tongs until nicely charred on all sides.
— Serve the charred leaves topped with the dressing and
pomegranate seeds, if using.

To Cook Indoors: Preheat a cast-iron griddle pan over a high
heat for at least 5 minutes, then cook the radicchio and chicory
on it for 5 minutes or so, or until charred.

English Mustard-rubbed Rib of Beef

Setup: Indirect cooking
Wood: Oak
Equipment: Tongs, drip tray,
probe thermometer
Prep time: 5 minutes
Cook time: 2½–3 hours
Serves: 8

---

150 g (5½ oz) English mustard
1 tablespoon celery salt
1 head of garlic, cloves
separated, peeled, and
crushed or grated
a few sprigs (about 10 g/¼ oz)
of rosemary, leaves finely
chopped
1 beef rib joint, with 2 or 3 ribs
(about 3.5 kg/7 lb 11 oz)
sea salt

I recommend cooking this if you want to show off, because it's huge, dramatic, and tastes amazing. It's also not difficult at all. The beef is not so much rubbed as smothered in a potent paste that combines some of my favourite British flavours: English mustard, rosemary and celery.

What happens is that the beef essentially roasts inside the barbecue, so you end up with tender, pink, smoky meat and an incredible savoury crust on the outside. It works as a centrepiece for a fairly traditional roast situation, as the most OTT buffet contribution ever, or, of course, as a top-tier sandwich ingredient. In fact, it's almost worth cooking this *just* for the leftovers.

— Combine the English mustard, celery salt, garlic and rosemary. Rub the mixture all over the meat, getting into every nook and cranny, then set aside while you light the barbecue.
— Prepare a barbecue for indirect cooking with the coals banked to either side, using a full starter chimney-full of coals. Position a drip tray in the centre on the base of the barbecue and fill it around 2.5 cm (1 in) full with water.
— Add a chunk of wood directly onto the hot coals and wait for it to smoulder. Put the beef on the grill in the centre, fat side up on the grill rack, over the drip tray. Put the lid on and leave the vents a quarter open. Cook for 2½–3 hours, aiming for a consistent temperature of 160–180°C (320–350°F) if you can. It can be hard to gauge this if you don't have an ambient thermometer though, so just make sure you turn the beef around halfway through, and use a prob thermometer to measure the internal temperature of the meat now and then. You'll need to top up the coals and add another chunk of wood around every hour or so. For medium-rare beef, remove it from the heat when a probe thermometer inserted into the thickest part of the meat registers 57°C (135°F).
— Rest the beef for 20 minutes before carving and serving sprinkled with sea salt.

To Cook Indoors: Preheat the oven to 180°C (350°F/gas 4). Cook the beef in a roasting tray for 25 minutes, then turn the oven down to 170°C (340°F/gas 3) and cook for 1½–2 hours until cooked to your liking.

A Smoky Barbecued Cowboy Chilli

Setup: Indoors, then indirect cooking
Wood: Oak or hickory
Equipment: Large saucepan or cooking pot that can go in the barbecue
Prep time: 20 minutes
Cook time: 2½ hours
Serves: 6–8

200 ml (7 fl oz/scant 1 cup) strong, hot filter coffee
1 dried mulato chilli
1 dried pasilla chilli
1 dried chipotle chilli
2 teaspoons coriander seeds
1 tablespoon cumin seeds
1 tablespoon neutral oil
750 g (1 lb 10 oz) chuck steak, diced
1 onion, diced
1 red (bell) pepper, diced
1 head of garlic, cloves separated, peeled and crushed
1 tablespoon dried oregano
250 ml (8 fl oz/1 cup) good-quality beef stock
400 g (14 oz) tin plum tomatoes
1 cinnamon stick
1 bay leaf
400 g (14 oz) tin white kidney beans, drained
1 tablespoon red wine vinegar
25 g (1 oz) dark chocolate (70% cocoa solids)

To serve
300 g (10 ½ oz) tortilla chips
300 g (10 ½ oz) sour cream
100 g (3 ½ oz) pickled jalapeños

I've been tweaking and tinkering with this recipe for a year or so now, and I think this is my favourite version. It can be started inside on the hob then moved onto the barbecue to infuse some smoke flavour but of course, you could just carry on cooking it indoors if you want to. It won't be as smoky, but it will still be flippin' fantastic.

This is very rich, with deep chocolate, fruit and coffee flavours from the chillies. I love it with a coal-baked jacket potato or rice, and sour cream, as well as the serving suggestion here.

— Pour the coffee into a bowl, add the dried chillies and soak for 30 minutes (put something like a small plate on top, to keep them submerged).
— Toast the coriander and cumin seeds in a dry frying pan over a medium heat until fragrant (keep giving the pan a shimmy about so they don't burn), then add to a spice grinder or pestle and mortar and grind or crush to a fine powder.
— Heat the oil in a large saucepan or casserole over a medium-high heat, and brown the diced meat in batches. Set aside.
— Heat a splash more oil in the pan, add the onions and pepper and cook over a medium heat for about 10 minutes until softened, scraping any flavour off the bottom of the pan.
— Remove the chillies from their coffee bath (save the coffee), remove their stalks, and give them a rough chop. Add them to the saucepan, along with the garlic, dried oregano and ground spices. Cook for a minute or so, stirring, then add the coffee. Return the browned meat to the pan and add the stock, tomatoes, cinnamon stick and bay leaf, and give everything a good mix.
— At this point, you can either transfer the chilli to the barbecue for the entire 2–2½ hours of cooking, or you can (as I often do), or simmer it on a low heat on the hob, covered, then give it a quick blast of smoke in the barbecue at the end. In this case, cook it for 1½ hours on the hob, then set up a barbecue for indirect cooking over medium heat with the coals banked to one side. Add a piece of wood to the lit coals and wait for it to smoulder, then place the chilli on the grill on the side with no coals for 30 minutes.
— When it's about 20 minutes from being ready, add the beans, vinegar and chocolate to the chilli. Serve with tortilla chips, sour cream and pickled jalapeños.

Smoky Roasted Roots
with Pistachio Butter

Setup: Indirect cooking
Wood: Oak, beech
Equipment: Tongs, disposable
foil tray (or another heatproof
tray that will fit inside the
barbecue)
Prep time: 5 minutes
Cook time: 1 hour
Serves: 4

---

3 medium carrots,
quartered lengthways
2 medium parsnips, peeled
and quartered lengthways
5 small beetroots (beets),
peeled and cut into 3 cm (1¼ in)
wedges
neutral oil, for cooking
the vegetables
150 g (5½ oz) shelled unsalted
pistachios
80 ml (2¾ fl oz/⅓ cup) cold water
2 tablespoons lime juice
2 tablespoons olive oil, plus
extra to serve
sea salt

I've never been particularly fussed about roasting root vegetables, to be honest, but cooking them with wood smoke like this concentrates their savoury richness and they're rendered wrinkly and tender, with colours super-saturated.

What really makes this special though is the pistachio 'butter' – a blend of nuts and lime juice that acts like a thick dressing, to be scooped up with each bite and also, inevitably, your fingers. You won't be surprised to hear that I advocate eating this with the Easy Barbecue Flatbreads on page 60 (truly, I am a flatbread addict).

— Prepare a barbecue for indirect cooking over medium heat, with the coals banked to one side.
— Put the vegetables into a disposable foil tray or other heatproof baking tray, add a splash of neutral oil and some salt, and mix.
— Add a chunk of wood directly on top of the lit coals and wait for it to smoulder. Place the tray of vegetables on the grill on the opposite side to the coals and put the lid on. Set the vents to a quarter open and cook for 1 hour, turning the tray around and mixing the vegetables once or twice during this time.
— Meanwhile, put the pistachios in a food processor and blend them as fine as possible. Keep the motor running while adding the water, the lime juice and a generous pinch of salt. Then (with the motor still running) gradually add the olive oil. Taste the pistachio butter to see if you want more salt or lime juice.
— Spread the pistachio butter onto a plate and top with the root vegetables, once ready. Add a final drizzle of olive oil and some crunchy salt, and serve.

To Cook Indoors: Preheat the oven to 180°C (350°F/gas 4). Put the vegetables in a roasting tray and combine with a splash of neutral oil and some salt. Mix. Cook for about 1 hour, turning halfway through, or until the vegetables are tender.

Smoky Celeriac Gratin
with Beer and Taleggio

Setup: Indirect cooking
Wood: Oak or beech
Equipment: Skillet or other heatproof dish that will fit in your barbecue, heatproof gloves
Prep time: 20 minutes
Cook time: 45 minutes–1 hour
Serves: 4–6

⅓ celeriac (celery root), peeled and cut into 3 mm (⅛ in) thick slices
1 head of garlic cloves, separated, peeled and thinly sliced
1 onion, peeled and thinly sliced
200 g (7 oz) Taleggio, sliced
300 ml (10 fl oz/1¼ cups) double (heavy) cream
200 ml (7 fl oz/scant 1 cup) stout
a piece of stale-ish sourdough (around the size of a large fist), torn into pieces
Parmesan, for grating on top
sea salt and freshly ground black pepper

This recipe combines the holy trinity of root vegetable, cheese and beer in a hot bubbling jumble made even dreamier given time on the grill.

Celeriac (celery root), very thinly sliced (a mandoline is useful for this job), is layered with onions, sliced Taleggio and – very important, this bit – chunks of stale sourdough. The bread soaks up all the 'sauce' underneath and goes super-crispy-crunchy on top. You will be living the dream. About that 'sauce': the whole thing is basically bathed in a mixture of cream and stout which brings toasty depth and of course, plenty of necessary fat to bind the whole thing together. It's probably the best gratin I've ever made, thanks to the way the smoke plays off the moodiness of the stout and earthy flavour of celeriac. Gimme a spoon and close the door behind you.

— Preheat a barbecue for indirect cooking over medium heat, with the coals banked to one side.
— In a skillet or other heatproof dish, layer up the celeriac (celery root), garlic, onions and taleggio, seasoning with salt and pepper as you go.
— Combine the cream and stout and pour on top of the vegetables and cheese. Season again and cover with a generous handful of grated Parmesan.
— Add a chunk of wood directly to the hot coals and wait for it to smoulder. Place the gratin on the grill on the opposite side to the coals and cook offset with the lid on and the vents a quarter open for 45 minutes–1 hour, rotating halfway through, until the gratin is cooked through. To get a nice brown top, place under a preheated grill for a few minutes, watching it carefully.
— Serve with a sharp salad.

To Cook Indoors: Preheat the oven to 180°C (350°F/gas 4) and cook for 45 minutes–1 hour, or until golden and cooked through.

Mussels
with 'Nduja, Thyme and Cider

Setup: Direct cooking
Equipment: Foil
Prep time: 20 minutes
Cook time: 8 minutes
Serves: 2–4, depending on
other dishes

1 kg (2 lb 4 oz) live mussels
4 garlic cloves, peeled and
smashed with the side of
a knife or something heavy
70 g (2½ oz) 'nduja
150 ml (5 fl oz/⅔ cup) dry cider
a few sprigs of thyme
sea salt

To serve
bread
lemon wedges

This will work anywhere you've got a little grill going and enough space to put the bag of mussels on it – it's great for beach or campsite cooking if you don't have a pot. White wine or stock works just as well as cider, and you could add some fresh parsley at the end of cooking, instead of the thyme. 'Nduja is a spicy Calabrian sausage that not only has heat, but plenty of fat, which means it melts down nicely over the shellfish.

— Prepare a barbecue for direct cooking over medium heat.
— Check through your mussels first, discarding any with broken shells, and giving any that are open a sharp tap on a work surface: if they don't close, chuck them away. You should also get rid of any that haven't opened after cooking.
— Make a parcel for the mussels by making a cross with two pieces of foil, then layering another two pieces on top to make a 'star' shape. Add the smashed garlic cloves, dot around half of the 'nduja, then add the mussels. Pour over the cider and dot the mussels with the remaining 'nduja. Add the thyme sprigs and season with salt.
— Close the foil parcel, sealing it well at the top, using another piece of foil if necessary.
— Place on the grill and cook for 8 minutes over direct heat with the lid on and the vents a quarter open, or until the mussels have all opened. Serve with bread and the lemon wedges.

To Cook Indoors: The mussels can just as easily be cooked in a pot on the hob, with a lid.

Beer and Mustard-braised Sausages
with Endives

Setup: Indirect cooking
Equipment: Tongs or
heatproof gloves, metal
roasting tray
Prep time: 10 minutes
Cook time: 30–40 minutes
Serves: 2–3

2 red or white chicory,
halved lengthways
neutral oil, for cooking
the chicory
1 large, curly Cumberland
sausage or 6 other sausages
1 litre (34 fl oz/4¼ cups) ale
3 tablespoons wholegrain
mustard
50 g (1¾ oz/3½ tablespoons)
butter
1 onion, thickly sliced
sea salt and freshly ground
black pepper
your choice of mustard,
to serve

It took me a while to get the hang of braising sausages;
they need quite a bit of flavour and richness in the broth
and absolutely must be crisped up at the end. This is a great
technique to use when you want to keep sausages warm, then
just finish them on the grill at the last minute. I like to make the
most of the beer bath by braising chicory in it at the same time.
The ale magnifies the bitterness of the chicory, so if you are
sensitive to bitterness and want something sweeter, replace
the ale with stock.

— Prepare a barbecue for indirect cooking over medium heat,
with the coals banked to one side.
— Brush the cut sides of the chicory with a little neutral oil and
char it, cut side down over direct heat for a few minutes until
nicely coloured.
— Place the charred chicory, sausage or sausages, ale,
wholegrain mustard, butter, onion and some salt and pepper
into a metal roasting tray and place on the grill, directly
over the coals, until simmering.
— Using heatproof gloves or tongs, move the tray slightly over
to the cooler side of the grill and cook with the lid closed and
vents half open for 30 minutes, rotating the tray halfway
through. The liquid should be simmering, so move it closer
to the coals if it isn't.
— Once the sausage or sausages are cooked through, they can be
removed from their beer bath and crisped up directly over the
coals before serving with the soft chicory and mustard.

A Sausage Sandwich

Setup: Indirect cooking
Equipment: Tongs,
roasting tray
Prep time: 10 minutes
Cook time: 30–40 minutes
Serves: 2–3

Beer and Mustard-braised
Sausages (page 238), prepared
without the endives
neutral oil, for cooking
2 large onions, thinly sliced
3 tablespoons mayonnaise
3 teaspoons Dijon mustard
1 baguette, soft centre
scooped out a bit for extra
sausage space, or 4 slices of
thick, fluffy white bread
any combination of English,
Dijon and wholegrain
mustards, for dipping
(I like all three)
ketchup, if you like

Everyone has their own preferences for a sausage sandwich
– all I can say is that this is mine. Of course, I don't always turn
to the barbecue when the craving strikes, but if I have the time
then this is worth the effort. I like to make a mustard
mayonnaise, then have a full trio of extra mustards on the side,
for dipping. Yes, you could also have ketchup.

— Cook the sausages according to the instructions, crisping
them up well at the end.
— Heat a splash of neutral oil in a frying pan over a medium
heat, add the onions and fry hard for 15–20 minutes until soft
and beginning to char in places – think more 'hot dog onions'
than 'slowly caramelised'.
— Combine the mayonnaise and Dijon mustard and spread
it onto the baguette or bread.
— Add the sausages (I leave them whole for the baguette,
but cut them in half lengthways for the sliced white). Add plenty
of onions and serve with your chosen dip arrangement.

Smoked Coronation
Turkey Sandwiches

Setup: Indirect cooking
Wood: Choose from beech,
apple or cherry
Equipment: Tongs, drip tray,
probe thermometer
Prep time: 20 minutes, plus
overnight brining
Cook time: 45-50 minutes,
plus resting time
Serves: 2

---

80 g (2¾ oz) sea salt
1 litre (34 fl oz/4¼ cups)
cold water
1 turkey drumstick
(about 1 kg/2 lb 4 oz)
sea salt and freshly ground
black pepper

Spice rub
1 tablespoon Madras
curry powder
1 teaspoon garlic powder
1 teaspoon onion powder
½ teaspoon freshly ground
black pepper
2 teaspoons cayenne
1 teaspoon light brown sugar
2 very generous pinches of salt

Turkey, for me at least, tastes a lot better smoked. While some barbecue enthusiasts smoke their whole turkey at Christmas, that's never been my thing; if I'm cooking Christmas dinner I'd rather have beef. Where smoked turkey really comes into its own is in sandwiches. I like to buy legs, which are easy to find (and, frankly, absolutely massive) and smoke them on their own just to make these sandwiches. A single leg will comfortably produce two well-stacked portions of sandwiches and smoked turkey is a lovely thing to have in the fridge anyway, for shredding into spicy noodle salads, making pies, soups... you know the drill.

This recipe is Coronation chicken, only with way more oomph in the form of spice, smoked meat and pickles. The recipe looks like a faff but it's pretty simple to put together while the turkey is smoking and anyway, you've probably realised by now that I don't mess about. Either make the sandwich right, or don't make the sandwich.

— The night before you want to cook the turkey, combine the 80 g (2¾ oz) salt with the litre of water and stir to dissolve. Place the turkey drumstick into a container and pour over the brine. Make sure the drumstick is totally submerged before covering and refrigerating overnight.
— The next day, rinse the turkey and pat dry. Combine all the spice rub ingredients and rub them all over the drumstick.
— Prepare a barbecue for indirect cooking with low-medium heat. I like to bank the coals on either side of the turkey with the drip tray on the base of the barbecue in the middle, but if your barbecue is smaller then go ahead and arrange them on one side with the drip tray on the other.
— Add a large chunk of wood to the hot coals and let it smoulder. Place the turkey on the grill over the drip tray. Close the vents down so there's just a small gap top and bottom.
— Cook for 45–50 minutes or until the turkey is cooked through (a probe thermometer inserted into the thickest part of the leg should read 73°C/163°F). Add another chunk of wood and/or a few more coals during cooking, if necessary, to keep the flow of smoke fairly constant.
— Make the chutney by combining the chutney ingredients with a splash of water in a small blender. Blend together until you have a smooth-ish chutney.

Coriander chutney

50 g (1¾ oz) coriander (cilantro)
leaves and stalks
1 tablespoon lime juice
1 green chilli
pinch of salt

Sandwich

3 tablespoons mayonnaise
2 teaspoons Madras curry
powder
squeeze of lime juice
1 tablespoon mango chutney
1 small red onion, finely
chopped
4 slices of very soft sliced
white bread (the Quick and
Easy Barbecued Naan recipe
on page 216 would also be
a powerful sandwich move)

— Once the turkey is cooked, rest for 15 minutes before
removing the meat from the leg and chopping it into small dice
(skin and all) – you want to make something that's really easy
to eat, so no big chunks. Put it in a bowl and stir through the
mayonnaise, curry powder, lime juice, mango chutney and red
onion. Season with salt and pepper.
— Spread a generous layer of the turkey mix onto two slices
of bread, spreading the other two with coriander chutney.
Close the sandwiches and eat!

To Cook Indoors: Preheat the oven to 180°C (350°F/gas 4).
Place the turkey into a roasting tray and cook for about
45 minutes, or until cooked through. Rest for 15 minutes.

Smoked Ham
(with two glazes)

Setup: Indirect cooking
Wood: Oak, beech, apple or silver birch
Equipment: Tongs, drip tray, roasting tray, probe thermometer
Prep time: 5 minutes
Cook time: 2½–3 hours, plus resting time
Serves: 8–10

Ham
3 kg (6 lb 8 oz) unsmoked, boneless, skin-on gammon, tied with string (leave this in place)
cloves, for studding

Whisky and marmalade glaze
150 g (5½ oz) marmalade
75 ml (2½ fl oz/5 tablespoons) whisky
50 g (1¾ oz/generous ¼ cup) light brown sugar
¼ teaspoon ground ginger
small grating of nutmeg
¼ teaspoon ground white pepper

Plum and fennel seed glaze
150 g (5½ oz) plum jam
pinch ground cinnamon
2 star anise
2 teaspoons fennel seeds
80 ml (2¾ fl oz/⅓ cup) water

This is a very simple way of cooking a ham on the barbecue. You're essentially roasting it as you would in an oven, but with an added dimension: smoke. You may need to soak the gammon before cooking (it's a gammon until it's cooked, when it becomes a ham), so check with your butcher to make sure.

You'll find two different glaze options below: whisky and marmalade, and plum and fennel seed – both add a sticky, caramelised coating to the top of the ham; personally I would never skip the glazing. The ham is beautiful sliced thickly for sandwiches, served as part of a buffet or Christmas spread. At my family home, we always eat ham on Christmas Eve.

— Prepare a barbecue for indirect cooking on low-medium heat, with the coals banked to either side and a drip tray positioned in the centre.
— Add a piece of wood directly to the lit coals, and wait for it to smoulder. Add 1 litre (34 fl oz/4 ⅓ cups) of water to the drip tray and place the gammon on the grill directly over it.
— Put the lid on and leave the vents ¼ open. Cook the gammon for 2–2½ hours, rotating once (you will need to top up the charcoal and wood once during this time), until a probe thermometer inserted into the ham registers 55°C (131°F).
— Remove the ham from the barbecue and carefully remove the skin with a knife, leaving the fat behind.
— Score the fat of the ham in a criss-cross pattern, taking care not to cut the meat. Stud each diamond with a clove.
— Put the ham into the roasting tray and brush with your glaze of choice. Return to the barbecue in the same position, cover again and cook for 20–30 minutes more, glazing it three times, until the ham registers 65°C (149°F) internal temperature (don't go further than this as the ham will start to dry out).
— Remove from the barbecue and allow to rest, wrapped loosely in foil, for at least 1 hour.

Whisky and marmalade glaze: Combine the ingredients in a saucepan and simmer over a low heat for 10–15 minutes until thickened.

Plum and fennel seed glaze: Combine the ingredients in a saucepan and simmer over a low heat for 10–15 minutes until thickened. Discard the star anise before glazing the ham.

Smoked and Braised
Ox Cheek Tacos

Setup: Indirect cooking
Wood: Oak
Equipment: Drip tray, tongs,
tortilla press
Prep time: 10 minutes,
plus 1 hour resting
Cook time: 5 hours
Serves: 6

900 g–1 kg (2 lb–2 lb 4 oz)
ox cheeks, any silvery
membrane removed
a little neutral oil
1 onion, chopped
4 garlic cloves, crushed
or finely grated
1 tablespoon of the rub
mixture
600 ml (20 fl oz/2½ cups)
beef stock

Spice and coffee rub
1 tablespoon light
brown sugar
2 tablespoons ground cumin
2 tablespoons paprika
1 tablespoon instant
coffee granules
1 tablespoon dried oregano
2 teaspoons freshly ground
black pepper
½ teaspoon ground cinnamon
2 tablespoons sea salt

Smoking then braising meat is a really fun way to deal with a cut that's a bit resistant. You get both smoke and tenderness and it's really foolproof, which is what you want when cooking simply, on a basic barbecue.

I've given these ox cheeks a slightly spicy coffee rub, then a long braise in beef stock, until they really give up. The salsa macha is a magical thing: full of chilli and peanut bits that make up a rich, smoky rubble. All this is lifted by nubbins of pickled kohlrabi, a vegetable that I love for its crisp freshness. Use daikon if you can't get hold of one. Combine all this with the melting, spiced meat and you've got a very pleasing winter taco situation.

— Combine all the ingredients for the spice rub in a bowl and reserve a tablespoon, setting it aside to use in the sauce.
— Rub the rest of the rub all over the meat and set aside at room temperature for 1 hour.
— Prepare a barbecue for indirect cooking on low heat, with the coals banked to either side and a drip tray positioned in the centre. Add around 1 litre (34 fl oz/4 ⅓ cups) of water to the drip tray and a chunk of wood to the coals and let it smoulder. Put the cheeks on the grill, directly over the drip tray, put the lid on and close down the vents so that they are just peeking open. Cook for 2 hours, topping up with more coals and another piece of wood as necessary.
— While the cheeks are cooking, make the salsa macha. Split the dried chillies and remove the seeds and stalks. Heat the oil in a small saucepan over a medium-low heat, add the garlic and cook for a couple of minutes until golden brown. Remove the garlic and discard it. Add the peanuts to the oil and cook for a couple of minutes until golden. Remove and set aside. Cook the chillies in the oil for a minute or two until slightly darker in colour, then set aside. Puree the fried peanuts and chillies in a food processor or pestle and mortar until gritty. Mix in the cooking oil, vinegar, oregano and a generous pinch of salt. Set aside.
— Make the pickled kohlrabi by combining the lime juice, salt and sugar in a bowl and stirring until the sugar and salt have dissolved. Add the kohlrabi and mix well. Set aside, stirring every now and then.
— Preheat the oven to 150°C (300°F/gas 2).

Salsa macha
3 dried ancho chillies
8 dried chillies de árbol
250 ml (8 fl oz/1 cup)
light olive oil
5 garlic cloves, peeled and
halved
100 g (3½ oz) unsalted peanuts
1 teaspoon dried oregano
1 tablespoon red wine vinegar
sea salt

Pickled kohlrabi
4 tablespoons lime juice
¾ teaspoon sea salt
2 teaspoons caster
(superfine) sugar
1 kohlrabi, peeled and
finely diced

Tortillas (makes ~35)
250 g (9 oz/2 cups) masa harina
large pinch of sea salt
about 300 ml (10 fl oz/1¼ cups)
warm water

To serve
200g sour cream
large bunch of coriander
(cilantro), leaves picked

— Heat the neutral oil over medium heat in a lidded casserole dish large enough to hold the ox cheeks., Add the onion and soften for about 10 minutes. Add the garlic and the reserved rub and cook, stirring for a minute or so, then add the ox cheeks and stock, put the lid on and transfer to the oven for 2.5 hours, or until completely tender.
— Make the tortilla dough by placing the masa harina and salt in a bowl and slowly adding the water, mixing with your hands. It should come together into a smooth mass and feel soft, without any lumps. Wrap the dough in a sealed container or using wax paper/cling film (plastic wrap) and let it sit for 30 minutes or so.
— Heat a cast-iron pan or non-stick frying pan (skillet) over a high heat. Pull off pieces of the dough and roll into balls roughly the size of a golf ball. Place a square of greaseproof paper into your tortilla press and put the ball on top. Top with another sheet of greaseproof and press. Cook in the hot pan until the edges start to look dry (a minute or so), then flip. The tortilla will start to puff up slightly and will have a speckled appearance when it is ready. Put it into a folded clean tea towel and repeat with the remaining masa. The tortillas can sit in the tea towel for a while, where they will stay soft and warm.
— After this time, you can remove the ox cheek and reduce the sauce if you like, or alternatively just pour some sauce over the cheeks when you shred them.
— Shred the ox cheeks, put back in the sauce and serve with the salsa macha, pickled kohlrabi, sour cream, tortillas and coriander (cilantro).

To Cook Indoors: You can simply omit the smoking part of the recipe, adding 3 tablespoons of the rub when softening the onion.

Coal-baked Potatoes
with Cacio e Pepe Butter

Setup: Direct cooking
Equipment: Foil, heatproof gloves, tongs
Prep time: 10 minutes
Cook time: 1–1½ hours
Serves: 4

4 baking potatoes
1 tablespoon black peppercorns
100 g (3½ oz/7 tablespoons) unsalted butter, softened
50 g (1¾ oz) pecorino, grated
sea salt

Cacio e pepe is the pasta dish that had a real moment, and there's something quite amusing – to me, at least – about taking the flavours and putting them on a jacket spud.

— Prepare a barbecue for direct cooking over medium heat. Once the flames have died down, spread out the embers. You want to cook them on glowing embers, not right in the fire.
— Prick a few holes in each potato with a fork, season with salt and wrap them individually in foil. Place them directly onto the embers and cook for 1 hour or so, turning them occasionally, until a skewer slips through with no resistance.
— While the potatoes are cooking, lightly toast the peppercorns in a dry frying pan (skillet) over a medium heat for a couple of minutes until fragrant (moving them around to make sure they don't burn), then coarsely crush in a pestle and mortar.
— Combine the peppercorns with the butter and Pecorino, then form the butter into a sausage and roll in cling film (plastic wrap) and cover before putting into the fridge to firm up.
— Once the potatoes are done, carefully unwrap them, split them open and serve them with the cacio e pepe butter.

To Cook Indoors: Preheat the oven to 180°C (350°F/gas 4). Prick the potatoes all over with a fork, rub with oil and season with salt. Cook directly on the oven rack for 1 hour – 1 hour 20 minutes, until the skin is crisp and the potatoes soft.

Winter Coleslaw

Setup: Indoors
Prep time: 15 minutes
Serves: 4

---

50 g (1¾ oz) pecans
2 ripe persimmons, topped
and tailed and thinly sliced
¼ small red cabbage, core
removed and cabbage very
thinly sliced (on a mandoline,
if you have one)
½ small red onion, thinly sliced
handful of mint leaves,
thinly sliced

Dressing
2 tablespoons lime juice
1 teaspoon honey
1 tablespoon olive oil
good pinch of salt

Persimmons are one of those fruits I never knew what to do with, but I've come to see them as a lifeline in the winter months when there's not much variety in the choice of British seasonal fruits, and their colour is so cheerful. However, a word of warning: they absolutely must be ripe. Unripe persimmons are incredibly tannic and will cause your mouth to dry and pucker. It's really unpleasant. Once ripe, they become like honey-custard sunshine in the mouth.

— Toast the pecans in a dry frying pan (skillet) over a medium heat until they start to smell fragrant. Move them around frequently, to prevent them burning. Set aside to cool then chop roughly.
— Combine the dressing ingredients in a bowl and mix well. Combine the sliced persimmon, cabbage, onion and mint leaves in another bowl and add the dressing. Mix well, add the pecans, and serve immediately.

Prep time: 15 minutes,
plus overnight salting and
10–14 days fermentation
Makes: 1.5 kg (3 lb 5 oz)

Vegetables

1 kg (2 lb 4 oz)
Brussels sprouts
500 g (1 lb 2 oz) carrots
1 daikon (about 600 g/1 lb 5 oz)
1 Chinese cabbage (about
850 g/1 lb 14 oz)
fine sea salt

Flavourings

2 large heads of garlic
(or 3 small), cloves separated
and peeled
5 cm (2 in) piece of ginger,
peeled
100 g (3½ oz) Korean chilli
flakes (gochugaru)
3 tablespoons white miso
4 tablespoons fish sauce

Brussels Sprout Kimchi

I posted a recipe for Brussels sprout kimchi online a couple of
years back and people went mad for it. I began receiving photos
of proud faces posing next to jars of fermenting brassica, and
tales of blooming dependency. Perhaps they were excited to
find another use for sprouts? They work perfectly in a kimchi,
of course, what with being mini cabbages and all*.

One of my favourite ways to eat sprout kimchi is in a Stilton
toastie after Christmas, when the cheeses are an assortment of
rapidly spoiling ends knocking around that chaotic part of the
fridge door. However, it's also great as a barbecue accoutrement
- have some with your smoked ham platter, or have them both
in a sandwich (yes, sandwiches again). Or, stuff some of this and
the odd-ends cheeses into the flatbreads on page 60 (which are
pretty much sandwiches, if you think about it).

*this may not be taxonomically correct.

— Trim the base of the sprouts, remove any loose leaves from
the outside, then slice them fairly thinly (don't worry too much,
some variation is fun).
— Peel the carrots and daikon, then cut them into thin
matchsticks or thin circles, ideally using a mandoline.
— Quarter the cabbage lengthways and trim away the thick
stem. Slice horizontally into roughly 2.5 cm (1 in)-thick pieces.
— Weigh the cabbage, carrots, daikon and sprouts all together
in a bowl, and calculate 5% of that weight (total weight of
vegetables $\times$ 0.05) – this is how much salt you will you need.
— Sprinkle the salt evenly over the vegetables, then massage
them with your hands until they start to soften and weep
liquid – about 5 minutes. Cover and leave overnight at
room temperature.
— The next day, give the vegetables a good rinse under
cold running water.
— Sterilise enough jars to accommodate the vegetables.
— Blend the garlic, ginger, Korean chilli flakes, white miso
and fish sauce in a food processor to a coarse paste.
— Mix the paste into the well-drained vegetables until it's fully
integrated, then transfer into sterilised jars, pressing down very
firmly with clean hands, until the juices are covering the
vegetables. Seal the jars and leave at room temperature. The
kimchi should start fermenting after a few days. Open the jar/s
to burp it every other day, and taste the kimchi after 10 days to
see how it's getting on. The kimchi will start to taste pleasantly
sour and slightly fizzy as it ferments, and this flavour will
increase in intensity as the process continues. It's up to you
when to halt that process. I generally transfer mine to the fridge
after 3 weeks, when I find the flavour is to my liking.

Setup: Indoors
Prep time: 15 minutes, plus 48
hours minimum pickling time
Makes: 500 g (1 lb 2 oz)

150 ml (5 fl oz/⅔ cup)
rice vinegar
350 ml (12 fl oz/1½ cups)
hot tap water
5 tablespoons caster
(superfine) sugar
2 tablespoons sea salt
500 g (1 lb 2 oz) Brussels
sprouts, stalks and any loose
outer leaves removed and
sprouts quartered
1 head of garlic, cloves
separated and peeled
10 white peppercorns

Pickled Brussels Sprouts

I first tried pickled Brussels sprouts in Vienna, in a small shop
run by two pickle and fermentation enthusiasts. I admired their
liberal use of garlic and while I originally sought to recreate
their recipe, I now generally pickle the sprouts in my standard
brine, only with lots of added garlic.

— Sterilise your jar/s first, as this is a quick process.
— Combine the rice vinegar, water, sugar and salt in a jug
and stir until the sugar and salt have dissolved.
— Pack the sprouts into the jar/s, layering them up with
the garlic and peppercorns.
— Pour over the brine, seal and refrigerate. The pickle will taste
good after 48 hours, and just gets better over a couple of weeks.
It will keep in the fridge for a couple of months.

Setup: Indoors
Prep time: 20 minutes, plus
about 10 days fermenting time
Makes: 1 large jar

125 g (4¼ oz) long red chillies,
stalks removed, halved and
deseeded
125 g (4¼ oz) Scotch bonnet
chillies
1 head of garlic, cloves
separated and peeled
500 g (1 lb 2 oz) raw honey
(see stockists on page 17)

Fermented Hot Garlic Honey

This is a pot of gold - literally - to keep on your kitchen counter
and experiment with. I love it squiggled over the Cheese and
Herb Flatbreads on page 64, and I wouldn't hesitate to include
it in dressings: try subbing it into the Grilled Peach and
Tomato 'Fattoush' on page 85, or the Winter Coleslaw on page
246. In fact, just drizzling it over lamb kebabs on top of
a whipped cool yoghurt would be very fun, or perhaps try
mixing it with lemon juice to use as a glaze...

This version is really spicy, I won't pretend otherwise.
You could replace the scotch bonnets with regular chillies,
if you like, but I do (as you well know by now) love their flavour.

— The honey is likely to be a little attached to its container,
so pop the jar in a saucepan of warmed water to melt it to
pouring consistency (don't let it get hot).
— Put the chillies and garlic cloves into a sterilised jar and pour
the honey on top, swirling to submerge everything. Seal the jar.
— Let the jar sit undisturbed for 24 hours, then turn it upside
down, to let the honey coat everything. Turn it back the other
way after another 24 hours, then turn again. Once everything
starts fermenting, there will be enough liquid to coat the chillies
and garlic, and you won't need to turn it anymore.
— Give it a taste after about 10 days - it will be very hot!
The honey will keep for up to a year in a cool, dark place.

Setup: Indoors
Prep time: 20 minutes
Cook time: 1 hour
Makes: about 1 kg (2 lb 4 oz)

2 pineapples
2 large red onions,
finely chopped
2 scotch bonnet chillies,
deseeded (if you like!) and
finely chopped
6 garlic cloves, crushed or
finely grated
200 g (7 oz/generous 1 cup)
light brown sugar
350 ml (12 fl oz/1½ cups)
white wine vinegar
1 teaspoon ground allspice
(ideally freshly ground from
around 12 allspice berries)
1 teaspoon ground ginger
2 teaspoons fresh
thyme leaves
2 teaspoons sea salt

Setup: Indoors
Prep time: 15 minutes,
plus 48 hours chilling time
Makes: 1.5 kg (3 lb 5 oz)

150 ml (5 fl oz/⅔ cup)
rice vinegar
350 ml (12 fl oz/1½ cups)
hot tap water
5 tablespoons caster
(superfine) sugar
2 tablespoons fine sea salt
1 large pineapple, trimmed,
peeled, core removed
and diced
1 lemongrass stalk, tough
outer layers removed and
inner part bruised
2 scotch bonnet chillies,
deseeded and thinly sliced
3 garlic cloves, peeled and
smashed with the side of
a knife (or something heavy)
a few white peppercorns

Jerk-spiced Pineapple Relish

I developed this lightly spiced, jerk-inspired relish as a friend for Christmas ham. I was always so taken with the pineapple relish my mum made every year (from a Thane Prince recipe in her book *Jams and Chutneys: Preserving the Harvest*) and I'd always wondered what a spiced version would be like, full of allspice and scotch bonnet chilli. Needless to say, it goes well with jerk chicken or pork, too. Thank you for the inspiration, Thane!

— Sterilise your jar/s first, as this is a quick process.
— Peel the pineapples and remove any tough 'eyes'. Cut them into quarters lengthways, then remove the tough core section from each quarter and dice the flesh into fairly small chunks.
— Put the pineapple into a large saucepan with all the other ingredients and cook for 1 hour over medium-low heat until thick, with a syrupy juice.
— Pack the relish into sterilised jars and seal. It will keep for about 6 months unopened, and a couple of weeks once you've popped the lid.

Scotch Bonnet Pickled Pineapple

Another partner for ham and jerk here... and a killer addition to a Ploughman's lunch or buffet. It's also very good on pizzas. Yes, I am very happy to eat pineapple on a pizza. I will be taking no further questions at this time.

— Sterilise your jar/s first, as this is a quick process.
— Combine the rice vinegar, water, sugar and salt in a jug (pitcher) and stir until the sugar and salt have dissolved.
— Pack the pineapple, lemongrass and scotch bonnet slices into the jar/s, along with the garlic and white peppercorns.
— Pour over the brine and refrigerate. They're good after 48 hours, and just get better over a few weeks. They'll keep in the fridge like this for a couple of months.

Acknowledgements

This book took years to form inside my head, and there's no doubt I'm in debt to the many different people who've influenced my cooking during that time. Thank you, all.

A huge thank you to all of the contributors who so generously gave time and recipes specifically for these pages: Max Bergius; Neil Robson; James Whetlor; Aliyu Dantsoho and Fatima Usman; Rosa Bulum and Ana Salam; Michelle Salazar de la Rocha and Sam Napier; Craig Evans; Bill and Jennifer Hawes; Liliane Nguyen; Ben Chapman; Saiphin Moore; Sally Butcher; Wasim and the team at Tayyabs; Sanjay Battychara; Andrea Oskis and her Auntie Androula; Makda Ghermai-Harlow and Jack; Mustafa Akpinar and Şiyar Akpinar.

Thank you to everyone at Hardie Grant but particularly Eve Marleau. Eve, you are the editor I always dreamed of finding; thank you for letting me write this book exactly as I envisaged it. Remember: ham is crucial.

To the best agent in the world, Kay Peddle – you made all of this happen! Thank you for working so hard, being endlessly supportive and sending me snacks in the post.

Thank you to stylist extraordinaire Valerie Berry: the woman, the myth, the legend! J'adore. Thank you also to brilliant assistants Hanna Miller, Songoo Kim and my cat pal Holly-dawn Middleton-joseph. Thank you too, Rachel Vere, for having exceptional taste in props and always bringing gingham into the room.

Laura Nickoll, I am so grateful for your keen editing eye – I learnt so much from you and will be a better recipe writer in the future because of your work. Thank you.

TEAM PIT! My babes Holly Catford and Rob Billington. I love you guys, thank you for coming on this journey with me. You are both so talented.

To Leah … MATE! Thank you for always supporting me in everything I do. I can't wait until we are two little old ladies and we can look back over stuff like this! I loves ya.

Thank you to mum and dad for supporting every single one of my careers… Look, I finally found the right one!

Finally, thank you to my family: Donald, Chaz and Delia. Donald, you had such a huge part to play in this book. I don't know how people write cookbooks alone because I could not have written this one without you. Thank you for all the shopping, testing and eating (and for managing my numerous meltdowns). This book is for you.

About the Author

Helen Graves is a food writer based in London. She is the editor of *Pit*, an independent magazine with roots in food and fire. She won Editor of the Year: Food & Drink at the British Society of Magazine Editors' Awards 2020 and has been shortlisted for 2021. You'll find her work in most major food and drink publications in the UK and beyond. This is her first full-length recipe book. helengraves.co.uk @foodstories

Published in 2022 by
Hardie Grant Books,
an imprint of Hardie Grant
Publishing

Hardie Grant Books (London)
5th & 6th Floors
52–54 Southwark Street
London SE1 1UN

Hardie Grant Books
(Melbourne)
Building 1, 658 Church Street
Richmond, Victoria 3121

hardiegrantbooks.com

Copyright text
© Helen Graves
Copyright photography
© Rob Billington

British Library Cataloguing-
in-Publication Data.
A catalogue record for this
book is available from the
British Library

Live Fire
ISBN: 978-1-78488-478-9

10 9 8 7 6 5 4 3 2 1

Publishing Director:
Kajal Mistry
Commissioning Editor:
Eve Marleau
Copy Editor: Laura Nickoll
Design and Art Direction:
Holly Catford/
Esterson Associates
Photographer: Rob Billington
Food Stylist: Valerie Berry
Prop Stylist: Rachel Vere
Proofreader: Lucy Kingett
Production Controller:
Katie Jarvis

Colour reproduction by p2d
Printed and bound in China
by RR Donnelley

FSC
www.fsc.org
MIX
Paper from
responsible sources
FSC® C144853

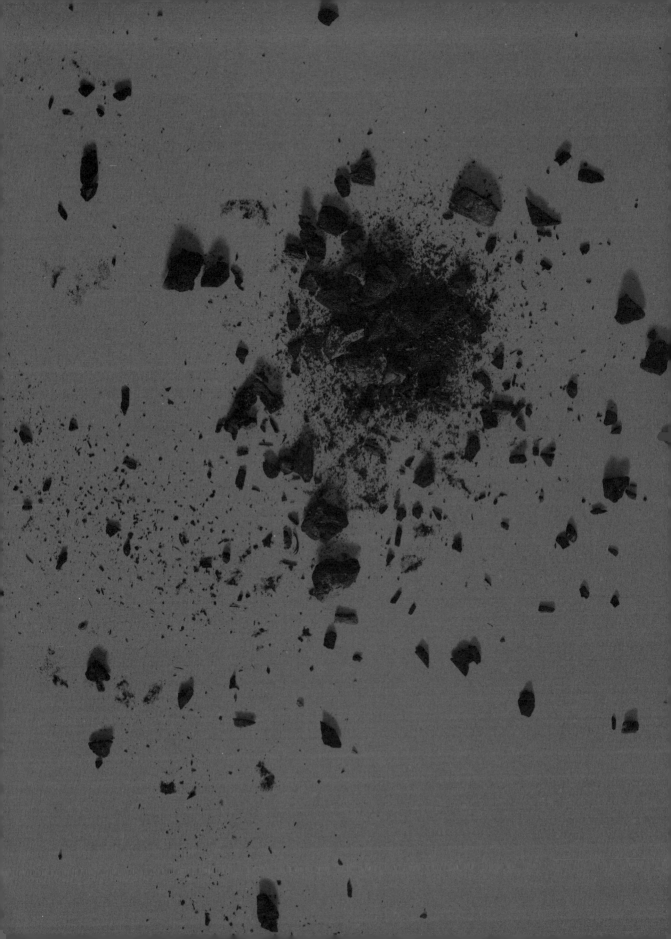